CW00539629

£13·99

THE
PSALMS

A new, cutting-edge translation

NICHOLAS KING

**kevin
mayhew**

First published in Great Britain in 2008 by Kevin Mayhew Ltd
Buxhall, Stowmarket, Suffolk IP14 3BW
Tel: +44 (0) 1449 737978 Fax: +44 (0) 1449 737834
E-mail: info@kevinmayhewltd.com

www.kevinmayhew.com

9 8 7 6 5 4 3 2 1 0

ISBN 978 1 84867 224 6
Catalogue No. 1501204

Cover design by Rob Mortonson
© Image copyright Mitzy. Used under licence from Shutterstock Inc.
Editor: Peter Dainty
Typeset by Richard Weaver

Set in Adobe Garamond and Trajan

Printed and bound in Great Britain

For HBC –
a song sung for the Lord

Contents

About the author

Nicholas King is a Jesuit priest who teaches New Testament at Oxford University. He is fond of playing squash and cricket. He is frequently in demand to lecture on biblical subjects, especially St Paul.

Introduction

Welcome to this translation of the psalms. The word 'psalm' comes to us from the Greek word *psallo*, which means to sing with a stringed instrument. The Hebrew equivalent is the word *mizmor*, which is found at the head of many psalms. The Hebrew title for the book, however, translates as 'Book of Praises', which gives it a rather different feel.

What follows in this book is a translation not from the Hebrew, such as you will find in almost every modern version, but from the Greek (known as the Septuagint, or LXX). There are two reasons why the Greek translation of the psalms is important to us today. In the first place, the LXX is our oldest witness to the text of the psalms. It is three centuries older than the text fixed by the Rabbinic scholars at Jamnia, and twelve hundred years earlier than the Masoretic Text (MT), the name given to the Hebrew text of the Bible to which vowels were added (Hebrew was originally written entirely in consonants, and vowels were invented later). Our earliest Hebrew manuscript is the Codex Leningradensis, which is early eleventh century BC, and dependent on revisions made by very capable Jewish scholars in the tenth century. Very often, the Greek manuscripts, which are much older, may therefore preserve an original meaning that the Hebrew has forgotten.

Secondly, the psalms are quoted with extraordinary frequency in the New Testament, and the version is usually that of the LXX. The Psalter, as far as New Testament authors are concerned, is the Greek translation of these hymns.

Psalms are difficult because they are poetry, and all poetry is difficult, especially when you try to translate it into another language. Inevitably, you lose some of the richness of imagery and expressions; and in the present case, you are reading a translation of a translation! In the poetry of the psalms, there are some very rare words, whose meaning we no longer know. So sometimes, the translator from Hebrew into Greek is clearly at a loss to know what a word means; at other times, however, he gives us a possible clue as to the meaning of the Hebrew. Very often, therefore, the LXX is good evidence for what the original text said. Another difficulty is that word-order in all poetry, and especially Hebrew poetry, is difficult; sometimes it is possible to translate the Hebrew in many different ways, and the Greek translator had to make a guess. Sometimes, too, the manuscripts are corrupt, and that poses another set of problems.

Psalms are hymns, originally written to be sung in the Temple; but the LXX psalms were clearly not to be sung in the Temple. You would not have been allowed to sing Greek there, for one thing. So this text was produced for those Jews who lived in the Diaspora around the Mediterranean, and had lost touch with their Hebrew roots. The Greek version of the psalms will have been intended for use in synagogues, and perhaps for people's private prayer and reading. That makes a difference to the text. Another difference is that the Hebrew of the psalms has a metre (though it took European scholars several centuries to discover it); the Greek version has no such metre, and in the translation I have not attempted to restore it, though I have tried to keep open the possibilities of a certain rhythm. Perhaps one day someone may set these psalms also to music?

It may be helpful to think of the psalms as 'a very old building' that has been lived in by a family for several centuries, or as a college at an ancient university, which has been inhabited by a community of students and teachers for half a millennium or more. In the course of time, many features of this building have been altered, or their original functions been forgotten; and they have been put to different purposes. So when the psalmist talks of 'my enemies', for example, we are no longer in touch with the original reference, and sometimes it is easier to pray such verses as a reference to those inner thoughts that upset us or alienate us. The great thing about living in such a building is its sense of lived history, and as you walk round the astonishing edifice that is the psalms, it may be helpful to be inspired by other members of the community who have prayed there before you. People are often inspired in this way when praying at the Basilica of the Holy Sepulchre in Jerusalem, or the Grotto at Lourdes: they find the place already hallowed by the prayers of other pilgrim-visitors. And as you walk prayerfully round the building, it may be helpful to notice on what a generous scale it is planned. Many of the psalms repeat familiar themes; Psalm 40:13–17, for example, reappears as the whole of Psalm 70. And Psalm 53 is almost identical to Psalm 14; but the editors thought it worth their while to include two very similar rooms in the building. Sometimes one of the rooms clearly had a function that we can no longer identify: so in Psalm 55 we read:

> If an enemy had reviled me, I should have put up with it;
> and if someone who hated me had spoken boastfully against me,
> I should have hidden from them.
> But you, my peer, my leader, my acquaintance,
> who sweetened food along with me;
> we walked in unity in God's house.

Clearly, this was a very important moment in the poet's experience of life; but we have no notion what the event was that gave rise to this sad reproach, mourning a loss of friendship. All we can do is make the room our own, and use it for our own purpose: finding Israel's God there.

Another factor that makes a difference to the text is the very different ways in which the songs are read; it is one thing if they are being sung in the Temple, another if you are searching through them to find predictions about the Messiah whom God is going to send, and another again if, like Christians, you think that the Messiah has already come. Consider, for example, the following extracts from Henry Williams Baker's version of Psalm 23:

The *King of love* my shepherd is…

And on his shoulder gently laid,
and home, rejoicing, brought me…

Thy Cross before to guide me…

Good Shepherd, may I sing thy praise…

In the above verses, the phrases printed in italics are not in the Hebrew original; they come from the New Testament, and Baker has, so to say, 'read Christ back into the psalm'. This is a perfectly legitimate procedure for a Christian reading of this text; but it is not there in the original.

Different again is the reading of many Christians today, especially monks and nuns, for whom the psalms are the official prayer of the Church, which they recite in Morning and Evening Prayer and at other times during the day. It helps them to bring their whole day together, and to structure it for God; for such people, the psalms have a quite different 'feel'.

A further difference is that the psalms have been collected into a single book, and that inevitably affects the way that we read them. They are also, of course, independent poems, but we cannot help noticing that the five doxologies (41:13; 72:18–19; 89:52; 106:48, and the whole of 146–150) that come at the end of certain psalms have the effect of dividing the collection into five 'books', perhaps on the model of the five books of Moses.

One difficulty about the LXX is that, as many readers will have noticed, the numbering is one short of the Hebrew version for most of the book. This is because the LXX has quite correctly put Psalm 9 and 10 together as a single psalm; they have also joined Psalms 114 and 115, to make LXX Psalm 113, and then turned Psalm 116:1–9 into Psalm 114, and 116:10–19 into 115. Then the number of 150 is attained by making Hebrew Psalm 147 into 146 (verses 1–11) and 147 (verses 12–20). Since the Latin Vulgate follows the LXX, the Catholic translations tended to go with that numeration; nowadays, however, most Bibles follow the Masoretic Text, and that is the policy that I have adopted. And, just for luck, the LXX adds a final psalm, which is also included here.

Another small difficulty about numbering concerns the verses. The Hebrew text includes headings as verse 1, and many modern versions exclude that from their calculation. In this version we shall follow this increasingly common practice, and not regard headings as part of the text; so if you find that a reference to the psalms does not seem to produce the result you want, it may be worth looking at the previous verse. I have kept the headings, because they are an important part of the existing text, but to indicate that they are not to be pronounced I have italicised them, so for public recitation they, and the mysterious 'Interlude' (see note on 3:2), are to be quietly ignored.

Throughout the translation I have adopted the policy of using inclusive language, that is to say, not speaking of 'man' or 'men' or 'the sons of men' when referring to all members of the human race. This has the undoubted benefit of making it clear that the particular text does not restrict itself to just one gender. It brings with it two difficulties, however. First, it obscures the fact that the society that produced these texts was a patriarchal one, that is to say it was run by the (male) head of the household, and that its texts are androcentric, that is to say, written from an exclusively male point of view. The second difficulty is that using inclusive language can sometimes make for very awkward English; but it is a price worth paying to avoid the appearance of excluding half the human race from God's sphere of attention. On the whole, I have not attempted to avoid male pronouns and adjectives for God; but we need to heed the warning of feminists that 'if God is male, then the male is God', and refuse to identify God with any gender. As you read, therefore, remember that God is not male, or at any rate no more male than female; and remember, too, that the assumption that God is masculine has often covered some very unattractive, and indeed ungodly, power-plays.

Enjoy this extraordinary collection of poems. Step aboard and listen to the ancient voices that have been singing them in the Jewish and Christian communities for upwards of 3000 years, and find your own story and your own journey to God written in them. There are psalms for every mood.

Nicholas King SJ
Feast of St Mary Magdalen 2009

BOOK ONE (Psalms 1–41)

Psalm 1   An introduction to the good life

1:1   Happy are those who have not walked in the counsel of the ungodly,
and have not stood in the path of sinners,
and have not sat on the seat of the pestilential;

2   but whose desire is the Law of the Lord,
and who will meditate on his Law day and night.

3   They shall be like the tree planted by streams of waters,
which shall give its fruit at the right time;
its leaf shall not fall off,
and whatever they do shall prosper.

4   Not so are the ungodly, not so;
[they are] like chaff which the wind casts from the face of the earth.

5   Because of this the ungodly shall not rise up in judgement,
nor sinners in the council of the just.

6   For the Lord knows the way of the just,
and the way of the ungodly shall perish.

Psalm 2   An introduction to the fate of the ungodly

2:1   Why did the nations rage, and the people meditate on empty things?

2   The kings of the earth approached;
and the rulers gathered into one place,
against the Lord and against his Messiah:

3   'Let us break their chains;
and let us hurl away their yoke from us'.

4   The One who dwells in [the] heavens
will laugh them to scorn;
and the Lord will hold them in derision.

5   Then God will speak to them in his anger;
in his rage he will throw them into disorder,

The interesting question about Psalm 1 is: why did they put this one first? What is your answer to that question? You may notice that neither this psalm nor the next has a title, which is uncommon among the psalms, and it may be that they are intended as an introduction to the whole collection.

It is a charming beginning to the collection of hymns, and encourages the pious not to think that they are wasting their time. The image of the tree by the water's edge speaks loudly in a dry climate like that of Israel. Jeremiah 17:7-8 makes powerful use of the idea.

1:1   *pestilential:* this is what the Greek says, translating a Hebrew word that means 'those who brag, scoff, speak boastfully'.

1:2   *meditate:* the idea here is that of reading the Law to oneself, partly out loud (the ancients did not, on the whole, read silently).

1:5   *the ungodly shall not rise up in judgement:* this does not refer to resurrection, though it was later read in this light. Rather it refers to the inability of the wicked to stand when God comes to judge.

council of the just: here the Greek uses a word from Athenian political theory to describe one of the major organs of democracy. It translates a Hebrew word that among other things means 'assembly' or 'congregation'.

2:1-2   *Why did the nations rage . . . against his Messiah:* these lines are quoted, in precisely this form, in Acts 4:25b-26, and applied to 'Herod and Pontius Pilate, with the Gentiles and the peoples of Israel' menacing the young Christian church.

2:1   *meditate on empty things:* as opposed to meditating on the Law in the previous psalm. These two psalms are closely connected. One presents the quiet image of a single person who is determined to follow what God wants; the second psalm offers the noisy image of those who are determined to oppose God.

2:2   *gathered into one place:* at least one perceptive scholar has suggested that there may be a reminiscence here of the story of the Tower of Babel in Genesis 11: the rulers gather together, just as the human race does in Genesis 11:2; they rebel against God ('Let us break their chains', verse 3; compare Genesis 11:4) and God puts an end to their folly in verse 5: 'in his rage he will throw them into disorder' (compare Genesis 11:8-9). Or is this just a pattern of the way humans relate to God?

Messiah: the Greek says 'Christ', which means the same thing ('Anointed One'), but would be misleading as a translation.

⁶ but I have been appointed King by him
on Sion, his holy mountain,

⁷ proclaiming the Lord's decree.
The Lord said to me,
'You are my son; I have begotten you today.

⁸ Ask of me, and I shall give you the nations as your inheritance,
and the ends of the earth as your possession.

⁹ You will shepherd them with an iron rod;
you will shatter them like a potter's vessel.'

¹⁰ And now, kings, understand:
be educated, all you who judge the earth.

¹¹ Serve the Lord with fear;
and rejoice [before] him in trembling.

¹² Accept discipline,
or the Lord may be angry and you be destroyed from the way of the righteous,
when his anger is suddenly kindled.
Happy are all those who trust in God.

Psalm 3   A lament – and God's response

A psalm of David, when he ran away from his son Absalom.

3:1 Lord, how those who afflict me have multiplied!
Many rise up against me.

² Many say to my soul:
'There is no salvation for you in your God'.

Interlude

³ But you, O Lord, are my protector,
my glory, you lift up my head.

⁴ With my voice I cried out to the Lord,
and the Lord heard me, from his holy mountain.

2:6   *I have been appointed King:* it is possible that the Greek is translating from a slightly different Hebrew text here; but it is clearly God's king who is speaking, not God in person. Or it may be that the translator found it hard to follow the change of person between verses 6 and 7.

2:7   *You are my son:* here it is impossible to use inclusive language without missing the point badly.

2:7   *You are my son; I have begotten you today:* Hebrews 1:5 quotes this with reference to Jesus. There may also be a hint of it in Mark's account of the baptism of Jesus (Mark 1:11), which reads 'You are my Son, the Beloved – with you I am well pleased', perhaps with an echo of Isaiah 42:1.

2:9   *shepherd them:* the Hebrew reads 'break them' or 'do evil to them'; but with a change of one consonant it can mean 'rule' or 'shepherd', and that may indeed be the original reading; it is certainly appropriate for a king appointed by God.

2:10   *you who judge the earth:* the Greek translation here perhaps echoes Wisdom of Solomon 1:1.

2:12   *the way of the righteous:* echoing the 'two ways' of Psalm 1:6.

Happy . . . are all those who trust in God: the poet drawing the moral of both these psalms.

3   **Heading**: *A psalm of David, when he ran away from his son Absalom:* this is the first of the titles affixed to many of the psalms; these headings are an indicator of the guesswork of later readers of the psalms, and cannot be taken as indicating the actual date of composition. 'Of David' is a less than literal rendering of a too-literal Greek version ('to David'). The events referred to are recounted in 2 Samuel 15–17 (see especially 15:12-18).

3:2   *There is no salvation for you in your God:* both the Greek and the Hebrew here have *'there is no salvation for him in his God':* this is the first of many examples in the psalms where the person switches abruptly. I have smoothed the translation by offering 'you . . . your' for 'him . . . his'. In English it is possible to ease the difficulty by the use of quotation marks; but there is nothing of the sort in the Hebrew. The difficulty will frequently reappear in the psalms.

Interlude: this is a possible translation of a Greek word, whose meaning nobody knows, which always translates the Hebrew word Selah, whose meaning nobody knows. Guesses range through 'pause', 'leading motif', 'lifting up one's voice (i.e. fortissimo?)', or 'prostration' or 'doxology', or even a Persian word meaning 'sound of the strings'. Probably it was added after the psalms were collected, to indicate a now irrecoverable musical instruction. We shall see the word a further 95 times in the LXX psalms, but will not comment on it again.

Interlude

5 I lay down and I slept;
and I arose, for the Lord will help me.

6 I shall not be afraid of tens of thousands of the people,
of those who are about me, who join in the attack against me.

7 Arise, O Lord, save me, O my God,
for you have struck all those who hate me without reason;
you have shattered the teeth of the wicked.

8 Salvation is the Lord's.
And may your blessing be on your people.

Psalm 4   An evening prayer

To the end. A song of David among the psalms.

4:1 When I called upon [God], the God of my righteousness heard me;
you opened a space for me in my tribulation;
have pity on me and hear my prayer.

2 How long [will] you people [be] hard of heart?
Why do you love emptiness and seek after falsehood?

Interlude

3 And know that the Lord has done wonderful things for his holy one;
the Lord will hear me when I cry to him.

4 Be angry, and do not sin;
speak in your hearts and on your beds be pierced.

Interlude

5 Offer a sacrifice of righteousness,
and hope in the Lord.

6 Many say, 'Who will show us good things?'
The light of your face has shone upon us, O Lord.

7 You have put gladness into my heart;
they have been filled with their corn and wine and oil at the right time.

8 In peace I shall lie down,
and at the same time I shall fall asleep
because you alone, Lord, make me live in hope.

3:7 *without reason:* this may represent an alternative Hebrew reading, differing by two letters from the existing Hebrew text, which means 'on the cheek'.

4 **Heading**: *To the end:* the Greek translator always renders in this way a Hebrew expression (*lammenatseah*) whose meaning is inaccessible to us. Some translators suggest 'for the leader'; the Aramaic translation has 'for praise'. Others argue for some kind of musical directive; others suggest that it is a matter of the correct attitude towards the merciful God. The fact is that we do not even know what verb it comes from.

4:1 *God of my righteousness heard:* the Hebrew probably read (although this depends what vowels we put in) 'O God of my righteous, hear'. Knowing precisely how to read the text will frequently be a problem; but we shall follow the option taken by the Greek translator.

4:4 *Be angry:* the Hebrew here reads 'tremble', but often in the sense of trembling with anger. Here it may mean 'get excited'.

be pierced: the Hebrew here reads 'be silent'. We have no easy way of telling what went on between the two versions.

4:5 *Offer a sacrifice:* literally 'sacrifice a sacrifice'; the Greek translates literally a Hebrew expression which sounds unnecessarily awkward in English.

4:6 *The light . . . has shone upon us:* the Hebrew, as it stands, which may not be what our translator read, has an imperative: 'lift up the light . . .'. It is possible that there is an echo here of Aaron's blessing at Numbers 6:26.

4:7 *they have been filled:* 'they' here is presumably the 'many' who were complaining in the previous verse. But it looks as though the translator has been tidying up here, and it is hard to know what Hebrew text he had in front of him.

at the right time: here the translator is doing his best with the Hebrew, which is probably mildly corrupt. Other Greek manuscripts suggest 'from their fruit'; but that is probably just an attempt to make sense of a baffling text.

Psalm 5 A morning prayer

To the end. For her who inherits, a psalm of David.

5:1 Give ear to my words, O Lord,
  take notice of my crying out.

2 Attend to the voice of my pleading,
  my King and my God;
  for it is to you that I pray, O Lord.

3 Early in the morning you will hear my voice;
  early in the morning I shall stand before you;
  and I shall gaze upon you;

4 for you are not a God who desires wickedness;
  nor shall the one who acts wickedly live with you.

5 Transgressors shall not remain before your eyes;
  you hate those who work lawlessness.

6 You will destroy all those who speak falsehood;
  the Lord abominates the man of blood, and the treacherous.

7 But I, because of the multitude of your mercy,
  shall enter your house;
  I shall bow down towards your holy shrine, in reverence for you.

8 O Lord, guide me in your justice, because of my enemies;
  make straight your way before me.

9 For there is no truth in their mouth;
  their heart is empty;
  their throat is an open tomb,
  with their tongues they have acted treacherously.

10 Judge them, O God, let them fall away from their plotting;
  according to the multitude of their impieties,
  drive them out, because they have provoked you, O Lord.

11 And let all that hope in you rejoice in you for ever;
  they shall exult, and you will dwell among them;
  and all those who love your name will boast in you.

12 For you will bless the just, O Lord,
  you have crowned us as with the weapon of your good pleasure.

---

5 **Heading:** *To the end:* see note on 4:1.

For her who inherits: the Hebrew here is a technical term, which might mean 'played on the flute' or 'against sickness'. But the Hebrew consonants could also mean something like 'to her who inherits'; or it might be the name of a tune: 'to be sung to "Inheritance".' We must get used to these uncertainties in translating the psalms.

5:1 *crying out:* the Hebrew here means something like 'murmuring', or perhaps 'imploring'.

5:2 *I pray:* the Greek here has 'I shall pray', reflecting a Hebrew tense that goes better into English as a present.

5:3 *I shall gaze upon you:* what human beings could not do. See Moses at Exodus 3:6; 33:20 (but contrast the special dispensation given to Moses and the elders at Exodus 24:9-11); and Samson's parents at Judges 13:23. There is a different view in the New Testament, of course: see Matthew 5:8.

5:7 *mercy:* translating a Hebrew word which means 'love', 'mercy', 'faithfulness', 'goodness', 'graciousness', 'steadfast love'.

5:11 *you will dwell among them:* the Greek word translated here by 'dwell' may well be echoed in John 1:14 'the Word . . . dwelt among us'. It is important to be attuned to these possible echoes.

5:12 *you have crowned us as with the weapon:* the Hebrew can mean this, as the translator has put it into Greek; but it is probably best translated as 'you surround us as with a shield', and the word for shield is the long shield that covers one's whole body, a powerful metaphor for God's faithful protection.

Psalm 6   The first 'Penitential Psalm'

To the end, among the hymns for the eighth. A psalm of David.

6:1 Lord, do not reprove me in your fury;
and do not punish me in your rage.

2 Have mercy on me, Lord, for I am weak;
heal me, Lord, for my bones are disturbed,

3 and my soul is very disturbed.
But you, O Lord, how long?

4 Turn, O Lord, rescue my soul,
save me for the sake of your mercy.

5 For in death there is no one who remembers you,
and in Hades who will sing your praises?

6 I am worn out with my groaning;
every night I shall make my bed awash;
with my tears I shall water my couch.

7 My eye is worn out with anger;
I have grown old because of all my enemies.

8 Depart from me, all you who work iniquity,
for the Lord has heard the sound of my weeping,

9 the Lord has heard my entreaty,
the Lord has welcomed my prayer.

10 Let all my enemies be ashamed and let them be very troubled;
let them be routed and utterly put to shame very soon.

Psalm 7   A prayer for deliverance from accusers

A psalm of David, which he sang to the Lord about the words of Cush, the Benjaminite.

7:1 O Lord my God, I have hoped in you:
save me from all those who pursue me, and deliver me,

2 otherwise like a lion he may seize my life,
with no one to pay the ransom, no one to save me.

---

6 **Heading**: *among the hymns for the eighth:* once again it is hard to be sure what the Hebrew means here, and our translator has done his best. It is clearly some kind of musical notation, and an intelligent guess is that it was 'with stringed instruments, on the eighth', which might refer to the eighth string, or perhaps to an eight-stringed instrument.

6:2 *my bones are disturbed:* this (more or less) is what both the Hebrew and the Greek say, but the general sense is, of course, that the singer is in enormous dismay.

6:5 *in death there is no one who remembers you:* it is only relatively late in the history of the Old Testament that the notion surfaces of a life that continues after death. For similar pessimism on this subject, see Ecclesiastes 9:5-6.

6:6 *I shall make my bed awash . . . water my couch:* this psalm is what scholars are accustomed to call an 'individual lament', so the imagery is understandable, but it is perhaps more moving in Hebrew and in Greek than in English, where it only just avoids comedy.

6:7 *worn out:* the Greek reads 'troubled' or 'disturbed', which is a gallant attempt at a Hebrew word whose meaning no one can be sure of, but is probably somewhere in the area of being 'cloudy' or 'dark'.

6:8 *Depart from me, all you who work iniquity:* this is quoted by Matthew at the end of the Sermon on the Mount (7:23) and by Luke (13:27). Oddly enough neither of them quotes this line precisely, but between them they get it all!

the Lord has heard the sound of my weeping: almost all the psalms of lament have this extraordinary moment. Virtually as the singer utters his complaint (and verse 8 showed him very low in morale, aged and practically on his deathbed), there comes to him a certainty that the Lord has heard his prayer.

7 **Heading**: *the words of Cush, the Benjaminite:* it is far from clear what this might refer to, possibly some story, known to the editors of the psalms, but not recorded in our existing biblical narrative. 'Benjaminite' is not quite what the translator wrote: he had son of Yemini, which more or less represents what the Hebrew has.

7:2 *he:* the switch from plural to singular is a bit confusing, but it is in both Hebrew and Greek. Presumably we are to think of something like 'the enemy' as the subject of the verb.

3 O Lord my God, if I have done this,
  if there is injustice in my hands,
4 if I have repaid with evil those who repaid me,
  may I then fall at the hands of my enemies, uselessly;
5 then let the enemy pursue my soul,
  and lay hold of my life, and trample it down into the soil,
  and make my glory dwell in the dust.

Interlude

6 Arise, O Lord, in your anger; be lifted up to the boundaries of my enemies.
  Awake, O Lord my God, in the decree which you commanded.
7 And the congregation of the peoples shall gather round you;
  and above it return to the heights.
8 The Lord will judge the peoples;
  judge me, O Lord, according to my righteousness,
  and according to my integrity which is upon me.
9 Let the wickedness of sinners be brought to an end;
  and you will direct the righteous,
  examining hearts and minds, O God.
10 My help from God is righteous,
  from God who saves the upright of heart.
11 God is a just judge, strong and long-suffering,
  not bringing on his wrath every day.
12 Unless you turn back,
  God will polish his sword; he has bent his bow, and made it ready.
13 And on it he has prepared vessels of death;
  he has got his arrows ready for those who are on fire.
14 Look! [the wicked] have had labour pains, bringing forth unrighteousness;
  they have conceived pain and brought forth iniquity.
15 They have made a hole and dug a pit;
  and they will fall into the trap that they made.
16 Their labour shall return on their own head,
  and their injustice shall come down on the crown of their head.
17 I shall give thanks to the Lord for his righteousness;
  and I shall sing to the name of the Lord Most High.

7:4 *uselessly:* the Greek here means 'empty', and is an attempt at translating a Hebrew word that has a notion of 'emptiness' about it, but here almost certainly means 'without cause'.

7:5 *my glory:* some have suggested 'my liver', in which case it would be another word for 'my soul'. But 'my glory' is perfectly possible in the psalms (see Psalm 3:3).

7:6 *boundaries:* this unexpected word is an alternative translation of a Hebrew word that almost certainly means 'anger'.

7:7 *the peoples:* here and in the next verse, this word almost certainly refers to the 'Gentiles'.

7:7 *above it return to the heights:* this, if not crystal clear in English, is what the Greek says. It is certainly a possible translation of the Hebrew, although the modern versions tend to go for something like 'take your seat on high'.

7:9 *hearts and minds:* Greek and Hebrew have 'hearts and kidneys', the seats, in that thought-world, of thoughts and emotions respectively. Exactly the same metaphor is used in Revelation 2:23.

7:10 *My help from God:* the Hebrew here has 'my shield is on God', which does not make much sense. Perhaps we should understand it as 'God is a shield above me'.

7:11 *bringing on his wrath every day:* the Hebrew here has 'a God who is indignant every day', and this may be a case where LXX has preserved the correct reading.

7:13 *he . . . his:* this is clearly God; but in 14-16 it is the wicked who are the subject, as the translation makes clear. In both the Hebrew and the Greek, however, there is a bewildering switch of reference, and we have to deduce when the psalmist is talking about God, and when it is the wicked who are in view.

7:17 *I shall give thanks to the Lord:* as so often in a psalm of lament, there comes this point, towards the end, when God has heard the petitioner's prayer. The confidence expressed in verse 1 here gets its reward.

Psalm 8   The glory of God, and of all creation

To the end. On the winepresses. A psalm of David.

8:1 O Lord, our Lord, how wonderful is your name in all the earth;
for your majesty is exalted above the heavens.

2 Out of the mouths of infants and babes at the breast
you have prepared praise because of your enemies,
to destroy the avenging enemy.

3 For I shall look upon the heavens, the work of your fingers,
the moon and the stars which you established.

4 What are humans that you remember them,
or their children that you take account of them?

5 You made them a little less than angels;
with glory and honour you crowned them.

6 You appointed them over the works of your hands;
you put all things under their feet,

7 sheep and all oxen, and all the beasts of the field,

8 birds of the air and fish of the sea,
the things that pass through the paths of the seas.

9 O Lord, our Lord, how wonderful is your name in all the earth!

Psalm 9–10   God saves the poor and the afflicted

To the end, about the secrets of the Son. A psalm of David.

9:1 I shall praise you, Lord, with all my heart;
I shall recount all your wonderful deeds.

2 I shall rejoice and exult in you;
I shall sing to your name, O Most High.

3 When my enemies are turned back,
they will be weakened, and perish before your face,

4 for you have maintained my right and my justice,
and you have sat on your throne judging justly.

5 You upbraided the Gentiles, and the ungodly were destroyed;
you wiped out their name for ages, for age upon age.

6 The enemy's swords have failed for ever;
and you have destroyed cities;
their memory is reduced to an echo,

7 but the Lord remains for ever;
he has prepared his throne for judgement.

---

8 **Heading**: *On the winepresses:* this is certainly one possible translation of the Hebrew, perhaps a reference to a 'Song of the Vintage'. We can no longer get back to the original reference.

8:2 *Out of the mouths of infants and babes:* quoted by Jesus at Matthew 21:16.

8:3 *For I shall look:* this is certainly a possible translation of the Hebrew, which could also mean 'when I look . . .'

the moon and the stars: so this is an evening prayer.

8:4 *humans . . . their children:* the attempt to use inclusive language here can lead us into awkwardness, but it is a price worth paying.

9 This psalm was originally an alphabetic psalm (although bits are now missing), and Psalm 10 was its continuation, as LXX correctly observes. We shall continue to number in accordance with the Masoretic Text, but with LXX in brackets after the MT numeration.

the secrets of the Son: this is the Greek translator's take on an untranslatable Hebrew *almuth-labben*, and it might mean precisely what he says here. Or it might be the name of a tune, to which the psalm is to be sung.

9:3 *will be weakened:* this, and 'they will perish', are reasonable translations of the Hebrew tense as it stands, but since this psalm is a thanksgiving for things that have already taken place, it is more likely that the poet understood these verbs as referring to a past event.

18

8 He will judge the world in righteousness;
    he will judge the peoples in uprightness.

9 The Lord was a refuge for the poor,
    a help at the right time when there is trouble.

10 And let those who know your name hope in you,
    for you did not abandon those who sought you out, O Lord.

11 Sing psalms to the Lord who dwells in Sion,
    proclaim among the peoples his doings.

12 For in seeking out blood he remembered them;
    he did not forget the cry of the poor.

13 Have mercy on me, O Lord,
    see my humiliation from my enemies,
    you who lift me up from the gates of death.

14 That I might proclaim all your praises
    at the gates of the daughter of Sion;
    I shall rejoice at your salvation.

15 The peoples are stuck in the destruction that they created;
    in the very trap that they had hidden,
    their foot is taken.

16 The Lord is known, when he does judgement,
    by the works of his hands the sinner is taken.

A song of Interlude

17 Let sinners be turned away into Hades,
    and all the nations who forget about God.

18 For the poor shall not be forgotten for ever;
    the expectancy of the needy shall not be destroyed for ever.

19 Arise, O Lord, do not let a mortal being prevail;
    let the nations be judged before you.

20 Appoint, O Lord, a lawmaker over them;
    let the nations know that they are only human.

Interlude

Psalm 10 (9:21-39)   God saves the poor and the afflicted

10:1 (9:21) Why, O Lord, do you stand far away?
    [Why] overlook us at the time when there is trouble?

2 When the ungodly behave arrogantly,
    the poor are set on fire;
    they [the ungodly] are taken by the plots that they are planning.

3 Because sinners sing their own praises,
    because of the desires of their soul;
    and the unjust call down blessings upon themselves.

4 The sinner has provoked the Lord,
    because of the abundance of his anger, they will not look for [God].
    'There is no God', in their eyes.

9:8 *He will judge the world in righteousness:* quoted by Paul in his speech to the Areopagus in Athens, Acts 17:31.

9:10 *proclaim among the peoples:* this refers to the message going out to the Gentiles; see the same word in verse 15.

9:16 *A song of Interlude:* the 'interlude' is our old friend *Selah;* the 'song' is the Hebrew word *higgaion*, which comes from a verb meaning to growl, or coo, or groan or mutter or even think or reflect. So it could mean a pause for reflection here, or perhaps a musical interlude, which is clearly the way the Greek has taken it.

10:2 *they:* presumably the wicked, though it does not say so.

5 Their ways are at all times defiled;
  your judgements are abrogated in their eyes.
  They will lord it over all their enemies.

6 For they said in their heart,
  'I shall not be shaken from generation to generation,
  I shall not suffer evil.'

7 Their mouths are filled with cursing and bitterness and guile.
  Under their tongue are suffering and grief.

8 They lie in wait with the rich in hidden places,
  to kill the innocent.
  Their eyes watch the poor.

9 They lie in ambush in a hidden place, like a lion in his den;
  They lie in ambush to plunder the poor,
  to plunder the poor when they drag them off.

10 God will bring them down in his trap;
   they will bow down and fall when they lord it over the poor.

11 For they said in their heart,
   'God has forgotten; he has turned away his face, so as never to look.'

12 Arise, Lord God; let your hand be raised up; do not forget the poor.

13 Why have the godless provoked God?
   For they said in their heart, 'God will not seek me out.'

14 You see [them], for you contemplate suffering and rage,
   to hand them over into your hands.
   Therefore the poor has been left to you;
   you were helping the orphan.

15 Break the power of the sinner and the wicked;
   their sin shall be demanded of them;
   and they will not be found because of their sin.

16 The Lord will reign for ever, and for ever and ever.
   You nations shall perish from his land.

17 The Lord has heard the desire of the poor,
   your ear has attended to the readiness of their heart

18 to give judgement for the orphan and the lowly,
   that people may cease from their boasting on earth.

Psalm 11 (10)   The Lord is my refuge

To the end. A psalm of David

11:1 In the Lord I have placed my trust;
   how will you say to my soul,
   'Depart to the mountains, like a sparrow'?

2 For see – the sinners have bent their bow;
  they have prepared arrows for their quiver,
  to shoot at the upright of heart on a dark night.

3 For they have destroyed what you fashioned;
  but what did the upright do?

11:1 *how will you say to my soul:* it seems that the petitioner has turned up to the sanctuary, asking what to do, and various people have apparently advised "fleeing to the hills", instead of trusting in God. The Judean hills with their inaccessible caves (such as those at Qumran where the Dead Sea Scrolls were hidden) and their steep hills and rocks, have always been places to hide from their enemies. This the petitioner is not prepared to do.

⁴ [They sang], 'The Lord in his holy Temple,
the Lord, whose throne is in heaven,
his eyes are looking upon the poor,
his eyes test the children of humans.'

⁵ The Lord tests the just and the ungodly;
but those who love injustice hate their own soul.

⁶ He will rain snares and fire and brimstone down on sinners,
and a stormy wind is a part of their cup.

⁷ For the Lord is just and loves righteous acts;
his face sees uprightness.

Psalm 12 (11)   God's message to those who are suffering

To the end; on the eighth, a psalm of David.

12:1 Save me, O Lord, for the holy have failed;
for truth has become scarce among human beings.

² Everyone has spoken emptiness to their neighbour;
their lips are treacherous, and they have spoken with a double heart.

³ Let the Lord destroy all treacherous lips, and all boastful tongues,

⁴ those who have said,
'We shall make our tongues strong;
our lips are our own – who is our Lord?'

⁵ 'Because of the wretchedness of the poor and the groaning of the needy,
now I shall arise,' says the Lord,
'I shall place them in safety;
I shall deal openly with them.'

⁶ The Lord's sayings are holy sayings;
silver tried and tested in the fire,
purified seven times in the earth.

⁷ You, O Lord, will guard us, and you will take care of us
from this generation, and for ever.

⁸ The ungodly walk about;
in accordance with your majesty,
you have greatly cared for us mortals.

Psalm 13 (12)   A lament by one on the point of death

To the end. A psalm of David

13:1 How long, O Lord, will you forget me? To the end?
How long will you turn your face away from me?

² How long shall I carry sorrows in my soul,
griefs daily in my heart,
how long shall my enemy be lifted up against me?

11:4 *[They sang]:* very often in the psalms the person switches; here for example, there is a change from describing what the wicked and the upright do, to talking about God. So 'they sang' is no more than a possible way of understanding the change, and it is in square brackets because it is not in the Hebrew.

upon the poor: the Hebrew just has 'his eyes are looking . . .', and it seems that the Greek translator felt that there was a gap to be filled. Some translations insert 'the world'.

11:6 *a part of their cup:* the idea of a 'cup' as metaphor for suffering is frequent in the Bible. See, of course, Jesus in Gethsemane (Mark 14:36 and parallels); and the question to the ambitious brothers, James and John (Mark 10:39), where those silly boys clearly do not know what they are asking for.

13:2 *sorrows:* the Hebrew original is a bit puzzling here. It is a word meaning 'counsel', 'advice', plans', but, with the addition of a single letter it could mean 'sorrows', and most editors opt for this solution.

3 Look upon me and hear me, O Lord my God,
   give light to my eyes, lest I sleep in death,
4 lest my enemy should ever say, 'I have prevailed against you';
   those who oppress me will rejoice if I am shaken.
5 I hoped in your mercy;
   my heart will rejoice in your salvation;
   I shall sing to the Lord who has shown kindness to me;
   and I shall play a tune to the name of the Lord, the Most High.

Psalm 14 (13)   God and the godless

To the end. A psalm of David

14:1 Fools say in their heart, 'There is no God.'
   They have wrought destruction and have met with loathing for their practices;
   there is none that does what is right,
   there is not even one of them.
2 The Lord looked down from heaven upon the children of Adam,
   to see if there were one who was wise,
   or who sought for God.
3 They have all turned aside together; they have become useless.
   There is no one who acts uprightly, not even one.
   Their throat is an open tomb;
   with their tongues they have behaved treacherously;
   there is a cobra's poison under their lips;
   their mouths are full of cursing and bitterness;
   their feet are quick to shed blood;
   affliction and distress are in their ways;
   and they do not know the way of peace.
   There is no fear of God before their eyes.
4 Will not all lawbreakers realise?
   They devour my people like the devouring of bread;
   they have not called upon the Lord.
5 They were fearful with dread, where there was no dread;
   for God is in the righteous generation.
6 You have dishonoured the plans of the poor;
   for God is their hope.
7 Who will supply Israel's salvation out of Sion?
   When the Lord restores his people's captivity,
   let Jacob exult, and Israel rejoice.

13:4 *I have prevailed against you:* the original has 'prevailed against him'.

14:1 *Fools say in their heart:* this psalm is more or less identical to Psalm 53.

14:3 *Their throat . . . before their eyes:* these lines have been inserted here (though not in Psalm 53), presumably on the basis of Romans 3:13-18, which is a patchwork of quotations from several different psalms, and presumably therefore by a Christian copyist.

14:5 *God is in the righteous generation:* that is what both the Hebrew and the Greek have, but modern versions are for some reason coy about this.

14:7 *restores his people's captivity:* this is what both the Hebrew and the Greek have. The sense, presumably is 'when God brings his people back from captivity'.

Psalm 15(14)   Who can be God's guest?

A psalm of David

15:1   Lord, who will dwell in your tent,
and who will camp on your holy mountain?

2   The one who walks without blame,
the one who does what is right,
the one who speaks truth from the heart,

3   the one who has not deceived with the tongue,
nor done any evil to their neighbour,
nor accepted any insult to those who are closest to them.

4   In their eyes the one who does evil is disdained;
they make an oath to their neighbour, and do not break it.

5   Those who have not lent out their money at interest,
who have not accepted bribes against the innocent;
those who act like this shall never be shaken.

Psalm 16 (15)   A quiet song of faith in the face of death

An inscription of David

16:1   Keep me safe, O Lord, for I have hoped in you.

2   I said to the Lord, 'You are my Lord,
for you have no need of my goods.'

3   For the saints who are in his land,
he has made all his desires marvellous among them.

4   The sicknesses [of the wicked] multiplied; after this they made haste.
No way shall I gather their gatherings of blood,
nor shall I recall their names on my lips.

5   O Lord [you are] the portion of my inheritance and of my cup;
you are the one who restores my inheritance to me.

6   The measuring-lines have fallen in the best places for me;
for my inheritance is best.

7   I shall bless the Lord who helped me to understand;
even until nightfall my heart instructs me.

15:1   *your tent:* we are to think here of the relatively spacious pavilions of Bedouin encampments rather than the constrained accommodation of modern backpackers.

15:2   *does what is right:* in both the Greek and the Hebrew, this phrase sounds like 'works righteousness'; modern translations are a bit shy of translating it in this way, possibly because of 16th century disputes that centred on this kind of terminology.

16   **Heading:** no one knows for certain what the Hebrew word *miktam* means, but it is possible that the Greek translation has preserved the original meaning. The Greek word means 'an inscription recorded on a pillar', the idea being that such an inscription would be indelible and permanent.

16:1   *I have hoped in you:* the Hebrew has 'I have taken refuge in you'.

16:2   *you have no need of my goods:* the Greek translator is doing his best with a very difficult Hebrew text, which may mean 'my prosperity rests with you alone', but is uncertain.

16:3   *he has made all his desires marvellous among them:* the Hebrew is difficult and probably corrupt, but the Greek may have preserved the correct reading here.

16:4   *The sicknesses [of the wicked] multiplied:* the change of tone is very abrupt here, even for the psalms. Clearly we are no longer speaking of the 'holy ones', but of their opponents, perhaps 'idol worshippers', so I have inserted [the wicked]. If that is the case, then a line or a half-line has dropped out at the beginning of this verse.

16:5-6   *portion . . . inheritance . . . measuring-lines:* all this vocabulary echoes the distribution of the land. See Joshua 13:23; 14:4-5; 15:13; 17:5.

8 I saw the Lord before me always;
   for the Lord is at my right hand, so that nothing might shake me.
9 Therefore my heart rejoiced and my tongue exulted,
   and still my flesh shall dwell in hope.
10 For you will not abandon my life to Hades,
   nor will you allow your holy one to see destruction.
11 You have made known to me the path of life;
   you will fill me with joy at your presence;
   delights at your right hand for ever.

Psalm 17 (16) Prayer of the innocent, suffering persecution

A prayer of David

17:1 Hear, O Lord of my righteousness,
   pay attention to my plea,
   give ear to my prayer, which is not [uttered] by deceitful lips.
2 Let my judgement come forth from your presence;
   let my eyes look upon uprightness.
3 You have tested my heart, you have visited it by night;
   you have tried me by fire; and no unrighteousness was found in me,
4 that my mouth may not speak of the deeds of mortals;
   through the words of your lips I have kept to rough ways.
5 Direct my steps in your paths,
   that my steps may not slip.
6 I cried out, for you heard me;
   O God, bend your ear to me, and listen to my words.
7 Show the wonders of your mercies,
   you who save those who hope in you,
   from those who resist your right hand,
8 guard me as the apple of your eye.
   Under the shelter of your wings you will shelter me
9 from the face of the ungodly who afflict me.
   My enemies have surrounded my life.
10 They have closed in their own fat;
   their mouth utters arrogance.
11 They throw me out, and now they have encircled me;
   they have set their eyes to turn to the ground.
12 They thought of me as though they were lions ready for their prey,
   and like a lion cub who lives in secret places.
13 Arise, Lord, intercept them, and overthrow them.
   Rescue my soul from the ungodly, your sword from the enemies of your hand.

16:8-11 *I saw the Lord before me . . . joy at your presence:* these verses are quoted in Peter's speech at Pentecost (Acts 2:25-28, 31), and in Paul's first speech, in the synagogue at Antioch in Pisidia (Acts 13:35).

17 **Heading:** *A prayer of David:* this accurately translates the Hebrew word, which is the overall title for the psalms, a reminder to us that as well as songs they are also prayers.

17:4 *I have kept to rough ways:* this is what the Greek says. The Hebrew may well mean 'I have kept/kept from the paths of the violent'.

17:10 *closed in their own fat:* this is the reading of both Greek and Hebrew. The sense is (perhaps) 'they have closed up their hearts'.

17:11 *They throw me out:* this whole verse is unintelligible in the Hebrew; but the Greek is an attempt to make sense of it.

> 14 O Lord, destroy them from the earth in their life,
> and their belly has been filled with your hidden things.
> They have been satisfied with sons,
> and they have left the remnant to their infants.
> 15 But I in my righteousness shall appear before your face;
> I shall be sated when your glory appears.

Psalm 18 (17)   The king's victory song

To the end. Of the Lord's servant David, what he said to the Lord, the words of this song in the day when the Lord delivered him from the hand of all his enemies, and from the hand of Saul.

18:1 And he said, 'I shall love you, Lord, my strength.
2 The Lord is my foundation and my refuge and my deliverer;
my God is my helper, and I shall hope in him;
he is my protector, and the horn of my salvation;
he is my defender.
3 I shall praise the Lord and call upon him;
and I shall be saved from my enemies.
4 The pains of death encircled me;
and the torrents of lawlessness threw me into confusion.
5 The pains of Hades encircled me,
and the snares of death intercepted me,
6 And in my affliction I called upon the Lord,
to my God I cried out;
from his holy Temple he heard my voice.
My cry shall come in before him, [shall come] to his ears.
7 Then the earth was shaken and started to tremble;
and the foundations of the mountains were disturbed;
and they were shaken, because God was angry with them.
8 Smoke went up in his wrath,
and fire burst into flame at his presence;
coals were kindled from it.
9 He made the heaven bow down;
he came down, and there was darkness under his feet.
10 He came upon the cherubim,
he was spread out, spread out on the wings of the winds.
11 He made darkness his hiding place;
his tent was in a circle about him,
dark water in clouds of air.
12 From the splendour that was before him,
his clouds passed, hail and coals of fire.
13 The Lord thundered from heaven,
the Most High uttered his voice.

17:14 *destroy them from the earth:* the Hebrew is very difficult here, and the Greek translator has done his best, but has come up with the impossible 'from a few, from the earth, divide them'. Nor does the rest of the verse improve matters at all.

18 **Heading:** *To the end . . . and from the hand of Saul:* this psalm reappears at 2 Samuel 22. This unusually lengthy

historical reference does not enable us to give it an accurate date.

18:7- *Then the earth was shaken and started to tremble:* here
16 begins the first of the many descriptions of a 'theophany' that we shall encounter in the psalms, the dramatic and terrifying appearance of God from out of his Temple. Read these verses with some care.

14 He sent forth his arrows and scattered them,
   he multiplied his lightnings, and confused them.

15 The springs of the waters appeared,
   and the foundations of the world were revealed,
   at your rebuke, O Lord,
   at the breathing of the breath of your anger.

16 He sent from on high and took me;
   he drew me out of the many waters.

17 He will deliver me from my powerful enemies,
   and from those who hate me;
   for they were stronger than I am.

18 They intercepted me on the day of my distress;
   but the Lord was my support.

19 He led me out into a broad space;
   he will deliver me because he delights in me;
   he will deliver me from my powerful enemies,
   and from those who hate me.

20 The Lord will reward me because of my righteousness,
   and because of the purity of my hands he will reward me.

21 For I have kept to the Lord's ways,
   and have not sinned against my God.

22 For all his judgements are before me,
   and I have not put aside his ordinances from me.

23 I shall be blameless with him;
   I shall be saved from my lawlessness.

24 The Lord will reward me because of my righteousness,
   and because of the purity of my hands in his sight.

25 With the holy you will be holy,
   and with the guiltless person you will be guiltless.

26 With the elect you will be elect,
   and with the crooked you will deal perversely.

27 For you will save a humble people,
   but you will humble the eyes of the arrogant.

28 For you, O Lord, will light my lamp,
   my God, you will lighten my darkness.

29 For by you I shall be rescued from a gang of pirates;
   with my God I shall leap over a wall.

30 As for my God – his way is blameless;
   the Lord's oracles are tested in the fire;
   the Lord is the protector of all those who hope in him.

31 For who is God but the Lord?
   Who is a God but our God?

32 God is the one who girds me with power,
   and has made my way blameless,

33 the one who directs my feet like the feet of a deer,
   and sets me on the heights,

18:20 *will reward me . . . will reward me:* the Greek here uses one word to translate two different Hebrew words, and I have followed the translator's lead.

18:21 *against my God:* literally, 'away from', the Greek sticking very close indeed to the sense of the Hebrew.

18:24 *The Lord will reward me . . . in his sight:* this verse is identical, apart from the final phrase, with verse 20.

34 who instructs my hands for war;
    you have made a bronze bow of my arms.
35 You gave me the shield of my salvation;
    your right hand gave me support;
    your discipline kept me upright to the end,
    and your discipline itself shall instruct me.
36 You made a broad place for my steps beneath me;
    my tracks did not weaken.
37 I shall pursue my enemies and overtake them,
    and I shall not turn back until they falter.
38 I shall afflict them, and they will be unable to stand;
    they shall fall beneath my feet.
39 You have girded me with power for war;
    you have hobbled under me all those who rose up against me.
40 You made my enemies show me their backs;
    you destroyed those who hated me.
41 They cried out, and there was no one to save;
    [they cried] to the Lord, and the Lord did not listen to them.
42 I shall grind them to powder, like dust before the wind;
    and like the mud of the streets I shall crush them.
43 You will deliver me from the arguments of the people;
    you will set me at the head of the Gentiles;
    a people whom I did not know became my slaves.
44 At the hearing of the ear they obeyed me;
    the children of foreigners lied to me.
45 Foreign children grew old, they limped away off their paths.
46 The Lord lives – and blessed be my God;
    may the God of my salvation be exalted.
47 It is God who gives me vengeance,
    who subdues peoples under me.
48 My deliverer from my angry enemies,
    from those who rise up against me,
    you will exalt me; from the unjust person you will deliver me.
49 Therefore I shall sing your praises among the nations, O Lord;
    and I shall play a melody to your name,
50 the one who makes great the deliverances of his King,
    who acts mercifully towards his Anointed One, towards David,
    and to his offspring for ever.'

Psalm 19 (18)   God is revealed in Creation and in the Law

To the end; a psalm of David

19:1 The heavens are telling the glory of God;
    and the firmament proclaims the work of his hands.
2 Day utters the word to day,
    and night proclaims knowledge to night.
3 There is no speech nor word
    whose voice is not heard.

18:44 *lied to me:* the Hebrew word here normally means 'to lie'; but it can also mean to 'feign obedience' or 'fawn', which accounts for some of the modern English versions.

19 This was probably originally two separate psalms, one celebrating God's glory in creation, and the other celebrating God's gift of the Law.

4 Their sound has gone out to all the earth,
and their words to the ends of the world;
[God] has pitched a tent for the sun.
5 He himself, coming forth like a bridegroom from his bridal chamber,
rejoices like a giant to run his race.
6 His going forth is from one end of the heavens,
and his goal is the other end of the heavens;
there is no one who can hide from his heat.

7 The Law of the Lord is perfect, restoring souls;
the Lord's testimony is reliable, giving wisdom to infants.
8 The decrees of the Lord are upright, giving joy to the heart;
the command of the Lord is a bright light, giving light to the eyes.
9 The fear of the Lord is pure; it endures for ever.
The judgements of the Lord are true, and are justified all together
10 they are more desirable than gold, more than many precious stones;
they are sweeter than honey or the honeycomb.
11 For your servant keeps them; in keeping them there is much reward.
12 Who will understand his transgressions?
Purify me from my hidden [faults].
13 From foreigners spare your servant;
if they do not lord it over me, then I shall be blameless,
and I shall be purified from a great sin.
14 And the sayings of my mouth,
and the meditation of my heart,
shall be pleasing before you for ever,
O Lord, my helper and my redeemer.

Psalm 20 (19)   A prayer for the king

To the end; a psalm of David

20:1 May the Lord hear you on the day of affliction,
may the name of the God of Jacob protect you,
2 send help to you from the sanctuary,
and support you from Sion,
3 remember all your sacrifices,
and honour your burnt offering.

Interlude

4 May the Lord give you your heart's desire;
and bring all your plans to fulfilment.
5 We shall exult in your salvation;
in the name of our God we shall be magnified.
May the Lord fulfil all your requests.
6 Now I know that the Lord has saved his Messiah;
he will listen to him from his holy heaven.
The salvation of his right arm comes with power.

19:4 *Their sound:* this is plainly the meaning of the Greek, and is probably what the Hebrew originally said.

19:13 *foreigners:* the Hebrew as it stands reads 'the insolent', which is only one letter different from the word for 'strangers' or 'foreigners'.

20:5 *magnified:* the Hebrew reads 'bannered' or 'raise the banners', which suggests a change of places of two consonants. It may well be that LXX has preserved the original reading here.

7   These people will glory in chariots;
    and those people will glory in horses;
    but we in the name of the Lord our God.

8   They have been hobbled and have fallen;
    but we have risen up and been restored.
    Lord, save your king, and listen to us on whatever day we call upon you.

Psalm 21 (20)   A prayer for the king is answered by God

To the end; a psalm of David

21:1   O Lord, the king shall rejoice in your power;
    in your salvation he shall greatly exult.

2   You have given him the desire of his soul;
    you have not deprived him of the prayer of his lips.

Interlude

3   For you have gone ahead of him with generous blessings;
    you have placed on his head a crown of precious stone.

4   He asked you for life, and you gave him
    length of days for ever and ever.

5   Great is his glory, because of your saving help;
    you will place glory and majesty upon him.

6   For you will give him blessing for ever and ever;
    you will make him rejoice with gladness in your presence.

7   For the king hopes in the Lord;
    and by the mercy of the Most High he shall not be shaken.

8   Let your hand be found by all your enemies;
    may your right hand find all those who hate you.

9   You will make them like a fiery furnace, at the time of your presence.
    The Lord will confound them with his anger;
    fire shall devour them.

10   You will destroy their fruit from the earth,
    and their seed from among humankind,

11   for they planned evils against you;
    they devised a plot which they will not be able to establish.

12   For you will turn their backs
    among your survivors you will prepare their faces.

13   O Lord, be exalted in your power;
    we shall sing and make music to your mighty deeds.

Psalm 22 (21)   Prayer to be delivered from suffering

To the end; according to 'The Deer of the Dawn', a psalm of David

22:1   My God, my God, pay attention to me; why have you abandoned me?
    The words of my transgressions are far from my salvation.

21:8 *Let your hand be found by all your enemies:* up to now the psalm has been a prayer for the king. At this point we hear God's response, an oracle delivered in the Temple.

21:12 *among your survivors:* the Hebrew has 'with your bow-string', which has one extra consonant.

22   **Heading**: *according to 'The Deer of the Dawn':* the Greek and Aramaic translations actually read something like 'the strength, or help' of the dawn, which would involve reading different vowels into the consonantal text. Probably the 'Deer of the Dawn' was the name of a well-known song, to which the words are to be sung.

This psalm was from the earliest stages important for Christians as they recounted the story of Jesus' death.

2 My God, I shall cry to you by day, and you will not hear;
   and by night, and it will not be foolishness for me.
3 But you dwell in the sanctuary;
   you are the praise of Israel.
4 Our ancestors hoped in you; and you rescued them.
5 They cried out to you, and they were saved;
   they hoped in you and they were not put to shame.
6 But I am a worm, and not a human being;
   reproached by humans, and an object of contempt for the people.
7 All those who saw me mocked me;
   they spoke with their lips and shook their heads, [saying,]
8 'He hoped in the Lord, let him save him,
   for he takes delight in him!'
9 For you are the one who brought me out of the womb,
   my hope since my mother's breasts.
10 I was cast on you since my birth;
   from my mother's womb you are my God.
11 Do not hold away from me,
   for trouble is near, and there is no one to help.
12 Many young bulls have encircled me
   fat bulls have surrounded me.
13 They have opened their mouths against me,
   like a lion that seizes [its prey] and roars.
14 Like water I am poured out,
   and all my bones are scattered;
   my heart has become like wax, melting within my belly.
15 My strength is dried up like a potsherd,
   my tongue is stuck to my throat;
   you have led me down into the dust of death,
16 for many dogs have encircled me,
   the assembly of those who do evil have surrounded me;
   they pierced my hands and my feet.
17 I counted all my bones;
   but they gazed on me, and they watched me.
18 They divided my garments among themselves;
   and over my clothing they cast lots.
19 But you, O Lord, do not delay [to come to] my assistance;
   pay attention to help me:
20 deliver my soul from the sword,
   and my only-begotten from the hand of the dog.
21 Save me from the mouth of the lion,
   and from the horns of the unicorns my lowliness.

22:2 *it will not be foolishness:* this is what the Greek says. It is possible that instead of *anoia* (foolishness) the Greek originally read *anesis* (indulgence). This might be the meaning of a difficult Hebrew word, which most modern commentators translate as 'silence' or 'rest'.

22:3 *you dwell in the sanctuary:* the Hebrew means something like 'you are the Holy One, you dwell on the praises of Israel'. Or, possibly, 'you are enthroned as the Holy One, [you are] the praise of Israel'.

22:12 *fat bulls:* the Hebrew here has 'strong ones of Bashan'.

22:16 *assembly:* the Greek says 'synagogue' here.

22:20 *only-begotten:* the Greek here offers a possible translation of the Hebrew word, one that would have readily spoken to Christians who saw the psalm as a foreshadowing of Jesus' death. That is certainly what the word means in the chilling story of the Binding of Isaac (Genesis 22:2, 12, 16). The word might also mean 'lonely' or 'deserted', but it is possible that the Greek has here preserved the most accurate translation.

22:21 *unicorns:* this, for some reason, is a standard LXX translation for a word that means 'wild oxen'.

22 I will declare your name to my brethren;
   in the midst of the assembly I shall sing praise to you.
23 You who fear the Lord, give him praise;
   all you offspring of Jacob glorify him;
   let all the offspring of Israel fear him.
24 For he has not despised nor has he been angry with the prayer of the poor;
   nor has he turned his face away from me;
   when I cried to him he heard me.
25 My praise comes from you in the great assembly;
   I shall repay my vows before those who fear him.
26 The poor shall eat and be filled,
   and those who seek him shall praise the Lord;
   their hearts shall live for ever and ever.
27 All the ends of the earth shall remember and return to the Lord;
   and all the families of the nations shall worship before you.
28 For the kingdom is the Lord's,
   and he will be master over the nations.
29 All the fat ones of the earth have eaten and worshipped;
   all those who go down into the earth shall fall before him; my soul lives for him.
30 My offspring shall serve him;
   the coming generation shall be declared to the Lord.
31 And they shall proclaim his righteousness to a people yet unborn,
   that the Lord has done it.

Psalm 23 (22) The Lord as shepherd, guide, and host

A psalm of David

23:1 The Lord shepherds me; and there shall be nothing lacking for me.
2 Into a place of green grass, there he has pitched my tent;
   on the water of repose he has fed me.
3 He has restored my soul;
   he has guided me on the paths of righteousness,
   for the sake of his name.
4 For even though I should walk in the midst of the shadow of death,
   I shall not fear evil, for you are with me;
   your stick and your rod, these have comforted me.
5 You have prepared before me a table,
   over against those who afflict me.
   You have anointed my head with oil;
   your cup is making me drunk, like the very best [wine].
6 Your mercy shall pursue me, all the days of my life;
   and my dwelling [shall be] in the house of the Lord,
   for length of days.

22:22 *I will declare your name:* in many psalms of lament there is a sudden change of mood like this. Many scholars understand that at this point an oracle from God is uttered by the priest, indicating that the prayer has been answered; in verse 2, the petitioner was complaining that God never answered prayers.

23:1 *The Lord shepherds me:* this lovely poem, many people's favourite in the canon of the psalms, is a work of great poetry in Hebrew, and in many English versions. The Greek translation, however, has not come up with a particularly lyric rendering, and this English version reflects that fact.

23:4 *your stick and your rod:* one possible interpretation is of these as instruments of corporal punishment which paradoxically express paternal affection in a culture such as this. Alternatively you may prefer to read it as a stick for support and a rod to ward off attackers.

Psalm 24 (23)   The Lord enters the sanctuary

A psalm of David, on the first day of the week

24:1   The Lord's is the earth and its fullness,
         the world and all who dwell in it.
   2   He founded it on the seas, and on the rivers he prepared it.
   3   Who will go up to the mountain of the Lord,
         and who will stand in his holy place?
   4   The one whose hands are innocent, and whose heart is pure,
         who has not taken their soul on the basis of vanity,
         and has not sworn to deceive their neighbour.
   5   Such will receive blessing from the Lord,
         and mercy from God their Saviour.
   6   This is the generation of those who seek him,
         seek the face of the God of Jacob.

Interlude

   7   'Lift up your gates, rulers, and be lifted up, eternal gates;
         the King of glory shall enter.'
   8   'Who is this King of glory?'
         'The Lord, mighty and powerful,
         the Lord, powerful in battle.
   9   Lift up your gates, rulers, and be lifted up, eternal gates;
         the King of glory shall enter.'
  10   'Who is this King of glory?'
         'The Lord of powers, he is the King of glory.'

Psalm 25 (24)   Asking God for forgiveness and help

A psalm of David

25:1   To you, O Lord, I have lifted up my soul;
   2   my God, I have trusted in you; let me not be put to shame,
         and do not let my enemies laugh me to scorn.
   3   For none of those who wait for you will ever be put to shame;
         all those who break the Law without purpose,
         let them be put to shame.
   4   O Lord, make me know your ways,
         and teach me your paths.
   5   Guide me in your truth,
         and teach me that you are God my Saviour;
         I have waited for you all the day.

---

24   **Heading**: *on the first day of the week:* this is not in the Hebrew, and presumably reflects a later usage. 'First day of the week' refers to Sunday, not the Sabbath.

24:3   *Who will go up to the mountain of the Lord:* the setting here seems to be a pilgrimage song, and a reminder that you have to be in a fit state to make your pilgrimage to the holy city and its Temple.

24:4   *has not taken their soul on the basis of vanity:* this is more or less what the Greek says, translating a Hebrew expression which may mean 'has not longed for vanity'. This is an example where the Greek, which has 'his soul', certainly preserves a correct text over against the Hebrew 'my soul'.

24:6   *face of the God of Jacob:* once again the LXX has preserved a correct reading. The MT has 'seek your face, O Jacob'.

24:7   *Lift up your gates, rulers:* the Hebrew here has the rather difficult 'lift up your heads, gates'; the Greek might be correct. The picture here is that of God in solemn procession coming to his Temple, and demanding entry; we must imagine a conversation between those outside, insisting on admission and those within, perhaps slightly disdainful. These verses are the key to the psalm.

24:10 *Lord of powers:* translating the Hebrew *YHWH Sabaoth*.

25:3   *none of those who wait for you will ever:* both Greek and Hebrew have 'all of those who wait for you will never . . .'

6 Remember your mercies, O Lord,
and your compassion, for they are from of old.
7 Do not remember the sins of my youth and of my ignorance;
in your mercy, remember me, for the sake of your goodness, O Lord.
8 The Lord is good and upright;
therefore he will instruct sinners in the way;
9 he will guide the meek in right judgement;
he will teach the meek his ways.
10 All the Lord's ways are mercy and truth
for those who seek his covenant and his testimonies.
11 For the sake of your name, O Lord,
pardon my sin, for it is great.
12 Who are the ones who fear the Lord?
He will instruct them on the way which they have chosen.
13 Their souls shall dwell in prosperity;
their offspring shall inherit the earth.
14 The Lord is the strength of those who fear him;
and the Lord's name [is the strength] of those who fear him;
and his covenant is to reveal to them.
15 My eyes are always on the Lord,
for he will draw my feet out of the snare.
16 Look upon me and have mercy on me,
for I am alone and poor.
17 The troubles of my heart have multiplied;
lead me out of my distress.
18 See my humiliation and my trouble;
and forgive all my sins.
19 See how my enemies have multiplied;
they have hated me with unjust hatred.
20 Guard my life and deliver me;
let me not be put to shame, for I have hoped in you.
21 The innocent and upright have joined with me,
for I waited for you, O Lord.
22 Redeem Israel, O God, from all its distress.

Psalm 26 (25)   Prayer of an innocent petitioner

Of David

26:1 Judge me, O Lord, for I have walked in my innocence;
hoping in the Lord I shall not weaken.
2 Try me, O Lord, and put me to the test,
examine my heart and mind by fire.
3 For your mercy is before my eyes,
and I delight in your truth.
4 I have not sat with the council of vanity,
and shall not go in with lawbreakers.
5 I hate the assembly of those who act wickedly;
I shall not sit with the impious.

25:8 *instruct:* literally, 'lay down the Law'. The Hebrew has 'teach', but the word is etymologically connected with Torah, or Law.

26:3 *I delight:* the MT here has a word that means 'I walk' or 'I live'.

33

6 I shall wash my hands in innocence,
  and I shall go around your altar, O Lord,
7 to hear te voice of praise, and to recount all your marvels.
8 O Lord, I love the beauty of your house
  and the place where your glory dwells.
9 Do not destroy my soul with the godless,
  nor my life with those who are bloodthirsty,
10 in whose hands are transgressions,
  their right hands are filled with bribes.
11 I have walked in my innocence;
  redeem me, and have mercy on me.
12 For my foot is set on righteousness;
  in the assemblies I shall bless you, O Lord.

Psalm 27 (26) Trusting confidently in God

Of David, before he was anointed

27:1 The Lord is my light and my saviour, whom shall I fear?
  The Lord is the protector of my life, of whom shall I be afraid?
2 When evildoers drew near to me, to eat up my flesh,
  those who afflict me, and my enemies, they stumbled and fell.
3 Even though an army were to array itself against me, my heart shall not fear.
  Even if war rise against me, even then I shall hope.
4 One thing I have asked for from the Lord, this I shall seek out:
  that I should live in the Lord's house, all the days of my life,
  to look at the delightfulness of the Lord, and to visit his Temple;
5 for he hid me in his tent on the day of my evils;
  he sheltered me in the hiding place of his tent; on a rock he set me on high.
6 And now, look: he has lifted up my head above my enemies.
  I went round and I sacrificed in his tent a sacrifice of joy;
  I shall sing and shall play the harp for the Lord.

7 O Lord, hear my voice, and the cry that I utter;
  have mercy on me, and hear me.
8 To you my heart has spoken;
  it has sought your face.
  Your face, O Lord, I shall seek.
9 Do not turn your face away from me;
  do not turn away from your servant in anger.

26:6 *I shall wash . . . around your altar:* the cleansing ritual is meant to demonstrate that the petitioner is clean. And the walk around the altar may be a way of asking for God's help; it was what the prophets of Baal did (in vain) in 1 Kings 18:26.

26:10 *bribes:* the Greek word here literally means *gifts;* the Hebrew can mean either gifts or bribes.

26:12 *set on righteousness:* the Hebrew here has 'stands on a level place'.

27 **Heading**: *Of David, before he was anointed:* 'before he was anointed' is not in the Hebrew.

27:5 *tent . . . hiding place . . . rock:* the poet here is entirely at home in the desert country of Palestine.

27:6 *sacrifice of joy:* the Greek word really means 'a loud noise'; but it is trying to translate a Hebrew word that can mean 'a scream' or 'a shout of alarm'; or, on the other hand 'a shout of jubilation', even a 'fanfare'. Faced with this richness, the Greek translator has done his best; but probably the context here demands something hinting at joy.

27:7 *O Lord, hear my voice:* normally the psalms of lament start with the petition, and the request for help from God, and then move on to express confidence in God. In this psalm, it is the other way round: verses 1-6 express confidence, and 7-14 give voice to the petition.

Be my helper; do not lay a curse upon me,
and do not abandon me, O God my Saviour.

10 Because my father and mother have forsaken me;
but the Lord has accepted me.

11 Instruct me, Lord, in your way,
and guide me on the right path, because of my enemies.

12 Do not hand me over to the desires of those who afflict me;
for unjust witnesses have risen up against me,
and injustice has told lies to herself.

13 I trust that I shall see the Lord's goodness in the land of the living.

14 Wait for the Lord; play the man,
let your heart be strong – and wait for the Lord.

Psalm 28 (27) A prayer for protection

Of David

28:1 To you, O Lord, I have cried out;
my God do not pass me over in silence,
for then I should be like those who go down into the Pit.

2 Listen to the sound of my prayer when I cry to you,
when I lift up my hands to your holy Temple.

3 Do not drag me away with sinners,
and do not destroy me with those who do evil,
those who speak peace with their neighbours,
but there is evil in their hearts.

4 Repay them according to their works,
and according to the wickedness of their practices;
repay them their recompense according to the works of their hands.

5 For they did not understand about the Lord's works,
nor about the works of his hands.
You will pull them down, and you will not build them up.

6 Blessed be the Lord, for he has heard the sound of my prayer.

7 The Lord is my help and my protector;
my heart has hoped in him, and I was helped.
My flesh revived, and I shall praise him willingly.

8 The Lord is the strength of his people,
and the saving refuge of his Messiah.

9 Save your people, and bless your inheritance,
and shepherd them and lift them up for ever.

27:12 *desires:* literally 'souls' or 'lives', but the Greek is translating a Hebrew word that can mean all these things, and also 'will' or 'desire'.

28:1 *my God:* the MT has 'my Rock', which neatly captures both God as protector and God as the place where the Temple is built.

28:3 *me:* the Greek, but not the Hebrew, has 'my soul'.

28:7 *I shall praise him willingly:* the Greek seems to have a different text in view. The MT reads 'my heart exults and with a song I shall praise him', which is a variation of just a few consonants in Hebrew.

28:8 *of his people:* this is not in the Hebrew text, but is quite likely to be the original meaning, preserved by LXX.

28:9 *people . . . inheritance . . . shepherd:* this is familiar OT language for the intimacy of the relationship between God and Israel.

Psalm 29 (28)   Hymn of praise to God

*A psalm of David at the Celebration of the Exodus and the Tabernacle
(or: At the Closing of the Festival of Tabernacles)*

29:1 Bring to the Lord, you sons of God,
    bring to the Lord young rams,
    bring to the Lord glory and power.

2 Bring to the Lord the glory of his name,
    worship the Lord in his holy court.

3 The voice of the Lord on the waters,
    the God of glory thunders,
    the Lord over many waters.

4 The voice of the Lord in power,
    the voice of the Lord in majesty.

5 The voice of the Lord who shatters cedars;
    the Lord will break the cedars of Lebanon.

6 The Lord grinds them to powder,
    Lebanon like a calf,
    and the beloved one like a young unicorn.

7 The voice of the Lord who cuts through flames of fire.

8 The voice of the Lord who shakes the desert;
    and the Lord will shake the desert of Kadesh.

9 The voice of the Lord who brings forth calves;
    and he will uncover thickets;
    in his Temple, everyone will say 'Glory!'

10 The Lord will dwell on the flood,
    and the Lord will sit as king for ever.

11 The Lord will give strength to his people;
    the Lord will bless his people with peace.

Psalm 30 (29)   A song of thanksgiving

To the end – a psalm to be sung at the dedication of the House of David.

30:1 I shall exalt you, O Lord, for you have lifted me up,
    and you have not made my enemies rejoice over me.

2 O Lord my God, I cried out to you,
    and you healed me.

3 O Lord, you led my soul up from Hades;
    you saved me from those who go down into the Pit.

4 Sing to the Lord, you his holy ones;
    sing praises to his holy name.

---

29 **Heading**: *at the Celebration of the Exodus and the Tabernacle:* this is not in the Hebrew, but may reflect the way the Exodus, or possibly the end of the feast of Tabernacles, was celebrated in Egypt.

29:1 *young rams:* literally 'sons of rams', following on 'sons of God'. This may be either an alternative translation of the Hebrew, or an attempt to avoid the theological implications of God having 'sons'.

29:2 *in his holy court:* this is what both the Greek and the Syriac read, an alternative to another word that they may have found difficult, but which Ugaritic parallels suggest mean 'revelation' or 'appearance'.

29:7 *who cuts through flames of fire:* this is the Greek translator's attempt at the Hebrew, which literally means 'who splits', which is often understood as 'flashes forth'.

29:10 *dwell . . . sit:* the translator here ingeniously translates the Hebrew word in both of its possible meanings.

30 **Heading**: *a psalm to be sung at the dedication of the House of David:* this presumably is a later heading, indicating that it was used at the service of Hanukkah after the Maccabean restoration in 165 BC. The psalm is much older than the 2nd century.

30:4 *to his holy name:* strictly speaking, the Greek reads 'to the memory of his holiness'; but the Hebrew word can signify both 'name' and 'memory'.

5 For there is anger in his rage, and life in his favour.
Weeping shall remain until evening, but joy until dawn.

6 As for me, I said in my prosperity, 'I shall never be shaken.'

7 Lord, in your pleasure you added power to my beauty;
but [then] you turned away your face and I became disturbed.

8 To you, O Lord, I shall cry out;
and to my God I shall make my entreaty.

9 What profit is there in my lifeblood,
in my going down to destruction?
Shall the dust give you praise, or proclaim your truth?

10 The Lord heard, and had mercy on me;
the Lord became my help.

11 You turned my mourning into dancing;
you tore up my sackcloth, and clothed me with gladness

12 that my glory may sing to you, and I shall not be pierced to the heart.
O Lord my God, I shall sing your praise for ever.

Psalm 31 (30) A prayer in distress

To the end; a psalm of David in terror

31:1 In you, O Lord, I have hoped – let me never be put to shame;
in your justice deliver me, and rescue me.

2 Turn your ear to me, make haste to rescue me;
be a God who protects me, and a house of refuge to save me.

3 For you are my strength and my refuge,
and for the sake of your name you will guide and support me.

4 You will lead me out of this trap which they have hidden for me;
for you are my protector.

5 Into your hands I shall entrust my spirit;
Lord God of truth, you have redeemed me.

6 You have hated those who persist with empty vanities;
but I have hoped in the Lord.

7 I shall rejoice and be glad in your mercy,
for you have looked upon my humiliation;
you have saved my life from its adversities.

8 You did not shut me up into the hands of the enemy;
you set my feet in a spacious place.

9 Have mercy on me, Lord, for I am afflicted;
my eye, and my soul, and my belly are troubled by anger.

10 For my life is worn out with pain,
and my years with groaning;
my strength has grown weak in destitution,
and my bones are troubled.

30:7 *you added power to my beauty:* this is what the Greek says. The Hebrew here is unintelligible and probably corrupt.

31 **Heading**: *in terror:* the Greek has a comment, not in the Hebrew, which literally means 'of ecstasy' (=standing outside oneself), which can refer to almost any strong emotion: dismay, astonishment, or terror. The last of these

seems best here, as it is the translation offered in verse 22 of a word that probably means 'alarm'.

31:6 *persist with empty vanities:* this is a possible translation of the Hebrew, but does not perhaps make it sufficiently clear that it is speaking of the worship of idols.

11 I have become a reproach among all my enemies,
and especially to my neighbours,
a source of dread to those who know me;
those who saw me outside fled from me.

12 I have been forgotten, out of mind like the dead;
I have become like a broken vessel.

13 For I heard the censure of many who dwelt around me,
as they gathered together against me;
they plotted to take my life.

14 But I have hoped in you, O Lord,
I said, 'You are my God.'

15 My times are in your hands;
deliver me from the hand of my enemies,
and from those who persecute me.

16 Let your face shine on your servant,
save me in your mercy.

17 O Lord, let me not be put to shame, for I have called upon you;
let the ungodly be put to shame,
and let them be brought down to Hades.

18 Let lying lips become dumb,
lips that speak iniquity, arrogant and scornful against the righteous.

19 How great is the abundance of your goodness, O Lord,
which you have stored up for those who fear you;
you have brought it to completion for those who hope in you,
in the sight of everybody.

20 You will conceal them in the secret place of your presence
from the troubles that humans inflict;
you will shelter them in your tent
from argumentative tongues.

21 Blessed be the Lord, for he has done wonderful works of mercy
in a city under siege.

22 But I said in my terror,
'I am cast out from the sight of your eyes;
therefore you listened to the sound of my prayer,
when I called upon you.'

23 Love the Lord, all you his holy ones,
for the Lord seeks for truth,
and repays those who overdo their arrogance.

24 Be courageous, and let your heart be strong,
all you who hope in the Lord.

Psalm 32 (31)　The second 'Penitential Psalm'

Of David – [a song] of instruction

32:1 Happy are those whose transgressions are forgiven,
and whose sins are covered over.

2 Happy is the one whose sins the Lord does not reckon up,
in whose mouth there is no guile.

31:21 *a city under siege:* the translator is doing his best. The Hebrew reads something like 'in the fortified city', which does not make sense. A possible emendation of the Hebrew would yield 'in times of oppression'.

32 **Heading:** *[a song] of instruction:* this is a standard LXX translation of the Hebrew word *maskil*, which probably means a song that is 'didactic', or 'artistically devised'. This is also the second 'penitential psalm'.

³ Because I kept silent, my bones grew old,
from my crying out all day long;
⁴ for day and night your hand was heavy upon me;
I turned to wretchedness while a thorn was fastened [in me].

Interlude

⁵ I made my sin known, and I did not conceal my transgression;
I said, 'I shall confess to the Lord my iniquity, against myself.'
And you forgave the impiety of my sin.

Interlude

⁶ Because of this, all your holy ones shall pray to you at an appropriate time;
but in the flood of many waters they shall not approach them.
⁷ You are my refuge from the trouble that surrounds me,
my joy, to redeem me from those who encircle me.

Interlude

⁸ I shall instruct you, and I shall guide you on this way where you are to go;
I shall fix my eyes upon you.
⁹ Do not be like horses or mules, who have no understanding;
with bit and muzzle hold their jaws tight,
those who do not come near to you.
¹⁰ Many are the scourges of the sinner;
but mercy surrounds those who hope in the Lord.
¹¹ Rejoice in the Lord, and exult, O you just;
and let them boast, all the upright in heart.

Psalm 33 (32)   A hymn of praise

Of David

33:¹ Rejoice in the Lord, you just;
praise befits the upright.
² Sing praise to the Lord on the harp,
on the ten-stringed lyre sing him songs.
³ Sing him a new song, play skilfully with a loud noise.
⁴ For the word of the Lord is upright,
and all his works are [done] in faithfulness.
⁵ The Lord loves mercy and judgement;
the mercy of the Lord fills the earth.
⁶ By the word of the Lord the heavens were established,
and by the breath of his mouth their entire host.
⁷ He gathers the waters of the sea like a bag,
who places the depths in his treasure chests.

32:4 *your hand was heavy upon me:* the metaphor here is from scourging or corporal punishment.

wretchedness while a thorn was fastened: so the Greek, which is probably to be preferred to the Hebrew. Thorns were often used for scourging in the ancient world, and this continues the metaphor. The Hebrew means something like 'my juice was overturned in a summer drought'.

32:6 *at an appropriate time:* the LXX here does its best with the Hebrew, which (possibly through a copyist's error) reads something like 'a time when he may be found'.

they shall not approach: 'they' is, presumably, the waters of the flood.

32:8 *I shall fix my eyes upon you:* so LXX. MT has 'counsel you', and it may be that the Greek has preserved the correct reading here.

32:9 *those who do not come near to you:* presumably the idea is 'so that they should be tamed and made to come near to you'.

33:7 *like a bag:* representing a Hebrew reading that is different by just one letter from the MT 'like a dam'.

8 Let all the earth fear the Lord;
   and let all who inhabit the world be shaken because of him.
9 For he spoke, and they came to be;
   he commanded, and they were created.
10 The Lord scatters the counsels of the nations;
   he brings to nothing the thoughts of the peoples,
   brings to nothing the counsels of rulers.
11 The Lord's counsel endures for ever,
   the thoughts of his heart from generation to generation.
12 Happy is the nation whose God is the Lord,
   the people whom he has chosen as his own inheritance.
13 The Lord observes from heaven;
   he sees all humankind.
14 From his prepared dwelling place
   he looks down on all those who dwell on the earth.
15 The one who fashioned their hearts alone,
   the one who understands all their works.
16 A king is not saved by a mighty army,
   and a giant shall not be saved from the abundance of his strength.
17 A horse is useless for safety,
   nor will it save by its great power.
18 Look! The eyes of the Lord are on those who fear him,
   those who hope in his mercy,
19 to deliver their lives from death,
   and to sustain them in [time of] famine.
20 Our soul waits for the Lord,
   for he is our help and our shield.
21 For in him our heart shall rejoice;
   and we have hoped in his holy name.
22 Let your mercy be upon us, O Lord,
   as we have hoped in you.

Psalm 34 (33) A (Wisdom) song of thanksgiving

Of David, when he changed his appearance before Abimelech, and he set him free, and he went off.

34:1 I shall bless the Lord at all times;
     his praise shall always be on my lips.
2   In the Lord my soul shall be praised;
     let the humble hear and be glad.

33:16 *giant:* this is a slightly unusual translation of a Hebrew word that can mean 'giant', but is more often better rendered as 'warrior' or 'hero' or even 'strong man'.

33:17 *useless:* literally, 'lying' or 'false'.

save by its great power: the Israelites were enormously impressed when they first came up against the military advantages of the cavalry and chariots, as the Romans were later to be impressed by the damage that elephants could wreak.

save: the Greek here reads 'shall be saved', which is a possible translation of the Hebrew, but the sense here seems to demand the active rather than the passive voice.

34 **Heading**: *Abimelech:* this is slightly mysterious, in that in the story related in 1 Samuel 21:11-15, when David pretended to be insane and therefore no threat, the king was Achish, not Abimelech. Oddly enough, the preceding passage (1 Samuel 21:1-5) is also cited with a wrong name, Abiathar instead of Ahimelech, in Mark 2:26.

This psalm is what is known as an 'acrostic' psalm, each verse in Hebrew starting with a different letter of the alphabet. The Greek has made no attempt to follow this, and neither shall we.

34:2 *shall be praised:* 'shall praise' would perhaps make more sense; the passive may be our translator's attempt to capture the grammatical mood of the Hebrew verb.

3 Magnify the Lord with me;
let us exalt his name for ever.
4 I sought the Lord, and he heard me,
and from all my sojourning he delivered me.
5 Approach him and be enlightened;
and your faces will not be ashamed.
6 The poor cried out, and were heard by the Lord,
and saved from all their troubles.
7 The angel of the Lord will encamp around those who fear him;
and he will deliver them.
8 Taste and see that the Lord is good,
blessed are those who hope in him.
9 Fear the Lord, all you his saints;
for those who fear him lack nothing.
10 The wealthy have become poor and gone hungry;
but those who seek the Lord will not lack for any good thing.

Interlude

11 Come here, children, and listen to me;
I shall teach you the fear of the Lord.
12 Who is the one who desires life,
who loves to see good days?
13 Keep your tongue from evil,
and your lips from speaking deceit.
14 Turn away from evil and do good;
seek for peace and pursue it.
15 The eyes of the Lord are on the just,
and his ears [turned] to their prayer.
16 The face of the Lord is on those who do evil,
to destroy their memory from the earth.
17 The righteous cried out, and the Lord heard them,
and from all their troubles he delivered them.
18 The Lord is near to the broken-hearted;
and he will save those who are humble in spirit.
19 Many are the afflictions of the righteous;
But from them all he will deliver them.
20 The Lord will guard all their bones;
not one of them shall be broken.
21 The death of sinners is evil,
and those who hate the righteous shall commit sin.
22 The Lord will redeem the lives of his servants;
none of those who hope in him shall commit sin.

34:8 *good:* in the Greek of the New Testament, this word would have sounded like the word for 'Messiah' or 'Christ', so a Christian reader would have heard 'that the Lord is Christ'.

34:10 *wealthy:* the Hebrew here has 'young lions', which does not make much sense, and is only a consonant away from one of two other words that the Greek translator may have had in mind. This is another place where LXX may have preserved the original meaning.

34:11 *Come here, children:* at this point, the psalm starts to sound like a Wisdom poem.

34:20 *not one of them shall be broken:* this is quoted, of course, in the Fourth Gospel's account of the death of Jesus, John 19:36.

Psalm 35 (34)   A prayer for protection against liars

Of David

35:1 Lord, pass judgement on those who wrong me,
    make war on those who make war on me.
2 Take up your buckler and shield,
    and arise to help me.
3 Bring forth a sword, and close in against those who persecute me.
    Say to my soul, 'I am your salvation.'
4 Let all those who seek my life be put to shame and embarrassed;
    let them be turned back, all those who plan evil against me.
5 Let them be as dust before the wind,
    and an angel of the Lord afflicting them.
6 Let their way be dark and slippery,
    and an angel of the Lord pursuing them.
7 For no reason they have hidden a snare's destruction,
    without cause they reviled my soul.
8 Let a snare that they know not come upon them;
    and let the trap which they concealed take hold of them,
    and let them fall into that very snare.
9 But my soul shall exult in the Lord,
    and delight in his salvation.
10 All my bones shall say, 'O Lord, who is like you?'
    You deliver the poor from the hands of those who are stronger than them,
    the poor and destitute from those who plunder them.
11 Unjust witnesses arose;
    they asked me things that I knew not.
12 They repaid me evil for good,
    and bereavement for my soul.
13 But I, when they troubled me, put on sackcloth,
    and I humbled my soul with fasting,
    and my prayer shall return to my bosom.
14 Like our neighbour or our brother, so I tried to please them,
    as one mourning and looking sullen, so I humbled myself.
15 But they rejoiced against me;
    and they gathered – they gathered, those scourges, against me;
    and I did not know it.
    They were scattered, but were not pierced to the heart.
16 They tempted me, they looked down their noses at me;
    they gnashed their teeth at me.
17 Lord – when will you look on?
    Restore my life from their wickedness,
    my only-begotten one from the lions.

35:3 *Bring forth:* the Greek here means 'pour out', an attempt presumably at the Hebrew, which means 'make empty'.

close in against: this, or *'lock up against'*, is the reading of both the Greek and the Hebrew, but some scholars suggest that the Hebrew word, with different vowels can be read as 'a battleaxe', which would make more sense here.

35:5 *before the wind:* more accurately, *'before the face of the wind'*.

35:16 *looked down their noses:* a more literal translation would be 'they disdained me disdainfully'.

35:17 *my only-begotten one:* this is a standard (and not wholly inaccurate) translation of a Hebrew word that also means 'unique' or 'lonely'. Christian readers will have thought of Psalm 22:13, 22, and its links with Jesus' crucifixion. And the reference to the 'lions' will have been of some interest to those Christians threatened with being thrown by Roman authorities to precisely those ravenous beasts. Also in the background, of course, is the story of the lions' den in Daniel 6:16-24.

18 I shall give you thanks, Lord, in a great assembly;
   among a mighty people I shall praise you.
19 Let not those who are unjustly hostile to me rejoice over me,
   those who hate me for no reason, and those who wink with their eyes.
20 For they spoke peace to me,
   and they devised trickery in their anger.
21 And they opened wide their mouths at me.
   They said, 'Bravo, bravo – our eyes have seen it.'
22 O Lord – you have seen; do not stay silent.
   Do not depart from me.
23 Awake, O Lord, and attend to my judgement, my God;
   and, O my Lord, to my just cause.
24 Judge me, O Lord my God, in accordance with your righteousness;
   and let them not rejoice over me.
25 Let them not say in their hearts, 'Bravo, bravo, our soul!';
   let them not say, 'We have swallowed him up.'
26 Let them be ashamed and embarrassed all together,
   those who rejoice at my misfortunes.
   Let them be clothed with shame and embarrassment,
   those who speak boastingly against me.
27 Let them rejoice and be glad, those who desire my righteousness;
   and let them say always, 'May the Lord be magnified,'
   those who desire peace for his servant.
28 And my tongue shall meditate on your justice,
   and all day long on your praise.

Psalm 36 (35)   Human wickedness and God's generosity

To the end. Of David, the Lord's servant.

36:1 The transgressor speaks to himself, in order to sin;
   there is no fear of God before his eyes.
2 For he has acted deceitfully before him,
   to find his iniquity and to hate it.
3 The words of his mouth are iniquity and deceit;
   he did not desire to understand how to do good.
4 He planned iniquity on his bed;
   he presents himself to every way that is not good;
   he is not offended by evil.
5 O Lord, your mercy is in heaven;
   and your truth reaches to the clouds.
6 Your righteousness is as God's mountains;
   your judgements like a great abyss;
   you will save humans and beasts alike, O Lord.
7 How you have multiplied your mercy, O God;
   the children of Adam will hope in the shelter of your wings.
8 They shall be intoxicated with the fatness of your house,
   and you will make them drink of the stream of your delights.

36:1 *there is no fear of God before his eyes:* these words are quoted at Romans 3:18, at the end of a long chain of Old Testament quotations which are intended to show how much God has done in Jesus for the human race.

36:2 *find his iniquity and to hate:* our translator is doing his very best with an extremely difficult, and perhaps corrupt, Hebrew text.

9 For with you is a fountain of life;
   in your light we shall see light.
10 Stretch out your mercy to those who know you,
   and your justice to the upright of heart.
11 Let not the foot of the arrogant come to me;
   nor the hand of sinners shake me.
12 There they fell, those who work iniquity;
   they were thrust out, and they will not be able to stand.

Psalm 37 (36) The Lord gives his reward

Of David

37:1 Do not fret over those who do evil,
   and do not be jealous of those who break the Law.
2 For like grass they shall quickly wither away,
   and like green plants they shall quickly fall away.
3 Hope in the Lord, and do good;
   dwell in the land and you will be looked after with its wealth.
4 Delight in the Lord,
   and he will give you the demands of your heart.
5 Reveal your way to the Lord;
   trust in him and he will act.
6 And he shall bring out your righteousness like the light,
   and your judgement like the midday [sun].
7 Be subject to the Lord, and entreat him;
   do not fret at the one who travels prosperously in their way,
   and the one who commits transgressions.
8 Cease from anger, and leave wrath aside;
   do not fret, so as to do evil.
9 For those who do evil shall be destroyed, and those who wait for the Lord,
   they shall inherit the land.
10 Just a little while, and the sinner shall not exist;
   you will seek his place, and you will not find it.
11 But the gentle shall inherit the earth,
   and they shall delight in the abundance of peace.
12 Sinners will watch out for the righteous,
   and will gnash their teeth at them.
13 But the Lord shall laugh at them;
   he foresees that their day will come.
14 Sinners have drawn their swords;
   they have bent their bow to cut down the poor and the needy,
   to slaughter the upright of heart.

36:9 *a fountain of life:* this idea is already in Jeremiah 2:13, and will reappear in John 4:14.

37:2 *like grass they shall quickly wither:* the idea of grass as an icon of perishability reappears at Psalm 92:7; 129:6.

37:3 *looked after with its wealth:* this is an admittedly slightly clunking translation of the Greek, which carries a hint of what shepherds do.

37:5 *Reveal:* this is what the Greek has. The Hebrew has a word that means to 'roll', although the English versions tend to opt for 'commit'.

37:9 *inherit the land:* or 'earth'. Originally this will have referred to the Holy Land; but for Christian readers the idea is picked up in the Beatitudes from the Sermon on the Mount (Matthew 5:5). For the full quotation, see verse 11 below.

37:12 *watch out for:* the Greek word can carry the meaning of a careful and malicious observation. The same Greek word is used of Jesus' opponents at Mark 3:2; Luke 14:1, 20:20.

15 Let their swords enter their own heart,
and let their bows be broken.
16 The little that the righteous person has
is better than the great wealth of sinners.
17 For the arms of sinners shall be broken;
but the Lord supports the righteous.
18 The Lord knows the ways of the blameless,
and their inheritance shall be for ever.
19 They shall not be put to shame in evil times;
and in days of famine they shall be sated.
20 For sinners shall be destroyed;
and, at the very moment when they are glorified and raised up,
the Lord's enemies are coming to an end;
like smoke they come to an end.
21 The sinner borrows, and will not repay;
but the just takes pity and gives.
22 For those who bless [the Lord] shall inherit the earth;
but those who curse [the Lord] shall be destroyed.
23 A person's steps are guided by the Lord;
the Lord will take pleasure in their journey.
24 When they fall they shall not be broken,
for the Lord supports their hand.
25 I was younger, and now I have grown old;
yet never have I seen the righteous abandoned,
nor their offspring looking for bread.
26 All day long they act mercifully and lend,
and their offspring will be a blessing.
27 Turn away from evil and do good,
and pitch your tent for ever.
28 For the Lord loves justice, and will not abandon his holy ones;
they shall be guarded for ever.
But the lawless shall be under attack,
and the offspring of the ungodly shall be destroyed.
29 But the righteous shall inherit the land,
and they shall pitch their tent upon it for ever and ever.
30 The mouth of the righteous shall utter wisdom,
and their tongue shall speak judgement.
31 The Law of their God is in their hearts;
and their steps shall not be tripped up.
32 The sinner observes the righteous,
and seeks to put them to death.
33 But the Lord will not abandon them into their hands;
nor will he condemn them when they are brought to trial.
34 Wait for the Lord, and keep to his way;
and he will lift you up to inherit the land;
when sinners are destroyed, you will see it.

37:16 *better than the great wealth of sinners:* this idea is a characteristic Wisdom notion. See, for example, Proverbs 16:8.

37:19 *sated:* this word is also used in Matthew's Beatitudes (Matthew 5:6).

37:20 *glorified and raised up:* these two words are both used in John's Gospel as a way of understanding Jesus' death – see, e.g., John 7:39; 17:1 ('glorified'); 3:14; 8:28; 12:32 ('raised up').

35 I saw the ungodly lifting themselves up on high,
raising themselves up like the cedars of Lebanon.

36 And I passed by, and look! They were no more;
I sought them, but their place could not be found.

37 Guard [your] innocence, and look to uprightness,
for the lover of peace will have a remnant.

38 But transgressors shall be destroyed all together;
the remnants of the godless shall be destroyed.

39 The salvation of the righteous comes from the Lord;
he is their protector in the time of trouble.

40 The Lord will help them and rescue them,
and will deliver them from sinners;
he will save them, for they have hoped in him.

Psalm 38 (37)   The third 'Penitential Psalm'

A psalm of David, for remembrance.
Concerning the Sabbath Day.

38:1 Lord, do not rebuke me in your anger;
do not discipline me in your wrath.

2 For your arrows are fixed in me;
and you have laid your hand upon me.

3 My flesh has no healing, in the face of your anger;
my bones have no peace, in the face of my sins.

4 For my iniquities have gone over my head;
like a heavy burden, they have weighed down upon me.

5 My bruises are stinking and rotten,
in the face of my folly.

6 I am wretched and bowed down to the end;
all the day I went around with a sullen expression.

7 For my loins are full of mockery,
and there is no healing in my flesh.

8 I was afflicted and utterly brought low;
I howled with the groaning of my heart.

9 O Lord, all my yearning is before you;
and my groaning was not hidden from you.

10 My heart is disturbed;
my strength has failed me, and the light of my eyes,
that too is no longer with me.

11 My friends and my neighbours drew near, facing me,
and my nearest of kin stood afar off.

12 They pressed upon me, those who sought my life;
and those who sought evil for me spoke empty words,
and practised deceits all the day long.

---

38   **Heading**: *for remembrance. Concerning the Sabbath Day:* 'For remembrance' is what the Greek says, and is an obvious translation of the Hebrew, though some scholars, basing themselves on the Aramaic translations, relate it to the frankincense offering. 'Concerning the Sabbath Day' is not in the Hebrew.

38:7   *my loins:* some Greek manuscripts have *psyche* (soul), but probably we should read, in accordance with the Hebrew and with the better Greek manuscripts, *psyai* (loins).

38:10   *that too:* a bit cumbersome in English, but it is what the Greek says, closely following the Hebrew.

38:11   *facing me . . . afar off:* the two Greek phrases represented here appear in similar proximity to each other in Mark's account of the Passion of Jesus: the first refers to the centurion who declared Jesus 'Son of God' (15:39), and the second to the brave women who witnessed Jesus' death (15:40).

13 But I was like a deaf person – I heard nothing;
and like a dumb man, not opening his mouth.

14 I was like one who does not hear,
one who has no reproofs in their mouth.

15 For in you, O Lord, I have hoped;
you will hear me, Lord my God.

16 For I said, 'May my enemies not rejoice over me';
and when my feet were shaken, they spoke boastfully against me.

17 For I am ready for scourges,
and my grief is before me all the time.

18 For I shall declare my iniquity,
and I shall be anxious about my sin.

19 But my enemies are alive, and they have prevailed against me;
those who hate me unjustly have multiplied.

20 Those who pay back evil for good accused me falsely;
because I pursued righteousness they abandoned me, the beloved,
like an abominated corpse.

21 Do not abandon me, Lord my God,
do not stay away from me.

22 Pay attention to me and help me,
Lord of my salvation.

Psalm 39 (38) A lament in the face of death?

To the end. For Jeduthun. A song of David.

39:1 I said, 'I shall guard my ways, so as not to sin with my tongue';
I set a guard on my mouth, while the sinner stood before me.

2 I was dumb and I humbled myself,
I was silent, [not speaking] good [words],
and my pain was rekindled.

3 My heart grew hot within me,
and in my meditation a fire would flare up;
I spoke with my tongue:

4 O Lord, make me know my end,
and the number of my days, what it is,
that I may know what I lack.

5 Look – you have made my days just a hand's breadth,
and my existence is as nothing before you;
but everything, including every living person,
is vanity.

Interlude

6 Nevertheless, human beings go their way like a shadow;
they are disturbed for no reason at all;
they lay up treasures, and do not know for whom they will gather them.

38:20 *the beloved, like an abominated corpse:* these words are not in all mss. of the Greek, nor in the Hebrew, but they are in some LXX mss, and should not be excluded.

39 **Heading:** *Jeduthun:* according to 1 Chronicles 16:41-42; 25:1-6; 2 Chronicles 5:12, one of David's musicians.

39:4-6 *my days just a hand's breadth:* this sense of the pointless brevity of human existence is not uncommon in the later Wisdom literature. See, for example, Psalm 90:12; Job 14:1; Ecclesiastes 6:12.

39:6 *like a shadow:* the Greek has 'in a statue/portrait/likeness', a very literal translation. The Hebrew word can mean that, but in this case it probably comes from a completely different word (but with the same consonants), which means 'shadow' or 'gloom'; that has to be the meaning here.

7 And now, what is my expectation?
Is it not the Lord?
And my existence comes from you.

8 From all my transgressions deliver me;
you have given me as a reproach to the foolish.

9 I was dumb, and I opened not my mouth;
because you are the one who made me.

10 Keep all your scourges away from me,
because of the might of your hand, I am finished.

11 You chastise us with reproofs for our iniquity;
you make our lives melt away like a spider's web,
but all of us are disturbed in vain.

Interlude

12 Listen to my prayer, O Lord, and turn your ears to my pleading;
do not be silent in response to my tears,
because I am a sojourner at your side,
and an alien, like all my ancestors.

13 Let me go, that I may recover,
before I depart and am no more.

Psalm 40 (39)   A thanksgiving and a prayer for help

To the end. A psalm of David.

40:1 I waited, I waited for the Lord, and he paid attention to me,
and he heard my pleading.

2 And he led me up out of the pit of wretchedness,
and from the muddy clay;
he set my feet upon a rock, and guided my feet,
and directed my steps.

3 And he put into my mouth a new song,
a hymn to our God;
many shall see, and shall fear,
and shall hope in the Lord.

4 Happy are those whose hope is the name of the Lord,
who have not looked upon vanities and lying frenzies.

5 O Lord, you have multiplied your wonderful deeds;
and there is no one who is like you in your thoughts.
I have proclaimed and have spoken;
your wonders are multiplied beyond number.

6 Sacrifice and offering you did not desire;
instead you prepared ears for me;
you did not demand holocaust and sin offering.

7 Then I said, 'Behold I have come –
in the scroll of the book it has been written about me.

8 I desired to do your will, O my God,
and your Law deep in my heart.'

39:7 *what is my expectation:* this is the meaning of the Hebrew ('what am I waiting for?'). The Greek uses a word that can mean 'expectation', but would normally be translated as 'endurance' or 'patience'.

40:6-8 *Sacrifice and offering . . . deep in my heart:* these verses in the LXX version are applied to Jesus at Hebrews 10:5-8, except that the rather difficult 'you prepared ears for me' has become 'you prepared a body for me', and is read as a reference to the incarnation.

9 I preached the good news of righteousness in the great assembly;
behold – I shall not prevent my lips [from speaking];
you know it, O Lord.

10 I have not concealed your righteousness in my heart;
I have spoken your truth and your salvation.
I did not hide your mercy and your truth from the great congregation.

11 But you, O Lord, do not remove your compassion far from me,
your mercy and your truth helped me at all times.

12 For evils beyond number have surrounded me;
my iniquities have overtaken me, and I was unable to see;
they are more than the hairs of my head,
and my heart has failed me.

13 Be pleased, O Lord, to deliver me;
give heed to help me.

14 May they be put to shame and embarrassed together,
those who seek my life to destroy it;
may they be turned backwards and put to shame, those who desire evil for me.

15 Let those who say 'Bravo, bravo,' to me,
immediately carry off shame as their prize.

16 Let all those who seek you, Lord, rejoice and exult in you;
let those who love your salvation always say,
'May the Lord be magnified.'

17 But I am poor and destitute; the Lord will take thought for me;
you my help and my protector, O my God –
do not delay.

Psalm 41 (40) A thanksgiving in time of sickness

To the end. A psalm of David

41:1 Happy are those who take notice of the poor and needy;
the Lord shall deliver them on the day of evil.

2 May the Lord guard them closely and give them life,
may the Lord bless them in the land,
and not hand them over to the hands of their enemy.

3 May the Lord help them on their bed of pain;
you have transformed their whole bed in their time of sickness.

4 I said, 'Lord, have mercy on me;
heal my soul, for I have sinned against you.'

5 My enemies have spoken evil against me:
'When will he die, and his name be destroyed?'

6 And if they came to see me, their heart spoke emptily;
they gathered iniquity to themselves;
they went out and talked.

7 All my enemies whispered together against me,
they devised evil against me.

40:13 *Be pleased, O Lord, to deliver me:* the rest of this psalm also appears as Psalm 70, but with a different name for God.

41:3 *transformed their whole bed:* this is the reading of both the Greek and the Hebrew, but scholars are far from agreed what it might mean. Probably the general idea is that God looks after the sick person, and makes them better, rather than (as a good nurse might) making their bed more comfortable.

41:4 *Lord, have mercy:* the Greek here and in verse 10 is precisely *Kyrie eleison.*

8   They put down an unlawful word against me,
'Now that he is lying [in bed], will he ever rise up again?'

9   For even the man of my peace, the one in whom I had hoped,
the one who had eaten my bread,
stabbed me in the back.

10   But you, O Lord, have mercy on me,
raise me up and I shall repay them.

11   By this I know that you were pleased with me,
that my enemy shall not rejoice over me.

12   But because of my innocence you helped me
and established me in your presence for ever.

13   Blessed be the Lord God of Israel for ever and ever.
May it be so, may it be so.

BOOK TWO (Psalms 42–72)

Psalm 42–43 (41–42) Longing for God – an exile's lament

To the end; [a song of] instruction, for the sons of Korah

42:1   Just as the deer longs for springs of water,
so my soul longs for you, O God.

2   My soul thirsts for God, the living God;
when shall I come and appear before the face of God?

3   My tears have become bread for me, day and night,
as it was said to me, each day, 'Where is your God?'

4   I remembered these things, and I poured out my soul within myself;
for I shall pass through in[to] the place of your wonderful tent,
to the house of God,
with a sound of rejoicing and thanksgiving,
the noise of those who keep the feast.

5   Why are you so very sad, my soul?
Why are you troubling me?
Hope in God, for I shall praise him,
my God, my salvation.

41:9 *the man of my peace:* this is the reading of both Hebrew and Greek. Scholars generally understand it as referring to an intimate friend, an ally in the covenant. It seems appropriate here to use the exclusively masculine language.

stabbed me in the back: this is the suggested understanding of a Hebrew and Greek expression which literally means something like 'lifted up the heel against me'.

the one who had eaten my bread, stabbed me in the back: John 13:18 has a different Greek translation of this same text.

41:13 *Blessed be the Lord God of Israel:* this doxology has nothing to do with the rest of this psalm. If you look at 72:18-20; 89:52; 106:48, and the whole of Psalm 150, you will find that in each case they bring to an end a 'book' of the psalms. So they were written as 'markers' at the time when the psalms were edited as a collection.

May it be so, may it be so: this is what the Greek says, correctly translating the Hebrew 'Amen and amen'.

42–43 These two psalms are undoubtedly a single poem, a lament in three parts. LXX inserts a heading between the two, which presumably means that the division had taken place by the time it was translated into Greek.

Heading: *sons of Korah:* we shall meet these again, in the headings of Pss. 44-49, 84, 85, 87, 88. According to 1 Chronicles (9:19; 26:1, 19) they are doorkeepers; but in 2 Chronicles 20:19 they are singers. At Exodus 6:21; Numbers 26:58 and 1 Chronicles 6:7 and 22 they are counted as Levites. The general drift is clear enough.

42:2 *appear:* this is the reading of both LXX and MT. The common translation 'when I shall I see the face of God' may indeed be the original version, which lost out because of the view that human beings cannot see God's face (see Exodus 33:20).

42:4 *your wonderful tent:* here LXX has understood the text better than MT.

42:5 *my salvation:* literally, in both Hebrew and Greek, 'the salvation of my face'.

6 My soul was troubled within me,
   therefore I shall remember you
   from the land of Jordan and Hermon,
   from the little mountain.
7 Deep calls upon deep, at the sound of your waterfalls;
   all your billows and your waves have gone over me.
8 By day the Lord will give commands to his mercy,
   and by night a song comes from me,
   a prayer to the God of my life.
9 I shall say to God, 'You are my helper – why have you forgotten me?
   Why do I go around with a sullen countenance,
   while my enemy oppresses me?'
10 While my oppressors crushed my bones,
   they reviled me, and said each day,
   'Where is your God?'
11 Why are you so very sad, my soul?
   And why are you troubling me?
   Hope in God, for I shall sing God's praises,
   the one who saves me, my God.

A psalm of David

43:1 Judge me, O God, and defend my case against a people that is not holy;
     deliver me from those who are unjust and deceitful.
2 For you, O God, are my strength;
   why have you repudiated me?
   Why do I go around with a sullen countenance,
   while my enemy oppresses me?
3 Send out your light and your truth;
   it is they who have guided me;
   they have led me to your holy mountain and to your tents.
4 And I shall come to the altar of God,
   to the God who gives joy to my youth.
   I shall sing praises to you with a harp, O God, my God.
5 Why are you so very sad, my soul?
   And why are you troubling me?
   Hope in God, for I shall sing God's praises,
   the one who saves me, my God.

42:6 *land of Jordan and Hermon:* presumably this is where we are meant to understand the lament as having been composed. The Hermon range (since the noun is in the plural in both Hebrew and Greek) is where the Jordan starts its journey down to the Sea of Galilee and the Dead Sea; so our poet is living up in the far north of the Holy Land.

the little mountain: so the Greek, and this is also the meaning of the Hebrew, which is however often transcribed as 'Mizar'.

42:11 *the one who saves me:* literally 'the salvation of my face', in both Hebrew and Greek. See also 43:5.

43:1 *defend my case:* the Greek here imitates the Hebrew and means something like 'justify my justification', a very strong way of expressing the poet's desire.

43:4 *my youth:* this is a possible, and perhaps an accurate, translation of a Hebrew word that could also mean 'my exultation'. An unexpected problem in translating this psalm is that Catholics above a certain age know it by heart in Latin (*ad Deum qui laetificat iuventutem meam*), and it is quite difficult to unthink that ancient memory, since the Latin followed the Greek quite closely.

Psalm 44 (43)   A national lament

To the end, for the sons of Korah. A psalm of instruction

44:1   O God, we heard with our ears,
  our ancestors told us of the works that you did in their days,
  in the days of old.

2   Your hand destroyed the nations;
  but you planted them;
  you dealt harshly with the peoples,
  and you expelled them.

3   For it was not by their sword that they came to inherit the land;
  nor was it their arm that saved them;
  it was your right hand, and your arm,
  and the radiance of your face,
  for you were pleased with them.

4   It is you who are my king and my God,
  you who command Jacob's deliverance.

5   Through you, we shall gore our enemies;
  and through your name, we shall scorn those who rise up against us.

6   For it is not in my bow that I shall trust,
  nor will my sword save me.

7   You saved us from those who oppressed us,
  and you put to shame those who hated us.

8   In God we shall make our boast, all day long;
  and in your name we shall give praise for ever.

Interlude

9   But now you have rejected us and put us to shame;
  and you will not go forth with our armies.

10   You turned us backwards in the face of our enemies,
  and those who hate us have plundered us at will.

11   You gave us as sheep to be eaten,
  and you have scattered us among the nations.

12   You sold your people for nothing,
  and there was no profit from their sale.

13   You made us a reproach to our neighbours,
  objects of scorn and derision for those about us.

14   You made us a byword among the nations,
  a reason for the peoples to shake their heads.

15   All day long, my shame is before me,
  and embarrassment has covered my face,

16   at the sound of those who reviled me and prattled,
  at the sight of the enemy who persecutes me.

44:2   *but you planted them:* this has to refer to the Israelites, of course, not to the Gentiles.

you expelled them: this is what the Greek says, translating a Hebrew verb that means 'you sent them', but which some scholars translate as 'you set them free'.

44:5   *gore:* this rather violent metaphor is what a bull does with its horn.

44:8   *we shall make our boast:* literally, 'we shall be praised', an attempt to render a Hebrew word that has connotations of both praising and boasting.

44:9-   *now you have rejected us . . . our belly clings to the earth:*
25   notice the freedom with which God's people feel able to rebuke the Almighty. In Jeremiah and in the Deuteronomic History there is a strong sense that the destruction of Jerusalem and the exile were the inevitable consequence of disobedience to God. See, for example, Jeremiah 5:7-9, 19; 16:10-13, and Judges 2:11-21.

44:10   *at will:* literally, 'for themselves', in both Greek and Hebrew.

52

17 All these things came upon us, and we had not forgotten you,
   nor did we sin against your covenant.
18 Our heart never turned back,
   and yet you turned our paths from your way.
19 For you have humbled us in a place of affliction,
   and the shadow of death has covered us over.
20 If we had forgotten the name of our God,
   and if we had spread out our hands to a foreign god,
21 would not God find this out?
   For God knows the secrets of the heart.
22 Because for your sake we are put to death all day long;
   we are reckoned as sheep for the slaughter.
23 Arise, Lord – why are you asleep?
   Do not reject us for ever.
24 Why do you turn away your face,
   why forget our destitution and affliction?
25 For our life is brought down to the dust,
   our belly clings to the earth.
26 Arise Lord, and help us;
   redeem us for the sake of your name.

Psalm 45 (44)   A royal wedding song

To the end; of those who will be changed; for the sons of Korah; a song of instruction. A song about the beloved.

45:1 My heart overflows with a good word;
   I speak my works to the king;
   my tongue is the pen of a speedy scribe.
2 You are the most handsome of men;
   grace is poured upon your lips;
   therefore God has blessed you for ever.
3 Gird your sword upon your thigh, O Mighty One,
   in your beauty and nobility,
4 and bend your bow, and be prosperous;
   and reign as king for the sake of truth and meekness and justice;
   and your right hand will wonderfully guide you.
5 Your arrows are sharpened, O Mighty One,
   peoples shall fall beneath you,
   in the heart of the king's enemies.

44:18 *you turned our paths from your way:* this makes the complaint even stronger than in the Hebrew, which probably reads 'we did not turn away from your path'.

45 **Heading**: *of those who will be changed:* this is the Greek attempt at a Hebrew word whose meaning is still uncertain. Often translated as 'lilies' (which would be the name of a tune), it may refer to a 'six-stringed instrument'. Or it could refer to a 'love song'.

45:1 *overflows:* or possibly 'vomits forth' or 'belches forth'. The Hebrew seems to mean 'is aroused'.

45:2 *the most handsome of men:* this is unmistakably addressed to the king, so we are not here abandoning the policy of using inclusive language. His wife's turn will come.

grace is poured upon your lips: Jesus' sermon in the synagogue at Nazareth evokes a similar response ('they wondered at the words of grace that marched out of his mouth', Luke 4:22).

45:4 *bend your bow:* the Greek here has opted for an alternative reading of the Hebrew text, which is in any case probably corrupt.

45:5 *in the heart of the king's enemies:* this is the reading of both the Greek and the Hebrew, but scholars are inclined to emend the text so that it reads 'the king's enemies lose heart'.

6   Your throne, O God, is for ever and ever;
     the staff of your kingdom is a staff of uprightness.

7   You have loved justice and loathed iniquity;
     therefore God, your God, has anointed you
     with the oil of gladness beyond your companions.

8   Myrrh and oil of myrrh and cinnamon flowers
     come from your garments,
     from your ivory palaces,
     from which they delight you,

9   the daughters of kings in your honour.
     The queen stands on your right,
     in a garment woven with gold, cunningly arrayed.

10   Listen, my daughter, and see; and bend your ear,
     and forget your people and your father's house,

11   for the king has desired your beauty;
     he is your lord.

12   The daughters of Tyre shall worship him with gifts;
     the affluent of the people will entreat your presence.

13   All her glory is that of the king's daughter,
     within, she is cunningly arrayed in golden tassels.

14   Virgins shall be brought to the king after her;
     her companions shall be brought to you.

15   They shall be brought in gladness and exultation;
     they shall be led into the king's Temple.

16   Instead of your ancestors children have been born to you;
     you will set them as rulers over all the earth.

17   They shall remember your name in every generation;
     therefore peoples will sing your praises for ever and for ever.

Psalm 46 (45)   Confidence in God's protection

To the end, for the sons of Korah, a psalm about hidden things

46:1   God is our refuge and strength, a help in the troubles that find us out.

2   Therefore we shall not fear when the earth is stirred, and the mountains are shifted in the heart of the seas.

3   The waters roared and were shaken;
    the mountains were shaken by his might.

Interlude

45:6 *the staff of your kingdom is a staff of uprightness:* notice how here, and in the next verse, the king is discreetly reminded that if he is to rule successfully and prosperously he has to operate justly. Israel never believed in mindless flattery of their monarchs; they always had to be reminded what God expected of them.

45:6-7 *your throne . . . your companions:* Hebrews 1:8-9 quotes these verses, more or less in this form, as part of a long series of OT citations aimed at demonstrating Jesus' superiority as Son of God.

45:7 *God has anointed you:* the verb here in Hebrew is that which gave rise to the word 'Messiah'; and the Greek is the source of the word 'Christ', so it is not surprising that the early Christians found here a reference to Jesus.

45:10 *Listen, my daughter:* now the poet turns to address the royal bride. She may not be entirely pleased with what she hears.

45:14 *Virgins shall be brought to the king after her:* this is now a description of the marriage ceremony. The virgins are the new queen's escorts, not additional lovers for the king.

45:17 *They shall remember your name in every generation:* this is echoed, of course, in Mary's Magnificat (Luke 1:48, 50).

46 **Heading:** *a psalm about hidden things:* this is what the Greek says. The Hebrew has *alamoth*, and no one knows what that means.

⁴ The torrents of the river gladden the city of God;
the Most High has made his tent holy.

⁵ God is in her midst; she shall not be shaken;
God will help her at the break of day.

⁶ The nations were troubled, kingdoms tottered;
he uttered his voice, the earth was shaken.

⁷ The Lord of hosts is with us,
the God of Jacob is our helper.

Interlude

⁸ Come and see the works of the Lord,
the portents he has placed on the earth.

⁹ He puts an end to wars, right to the ends of the earth;
he will shatter the bow and splinter the spear;
he will burn shields with fire.

¹⁰ Stop and realise that I am God.
I shall be exalted among the nations,
I shall be exalted upon the earth.

¹¹ The Lord of hosts is with us,
the God of Jacob is our helper.

Psalm 47 (46)   The Lord as King

To the end, a psalm for the sons of Korah

47:¹ All you nations, clap your hands,
shout aloud to God with a sound of exultation.

² For the Lord Most High is to be feared,
a great King over all the earth.

³ He has subdued peoples under us, and nations under our feet.

⁴ He has chosen his inheritance for us,
the glory of Jacob whom he loved.

Interlude

⁵ God has gone up with a shout,
the Lord with the sound of a trumpet.

⁶ Sing a melody to our God,
sing a melody;
sing a melody to our King,
sing a melody.

⁷ For God is King of all the earth,
sing a wise melody.

46:4 *torrents of the river gladden the city:* there is no river in Jerusalem, of course, only the Gihon Spring and (when it is flowing) the Wadi Kedron. Scholars suggest that what we have here is the transference to Jerusalem of imagery belonging to the eschatological Garden of Eden (see Genesis 2:10). Jerusalem has become assimilated to Paradise, invincible, despite the threat of the menacing waters. Something of this sort is going on in Ezekiel's vision of the waters flowing out of the Jerusalem Temple (Ezekiel 47:1-12, taken up in Revelation 22:1-2, the waters of life flowing from the New Jerusalem. Notice how the imagery of Ezekiel and Genesis is taken up in this passage).

46:10 *Stop and realise:* this is what the translator has done with the familiar 'be still and know . . . '

47:5 *God has gone up with a shout:* for a glimpse of what this might mean, see 2 Samuel 6:15, the account of David bringing the Ark into the Temple.

47:7 *sing a wise melody:* this is what the Greek says, although it could more literally be translated 'pluck the strings in an intelligent way'. It translates two Hebrew words, the first of which means 'pluck the strings (and make music)'; the second, *maskil*, probably means 'a didactic poem', but our translator knew that there was a connection with the idea of intelligence.

8 God reigns over the nations,
God sits on his holy throne.

9 The rulers of the people have gathered with the God of Abraham;
the mighty of the earth have been greatly exalted.

Psalm 48 (47)   The splendour of the city of God

A psalm. Of a song. For the sons of Korah. On the second day of the week.

48:1 Great is the Lord, and much to be praised,
in the city of our God, on his holy mountain.

2 Well planted, to the joy of all the earth,
are the mountains of Sion, the sides of the north,
the city of the great King.

3 God is known in her palaces,
when he comes to her help.

4 For, see, the kings have gathered,
they came together.

5 When they saw, they were so astonished;
they were disturbed, they were shaken.

6 Trembling seized them, the agony as of a woman in labour.

7 With a violent wind, you will shatter the ships of Tarshish.

8 As we have heard, so we have seen in the city of the Lord of hosts,
in the city of our God.
God has laid its foundations for ever.

Interlude

9 We have thought of your mercy, O God,
in the midst of your Temple.
As your reputation, O God,

10 so your praise reaches to the ends of the earth;
your right hand is full of justice.

11 Let Mount Sion rejoice,
let the daughters of Judah exult,
because of your judgements, O Lord.

47:9 *with the God of Abraham:* MT here has 'the people of the God of Abraham'. It may be that the Greek here preserves the correct reading; or since the word for 'with' and the word for 'people' have the same consonants in Hebrew, it may be that both words were in the original, and one dropped out by a scribal error.

the mighty of the earth have been greatly exalted: so LXX; MT reads something like 'the shields of the earth belong to God; he has been greatly raised up'.

48 **Heading**: *On the second day of the week:* i.e. Monday; but the text gives us no clue why this song should be sung on a Monday.

48:2 *Well planted:* this is a scholarly guess at the meaning of a particularly impenetrable Greek phrase. The Hebrew here reads 'lovely in height'.

the sides of the north: it is hard to see what to make of this. The thing to remember is that the poet is praising God's city, which he sees as the centre of the world. But it is also possible that the word translated 'north' was originally understood as 'the sacred mountain'. We can no longer confidently say what it means; but we do know that God is being praised here.

48:3 *comes to her help:* this is the key point. The next verses describe an attack that will be made on the city: God will defend Jerusalem, come what may.

48:4 *the kings have gathered:* some manuscripts here have 'the kings of the earth', possibly because of the use of that phrase in Ps 2:2.

48:7 *violent wind:* the Hebrew here has 'east wind'.

ships of Tarshish: a bit mysterious. Ships obviously could not threaten Jerusalem, and scholars are no longer agreed on where Tarshish might be. The word may well mean a 'refinery'. 1 Kings 10:22 suggests that Tarshish ships were the best and biggest around.

48:8 *As we have heard, so we have seen:* in other words, the singer's experience matches the traditions passed down about God's exploits.

48:10 *justice:* this is a respectable translation of both the Greek and the Hebrew, but the context makes it clear that something wider is meant here, including the notion of God's 'victory' (cf. the word 'judgements' in verse 11 below).

12 Go round about Sion, and embrace it,
    give a full account of her towers,
13 turn your thoughts to her power,
    give an accurate observation of her palaces,
    so that you may give an account to the next generation.
14 For this is God our God,
    for ever and for ever.
    God himself will shepherd us for ever.

Psalm 49 (48)   A wisdom psalm

To the end, a psalm for the sons of Korah

49:1 Hear these things, all you nations,
    turn your ear, all you who dwell on earth,
2 you low-born and high-born,
    rich and poor alike.
3 My mouth shall speak wisdom,
    and the meditation of my thoughts shall speak understanding.
4 I shall turn my ear to a proverb;
    I shall open up my riddle on a stringed instrument.
5 Why should I be fearful on an evil day?
    The lawlessness of my pursuers shall encircle me,
6 those who trusted in their power,
    and who boast in the abundance of their riches.
7 A brother (or sister) cannot redeem a person;
    no one shall give God a ransom offering,
8 or the price of the redemption of their life,
9 even if they laboured for ever;
    and live to the end;
    so that they shall not see destruction.
10 When they see the wise perishing,
    the fool and the senseless alike shall die,
    and they shall leave their wealth to others.
11 And their graves are their homes for ever;
    their dwelling places from generation to generation,
    they called their names down on their lands.
12 People who are honoured do not understand;
    they are compared to senseless cattle;
    they are just like them.

48:14 *For this is God our God:* this is the clue to the entire psalm. What counts is not the undoubted beauty and power of Jerusalem, but God's faithfulness and power.

49:2 *low-born and high-born:* literally 'earth-born and sons of human beings'. The Hebrew is equally problematic, 'the sons of Adam and the sons of a man'; but the second half of the verse, the contrast between 'rich' and 'poor' makes clear what it must mean. All humans, the Wisdom tradition reminds us, are equal before God.

49:3 *wisdom . . . understanding:* now it becomes a bit clearer – this is a poem in the Wisdom tradition.

49:4 *turn my ear to a proverb:* the point here is that the singer is of the view that God can speak through a 'proverb', that characteristic product of the Wisdom tradition of the Ancient Near East. God is not, for our psalmist, limited to speaking only through the 'Law and the Prophets'.

49:5 *my pursuers:* LXX reads 'my heel', which is one possible translation of the (slightly obscure) Hebrew word, which can also mean 'hoof', 'footprint', 'rearguard', and perhaps also 'bumpy terrain' and 'sly'.

49:7 *brother (or sister):* this is the reading of both Greek and Hebrew; modern versions tend however (often without telling you) to emend to a very similar Hebrew word that means 'indeed'.

49:11 *called their names down on their lands:* this is a form of legal conveyancing for the wealthy; but the point here, of course, is that they cannot 'take it with them'.

13 This way of theirs trips them up,
and yet later on they will delight in their mouth.

Interlude

14 Like sheep they are placed in Hades, Death shepherds them,
and the upright shall lord it over them early in the morning.
Their help shall grow old in Hades, shall fall away from their glory.

15 But God will ransom my life from the power of Hades,
when he accepts me.

Interlude

16 Do not be afraid when someone becomes wealthy,
and when the glory of their house increases.

17 For when they die they shall not take it all with them,
nor does their glory go down with them.

18 For their soul shall be blessed in their lifetime;
they shall praise you when you do good to them.

19 Yet they shall go into the generations of their ancestors;
they shall never look upon the light.

20 People who are honoured do not understand;
they are compared to senseless cattle;
they are just like them.

Psalm 50 (49) The people of God in the dock

A psalm of Asaph

50:1 The God of gods, the Lord has uttered, and has summoned the earth,
from the rising of the sun to its setting.

2 From Sion the majesty of his beauty will come forth;
God, our God will shine forth visibly

3 and will not be silent;
a fire shall burn before him,
and about him a very great storm.

4 He shall summon the heaven above,
and the earth, in order to judge his people.

5 Gather his holy ones before him,
those who made a covenant with him by sacrifice;

6 the heavens shall declare his righteousness.
For God is judge.

Interlude

49:14 *Their help shall grow old:* the text is impossible to reconstruct here, both in Hebrew and in Greek; but the general picture is that of the wealthy being guided by Death down to Hades, without their realising it.

49:15 *God will ransom my life:* is this what the psalmist is saying (i.e. trusting that God will spare him, but not the wicked, from death)? Or are we to hear the wealthy insisting right up to the last moment that 'God will see me right'? It is impossible to tell; generally, it is supposed that you do not find evidence of a belief in life after death in Israel until the 2nd and 1st centuries BC, with the books of Daniel, 2 Maccabees, and Wisdom.

49:18 *For their soul shall be blessed:* the precise meaning here may be obscure, but the gist is clear enough, that the wealthy are going to congratulate themselves on how much God loves them, whereas in fact they are going to die, just like everybody else.

50:2 *will shine forth visibly:* the Hebrew says simply 'will shine forth'. Notice throughout this psalm the absolute superiority of God. We shall not understand either Israel's religion or God himself unless we grasp that the Creator is infinitely above us.

7 'Hear, my people, and I shall speak to you;
Israel, and I shall testify against you.
I am God, your God.

8 I shall not reprove you for your sacrifices;
your whole burnt offerings are always before me.

9 I shall not accept young bullocks from your house,
nor young he-goats from your flocks.

10 For all the wild beasts of the forest are mine,
animals on the mountain, and cattle.

11 I know all the birds of the air,
and the beauty of the field is mine.

12 If I get hungry, no way shall I tell you;
for the world is mine, and all that is in it.

13 Am I going to eat the flesh of bulls,
or drink goats' blood?

14 Offer God a sacrifice of praise,
and pay your vows to the Most High.

15 And call on me on the day of trouble,
and I shall deliver you, and you will glorify me.'

Interlude

16 And to the sinner, God has said,
'Why do you recite my ordinances,
and take my covenant on your lips?

17 But you hate discipline, and you have flung my words out behind you.

18 If you saw a thief, you would run along with him;
and you have thrown in your lot with adulterers.

19 Your mouth has increased wickedness,
and your tongue has framed deceit.

20 You have sat and spoken against your brother (or sister),
you raised a stumbling block against your own mother's child.

21 You have done these things – and I was silent;
you had the wicked thought that I would be like you!
I shall reprove you, and I shall show you to your face.'

22 (Understand these things, you who forget God;
otherwise God may plunder you, with no one to rescue you.)

23 'A sacrifice of praise will glorify me,
and there is the way by which I shall show them God's salvation.'

50:10 *cattle:* the same word in Hebrew can mean 'cattle/oxen' and 'thousand(s)', which accounts for some of the English translations.

50:11 *the beauty:* the Hebrew has a word that means something like 'insects'. The general point remains the same, of course, that Israel's God is the God of all creation.

50:18- *thief . . . adulterers . . . deceit:* the person whom God is
19 accusing has disobeyed three of the Ten Commandments.

50:22 *Understand these things:* I take this to be a severe warning, interjected by the psalmist into God's speech.

50:23 *there is the way:* here the Greek exactly translates the Hebrew as we have it; but by changing one consonant in Hebrew you can have 'those who are perfect in the way', which is very likely the original reading.

Psalm 51 (50)   The *Miserere*

The fourth 'Penitential Psalm'

To the end. A Psalm of David, when Nathan the prophet went to him, because he had gone in to Bathsheba.

51:1   Have mercy on me, O God, in your great mercy,
    and in your compassion wipe out my iniquity.

2   Wash me more and more from my transgression,
    and purify me from my sin.

3   For I know my transgression,
    and my sin is always before me.

4   Against you alone I have sinned;
    I have done what is wicked in your sight,
    that you may be justified in your words,
    and may conquer when you judge.

5   For, see, I was conceived in transgressions,
    and in sin my mother longed for me.

6   For, see, you love truth;
    you have revealed to me the obscure and hidden details of your wisdom.

7   You will sprinkle me with hyssop, and I shall be purified;
    you will cleanse me, and I shall be whiter than snow.

8   You will make me hear rejoicing and gladness;
    the bones that have been humbled shall rejoice.

9   Turn your face away from my sins,
    and wipe away all my iniquities.

10   Create a pure heart in me, O God,
    and renew an upright spirit within me.

11   Do not thrust me away from your presence;
    and do not remove you holy spirit from me.

12   Restore the joy of your salvation to me,
    and strengthen me with your authoritative spirit.

13   I shall teach transgressors your ways,
    and the godless shall turn back to you.

14   Deliver me from bloodshed, O God, the God of my salvation;
    my tongue shall rejoice at your justice.

15   O Lord, you will open my lips,
    and my mouth shall declare your praise,

16   for if you wanted sacrifice, I would have given it;
    you will not take pleasure in whole burnt offerings.

17   A broken spirit is a sacrifice to God;
    God will not despise a heart that is broken and humbled.

18   O Lord, in your pleasure give comfort to Sion;
    and let the walls of Jerusalem be rebuilt.

---

51 **Title: The *Miserere*:** This is so called because it is the first word in Latin of this, the most famous of the Penitential psalms.

Heading: *A Psalm of David:* This cannot be quite accurate; a number of factors suggest a post-exilic date for this well-known psalm: the reference to the rebuilding of Jerusalem's walls, for example, and the notion of individual, personal repentance from sin. The last two verses of the psalm suggest that it was written in the Exile, when animal sacrifices were no longer possible, but the poet looks forward to a time when they will be reinstated. You can see, however, why it was attributed to David (look at 2 Samuel 11:1–12:25 for the well-crafted story to which the heading refers).

51:1 Have mercy on me, O God: the opening of one of the best known psalms in the book, thanks to its regular liturgical usage.

51:10 *within me:* so the Hebrew; the Greek literally means 'in my inmost parts'.

¹⁹ Then you will be pleased with a sacrifice of righteousness,
an offering and whole burnt offerings;
then they shall offer up young bulls on your altar.

Psalm 52 (51)   Prophetic oracle against the rich and corrupt

To the end; a song of instruction. Of David. When Doeg the Idumean came and told Saul, and said to him 'David has gone to the house of Abimelech'.

52:1 Why, O powerful one, do you boast of evil-doing, iniquity all day long?
2 Your tongue has planned injustice;
like a sharpened razor you have contrived deceit.
3 You have loved wickedness more than goodness,
injustice more than speaking justice.

Interlude

4 You have loved all the words of destruction, [and] a deceitful tongue.
5 Therefore God will destroy you for ever,
to pluck you up and remove you from your tent,
and your root from the land of the living.

Interlude

6 And the just shall see and shall fear;
and they shall laugh at him, and say,
7 'Look – a man who did not make God his helper,
but hoped in the abundance of his wealth,
and sought his strength in vanities.'
8 But I am like an olive tree, fruitful in God's house;
I have trusted in God's mercy for ever and for evermore.
9 I shall praise you for ever,
for you have acted,
and I shall wait for your name,
because it is good before your holy ones.

Psalm 53 (52)   God and the godless

To the end. A psalm of David
To the end; according to Mahalath. A song of instruction. Of David.

53:1 Fools say in their heart, 'There is no God.'
They have destroyed themselves, and have met with loathing for their practices;
there is none that does what is right,
there is not even one of them.
2 God looked down from heaven upon the children of Adam,
to see if there were one who was wise,
or who sought for God.

52   **Heading:** *Doeg the Idumean:* for this story, see 1 Samuel 22:6-19, where Doeg betrays Ahimelech (or Abimelech), and then murders him and all the rest of the priests, after Ahimelech had (rather nervously) allowed David to eat the show-bread, and take the sword that had belonged to Goliath (see 1 Samuel 21:2-10).The story is also referred to at Mark 2:26, but there Mark makes Abiathar the high priest, not Ahimelech. Our heading does not really fit the bill; the editors of the psalms were determined to make David the author of as many of the psalms as possible, and to fit them into the known circumstances of his life.

52:4   *destruction:* the word originally means 'drowning'.

52:8   *I am like an olive tree:* as so often, the psalm ends in a song of quiet confidence in God, against all probability. For a similar image of the flourishing of those who pay attention to God, see the 'tree' at Psalm 1:3.

53   **Heading:** *God and the godless:* this psalm is virtually identical to Psalm 14. LXX has one or two additions, mainly in verse 4.

Mahalath: probably a tune recommended for this song, but we cannot be sure.

3 They have all turned aside together; they have become useless.
There is no one who acts uprightly, not even one.
4 Will not all lawbreakers realise?
They devour my people as though they were eating bread;
 they have not called upon the Lord.
5 There they shall be fearful with dread, where there was no dread;
for God is in the righteous generation.
You have dishonoured the plans of the poor;
for God scattered the bones of those who try to please fellow humans;
they were put to shame, for God disdained them.
6 Who will supply Israel's salvation out of Sion?
When the Lord restores his people from captivity,
Jacob shall exult, and Israel rejoice.

Psalm 54 (53) God is my helper

To the end; among hymns of instruction. Of David, when the Ziphites came and told Saul, 'Look – has not David taken refuge with us?'

54:1 O God, save me by your name, and judge me with your power.
2 O God, listen to my prayer, turn your ears to the words of my mouth,
3 for foreigners have risen up against me,
and the powerful have sought my life;
they have not placed God before them.

Interlude

4 For look – God helps me,
and the Lord is the protector of my life.
5 He will return evil on my enemies;
in your truth destroy them utterly.
6 I shall willingly sacrifice to you;
I shall praise your name, O Lord, for it is good.
7 For you have delivered me from every trouble,
and my eye has looked upon my enemies.

Psalm 55 (54) Uttering one's worst feelings

To the end; among the hymns of instruction. Of David.

55:1 Give ear, O God, to my prayer, and do not disregard my petition.
2 Pay attention to me, and listen to me;
I was grieved in my conversation; and I was troubled,
3 because of the voice of the enemy, and because of the sinner's oppression,
for they visited iniquity upon me,
and in their wrath they were angry with me.

53:3 *There is no one who acts . . . not even one:* after this line in Psalm 14 LXX adds, 'Their throat is an open tomb; with their tongues they have behaved treacherously; there is a cobra's poison under their lips; their mouths are full of cursing and bitterness; their feet are quick to shed blood; affliction and distress are in their ways; and they do not know the way of peace. There is no fear of God before their eyes.'

54 **Heading**: *Ziphites came and told Saul:* the story is told at 1 Samuel 23:19ff. It is hard to see a connection between

this psalm and the story, but it is worth noticing that in 1 Samuel 23:15 and in verse 3 of our psalm there is a reference to 'seeking life', and that may have led an editor, determined to find a connection between David's life and a song he wished to attribute to the king, to opt for this one.

55 **Heading**: *Uttering one's worst feelings:* we should take courage here from the psalmist's willingness to 'let it all hang out'; he is really cast down, apparently for good reason. And he does not mind who knows it.

4 My heart was disturbed inside me,
  and the fear of death fell upon me.
5 Fear and trembling came upon me,
  and darkness covered me.
6 And I said, 'Who will give me wings like a dove,
  that I may fly away and be at rest?'
7 Look – I have travelled far in my flight,
  and made my lodging in the desert.

Interlude

8 I waited for the one who saves me from discouragement
  and from the storm.
9 O Lord, destroy and divide their tongues,
  for I have seen iniquity and contradiction in the city.
10 Day and night they will go round the city;
  and on her walls are lawlessness;
  and there is trouble in her midst – and injustice.
11 Usury and deceit have not left the city's streets.
12 For if an enemy had reviled me, I should have put up with it;
  and if someone who hated me had spoken boastfully against me,
  I should have hidden from them.
13 But you, my peer, my leader, my acquaintance,
14 who sweetened food along with me;
  we walked in unity in God's house.
15 Let death come upon them, and let them go down alive to Hades,
  for there is wickedness in their dwelling places, in the midst of them.
16 As for me, I cried to God, and the Lord heard me.
17 Evening and morning, and at noon,
  I shall recount and I shall tell;
  and he will listen to my voice.
18 He will redeem my life in peace from those who draw near to me;
  for they were with me in great numbers.
19 God will hear and will humble them,
  The One who exists before the ages.

Interlude

  For there is no change; and they did not fear God.
20 He stretched out his hand to repay;
  they defiled his covenant.
21 They were scattered because of the anger of his face,
  and his heart drew near; his words were smoother than oil;
  and yet they are arrows.

55:8-9 *I waited . . . in the city:* these verses are impenetrable in Hebrew; our translator has done his gallant best.

55:13 *my peer, my leader, my acquaintance:* this is what it says, in both Hebrew and Greek. We have no way of determining who the psalmist is referring to; but it makes this song accessible to anyone who has had experience of betrayal by a friend.

55:19 *there is no change:* this is what both the Greek and Hebrew have. What it means varies according to which scholar you have been talking to. Some speak of an 'exchange of prisoners', an important part of conducting wars in the Ancient Near East. Others think of people failing to alter the way they conduct their lives in response to God's invitation. We cannot be clear what the original Hebrew said, never mind what it meant.

55:21 *they were scattered:* the Hebrew has 'they were divided', which is not very far away.

anger: here the Hebrew has a word that means something 'curdlike', hence 'soft as butter' in many English versions. But it is likely that LXX has preserved the correct reading here.

arrows: the Hebrew here has 'unsheathed swords', which is at least in the same area.

22 Cast your care upon the Lord;
and he will sustain you;
he will not allow the just to be shaken.

23 But you, O God, will lead them down to the pit of destruction;
they are bloodthirsty and treacherous people;
they shall not live out half their days;
but I shall hope in you, O Lord.

Psalm 56 (55) Trusting in God

*To the end, for the people who had travelled far from the holy places;
for David as an inscription, when the foreigners seized him at Gath.*

56:1 Have mercy on me, O God, for they have trampled me down;
all day long, they have made war on me and afflicted me.

2 My enemies have trampled me down, all day long;
for they are many who make war on me from on high.

3 I shall be afraid by day; but I shall hope in you.

4 In God I shall praise his words; I hope in God,
I shall not fear what flesh can do to me.

5 All day long they abominate my words;
all their thoughts are against me for evil.

6 They shall live nearby and conceal themselves;
they will watch my steps, just as they have lain in wait for my life.

7 On no account will you save them,
in anger you will bring down the peoples, O God.

8 I have proclaimed my life to you;
you set my tears before you just as [it said] in your promise.

9 My enemies shall turn back
on the day when I call upon you.
Behold, I know that you are my God.

10 In God (I shall praise [his] word),
in the Lord (I shall praise [his] message),

11 in God I put my hope;
I shall not fear – what can humans do to me?

12 On me, O God, are the vows which I shall repay you,
[the vows] of your praise.

13 For you delivered my life from death,
and my feet from slipping,
to be pleasing to God in the light of the living.

56 **Heading**: *people who had travelled far from the holy places:* the original Hebrew probably indicated a tune to which the psalm was to be sung. The LXX translator is clearly working on the same Hebrew consonants, and doing his best with a very difficult line.

inscription: see note on Psalm 16, Heading

when the foreigners seized him at Gath: this is a later addition to the psalm, added in order to maintain the fiction that David wrote all the psalms. The story referred to is that at 1 Samuel 21:11-15, when David ends up pretending to be mad, so as to diminish any sense of menace to the Philistines.

56:4 *praise his words:* The Greek here actually has 'my words', possibly because the translator has misread the Hebrew, which would be only one (very similar) letter different.

56:7 *On no account will you save them:* this is one way of taking the Greek, which is trying to translate a Hebrew expression that means, probably 'because of the idol they will save themselves'. The Greek might therefore better be read as 'Because of the Nothing you will save them'.

56:10 *praise [his] word . . . praise [his] message:* the translator has made a gallant attempt at rendering the Hebrew, which reads, 'In God I shall praise a word, in YHWH I shall praise a word', using the same word each time for 'word'; it is not clear quite what it means, but the translator has at least introduced a variation, in that he uses two words for 'word' (*rhema* and *logos*).

56:12 *[the vows] of your praise:* here the translator has made another gallant attempt, reading a slightly unusual Hebrew 'praises' as a genitive, 'of your praise'.

Psalm 57 (56) A prayer for rescue

To the end. 'Do not destroy'. Of David. For an inscription.
When he fled from the presence of Saul, into the cave.

57:1 Have mercy on me, O God, have mercy on me;
for in you my soul has trusted,
and under the shadow of your wings I shall find hope,
until wickedness passes away.
2 I shall cry to God the Most High,
to the God who has been my benefactor.
3 He sent from heaven and he saved me;
he handed over to reproach all those who trampled over me.

Interlude

God sent out his mercy and his truth.
4 And he delivered my soul from the midst of lions' cubs;
I slept disturbed.
Human beings – their teeth are spear and arrows;
and their tongue is a sharp sword.
5 Be exalted above the heavens, O God;
and let your glory be over the whole earth.
6 They have prepared a trap for my feet;
and they have made my soul bow down.
They dug a pit before my face, and they fell into it!

Interlude

7 My heart is ready, O God, my heart is ready.
I shall sing and I shall play on the harp.
8 Awake, my glory, arise lyre and harp;
I shall awake at dawn.
9 I shall praise you among the peoples, O Lord;
I shall play on the harp for you among the Gentiles.
10 For your mercy has been made great, even as high as the heavens;
and your truth reaches to the clouds.
11 Be exalted as far as the heavens, O God,
and may your glory be over all the earth.

Psalm 58 (57) Against corrupt judges

To the end. 'Do not destroy'. Of David.
For an inscription.

58:1 If indeed you speak what is right,
then you human beings should judge uprightly.
2 For you work iniquity in your heart, injustice in the land;
and your hands weave injustice.

---

57 **Heading**: *'Do not destroy'*: this is almost certainly the name of the tune to which the psalm is to be sung.

When he fled from the presence of Saul: This historical reference is to the events narrated in 1 Samuel 22 and the following chapters, when David has to take refuge in the wilderness, in the cave of Adullam.

57:2 *my benefactor:* this translation of a Hebrew word that really means something like 'requite' or 'repay' may be influenced, consciously or unconsciously, by the fact that some of the Ptolemy rulers of Egypt gave themselves the name of 'Euergetes', or 'Benefactor'.

58:1 *human beings:* this is what the Greek has ('sons of men'); but the Hebrew actually has 'gods'. This is one of the three psalms (83 and 109 are the others) that do not appear in the Catholic liturgy, nor in the Office, presumably because the tone is so unrelievedly negative.

3 Sinners have been estranged from the womb;
from the belly they have gone astray;
they have told lies.
4 Their rage is like that of the snake,
like that of the adder that is deaf and stops her ears.
5 She does not hear the voice of charmers,
nor heed the drug prepared by the wise.
6 God has crushed their teeth in their mouth;
the Lord has crushed to pieces the molars of lions.
7 They shall be set at naught like water that passes through;
he will bend his bow until they grow weak.
8 Like melted wax they shall be destroyed;
the fire fell on them, and they did not see the sun.
9 Before your thorns take notice of the bramble,
he will drink you down like the living, like victims of his anger.
10 The just shall rejoice when they see [God's] vengeance on the ungodly;
he will wash his hands in the sinner's blood.
11 And people shall say, 'Indeed there is a reward for the righteous;
indeed there is a God who judges them on earth.

Psalm 59 (58) **A prayer for deliverance from enemies**

To the end. 'Do not destroy'. Of David.
For an inscription. When Saul sent and guarded his house, in order to kill him.

59:1 Deliver me from my enemies, O God,
and ransom me from those who rise up against me.
2 Deliver me from those who work iniquity;
and save me from the bloodthirsty.
3 For behold they have hunted after my life;
the powerful have made an attack upon me;
it was not my iniquity, nor my sin, O Lord.
4 Without any iniquity of mine they ran straight ahead;
arise to meet me, and see.
5 And you, Lord of hosts, God of Israel, pay heed, and examine all the
Gentiles;
show no pity on those who do iniquity.
Interlude
6 They will return at evening;
and they will be as ravenous as a dog, and they will encircle the city.
7 Behold they shall prophesy with their mouth,
and a sword is on their lips: 'Who has heard [us]?'
8 And you, O Lord, will laugh them to scorn;
you will disdain all the nations.
9 My strength, I shall watch out for you,
for you, O God, are my helper.
10 My God – his mercy will go before me;
God will show me it among my enemies.

---

59 **Heading**: *When Saul sent and guarded . . . in order to kill him:* this refers to the episode recounted at 1 Samuel 19:11-18.

59:9 *I shall watch out:* literally, 'I shall guard', which is a common LXX translation of this particular Hebrew word.

¹¹ Do not kill them, or they may forget my people;
   scatter them by your power, and bring them down, O Lord my shield.

¹² [. . .]the sin of their mouth, and the word of their lips,
   and let them be taken because of their arrogance,
   and because of their cursing and falsehood
   let their destruction be proclaimed,

¹³ by the wrath of destruction – and they shall not exist.
   And they will know that God is Lord over Jacob and of the ends of the earth.

   Interlude

¹⁴ They will return at evening, and they will be as ravenous as a dog;
   and they will encircle the city.

¹⁵ They shall scatter to find food,
   and if they are not satisfied then they shall growl.

¹⁶ But I shall sing to your power,
   and I shall rejoice at your mercy in the morning.
   For you have been my protector, and my refuge on the day of my affliction.

¹⁷ My helper, I shall sing to you;
   you are my protector,
   O God, my mercy.

Psalm 60 (59)   A prayer for God to defeat the enemy

*To the end. For those who will be changed. For an inscription. Of David
(for teaching).*
*When he had burnt Syrian Mesopotamia and Syrian Soba, and Joab had
returned and had struck the Valley of the Salts, twelve thousand people.*

^{60:1} O God, you rejected us and destroyed us; you were enraged with us –
   but you have had pity on us.

² You have shaken the earth and troubled it;
   heal its wounds – for it has been shaken.

³ You have shown difficult things to your people;
   you have made us drink the wine of stupefaction.

⁴ You gave those who fear you a sign,
   to flee from before the bow.

   Interlude

⁵ That your loved ones may be rescued,
   save with your right hand, and listen to me.

⁶ God has spoken in his holy place,
   'I shall rejoice, and I shall divide up Shechem,
   and I shall measure out the Valley of Tents.

---

60   **Heading:** *For those who will be changed:* see note on the
heading of Psalm 45.

When he had burnt Syrian Mesopotamia: it looks as
though this attempt to find a historical setting to the
psalm links it with the story told in 2 Samuel 8 (see
especially verse 13, but notice that the numbers there are
eighteen thousand), and see also 2 Samuel 10:13, 18. It
is very hard to determine a date for the composition of
this psalm. Many scholars locate it in the time after the
Exile, when the boundaries of Israel were comparatively
limited. This is how they express their hope in God.

Valley of the Salts: probably the valley of the Arabah,
which goes down from the Dead Sea to the Gulf of
Aqabah.

60:4   *flee from before the bow:* in the culture that produced our
psalms, bow and arrow was 'state-of-the-art' technology,
and, because of its use for long-range killing, quite
terrifying for those who had not yet developed adequate
armour.

60:6   *Valley of Tents:* this is a literal translation of the 'Valley of
Succoth', across the Jordan, in the hills opposite
Shechem. Implicitly there is a claim here to extend
Israel's borders beyond their traditional boundaries.

7 Mine is Gilead, and mine is Manasseh;
and Ephraim is the strength of my head. Judah is my king.
8 Moab is the cauldron of my hope;
over Edom I shall stretch out my sandal;
the foreigners have been subjected to me.
9 Who will lead me into the fortified city?'
10 Is it not you, O God, who has rejected us?
And will you not go forth, O God, with our armies?
11 Give us help in our time of trouble;
for human deliverance is useless.
12 In God we shall do mighty deeds,
and God will bring to nothing those who afflict us.

Psalm 61 (60)   God is the rock

To the end; among the hymns of David.

61:1 O God, hear my entreaty, pay attention to my prayer.
2 From the ends of the earth I have cried out to you;
when my heart was weary, you lifted me up on a rock.
3 You guided me, because you were my hope,
a tower of strength in the presence of the enemy.
4 I shall dwell in your tent for ever;
I shall be sheltered under the shelter of your wings.

Interlude

5 For you, O God, have heard my prayers;
you have given an inheritance to those who fear your name.
6 You shall add days to the days of the king,
his years like generation upon generation.
7 He will remain for ever before God;
God's mercy and truth who shall seek out?
8 So I shall sing to your name for ever and ever,
to fulfil my vows, day after day.

Psalm 62 (61)   A song of trust in God alone

To the end; according to Jeduthun. A psalm of David

62:1 Shall not my soul submit to God?
For from [God] is my salvation.
2 For he is my God and my Saviour,
my helper, I shall not be shaken any more.
3 How long will you attack a person;
you are all killing, as though with a bowed wall or a broken hedge.

60:8 *cauldron . . . sandal:* it may be helpful to observe that these are both symbols of slavery: the cauldron is understood as a washbasin held by slaves, and the sandal is stretched out over enemies who have been defeated, so they are symbolically 'under his feet'.

60:9 *fortified city:* both the Hebrew and the Greek here have 'city of fortification'.

61:6 *like generation upon generation:* this translation assumes that the Greek, which reads 'until a day of generation and generation', has misread one consonant in the Hebrew text.

62 **Heading:** *Jeduthun:* according to 1 Chronicles 9:16; 16:38, 41-42; 25:1, 3, 6; and 2 Chronicles 5:12 Jeduthun was a Levite, a prophet and a music maker in the time of David. Presumably he wrote, or had attributed to him, the tune to which this psalm was to be sung.

4 However they plotted to repel my honour;
they ran with falsehood;
with their mouth they uttered blessings,
but with their heart they were cursing.

Interlude

5 However, submit to God, O my soul,
for from him comes my endurance.
6 For he is my God, and my Saviour, my helper;
I shall never run away.
7 My salvation is in God, and my glory.
[He is] the God of my help,
and my hope is in God.
8 Hope in him, all you gathering of the people,
pour out your hearts before him.
God is our help.

Interlude

9 But ordinary people are nothing;
people are false in their balances,
so as to act unjustly.
They are together made of nothingness.
10 Do not put your hope in injustice;
do not long for booty;
if wealth comes pouring in, do not set your heart on it.
11 God has spoken once; these two things have I heard,
that power belongs to God,
12 and to you, O Lord, belongs mercy.
For you will repay each of us according to our works.

Psalm 63 (62) **Longing for God**

A psalm of David, when he was in the wilderness of Judaea.

63:1 O God, my God, I rise early to seek you;
my soul is thirsting for you.
How often has my flesh [yearned] for you,
in desolate and untrodden and waterless land!
2 So I have appeared before you in the sanctuary,
to see your power and your glory.
3 Because your mercy is better than life,
my lips shall praise you.
4 So I shall bless you in my life;
in your name I shall lift up my hands.

62:8 *gathering:* literally, 'synagogue', possibly because of a misreading of a Hebrew word for 'time'. The Hebrew reads 'at all time, O people'.

62:11 *once; these two things:* these numerical riddles are thought to be characteristic of wisdom literature.

63 **Heading:** *when he was in the wilderness of Judaea:* this is, presumably, what is recounted at 1 Samuel 23:14 or 24:2.

63:1 *[yearned]:* The translator here seems to have misread the Hebrew 'yearned' for a word with identical consonants meaning 'how often'.

63:2 *I have appeared:* that is what the Greek has, but the Hebrew implies that the psalmist has had a vision of God, not that God has seen him.

5 May my soul be filled with fatness and abundance;
  and my mouth will praise you [with] lips of joy.

6 If I remembered you on my bed,
  in the early morning I would meditate on you.

7 For you were my helper,
  and under the shadow of your wings I shall exult.

8 My soul has kept close behind you;
  your right hand has given me support.

9 While they sought my life, in vain;
  they will enter the lowest parts of the earth.

10 They shall be handed over to the hands of the sword,
  they shall be portions for foxes.

11 But the king shall rejoice in God;
  all those who swear by him shall be praised,
  for the mouth of those who utter injustice was blocked up.

Psalm 64 (63) A confident lament

To the end. A psalm of David.

64:1 Hear my voice, O God, when I make my entreaty;
  deliver my soul from fear of the enemy.

2 You have sheltered me from the swarm of those who do evil,
  from the crowd of those who wreak iniquity,

3 those who sharpen their tongues like a sword,
  and have bent their bow – a bitter thing,

4 to shoot in secret at the blameless;
  they will shoot suddenly at him – and they shall not fear.

5 They have strengthened an evil word for themselves;
  they have described how to conceal traps;
  they have said, 'Who will see them?'

6 They have searched out iniquities,
  they have fainted while searching out carefully;
  a person shall approach – and their heart is deep.

7 And God shall be exalted;
  their wounds have become a child's arrow.

8 Their tongues have become utterly weak,
  all those who looked upon them were troubled.

9 Everyone was afraid, and they proclaimed God's works;
  and they understood God's deeds.

10 The just shall rejoice in the Lord;
  they shall hope in him,
  and all the upright of heart shall be praised.

63:5 *fatness and abundance:* in a society that had to scratch hard for a living, these two words, which mean very much the same thing in both Hebrew and Greek, would be regarded as a good thing, rather than as in health-conscious and over-fed societies, a bad thing.

my mouth will praise you [with] lips of joy: the Hebrew means more or less exactly what the Greek translation takes it to mean. For English it is necessary to add the word 'with'.

64:6 *they have fainted . . . their heart is deep:* the translator is doing a gallant job with some fairly impenetrable Hebrew. The same is true, you might feel, of the verses on either side here.

64:7 *a child's arrow:* this is a strikingly effective image for those who will fail in their rebellion against God, but it probably comes from misreading the Hebrew word for 'suddenly'.

Psalm 65 (64)   **Thanksgiving for God's generosity**

To the end; a psalm of David. A song of Jeremiah and Ezekiel, as a result of the business of the Exile, when they were about to go out.

65:1   A hymn is fitting for you, O God, in Sion,
       and a vow shall be repaid to you in Jerusalem.
   2   Listen to my prayer; all flesh shall come to you.
   3   The words of the lawless have been too strong for us;
       but [we ask you to] pardon our sins.
   4   Blessed are those whom you have chosen and taken to yourself;
       they will dwell in your courts.
       We shall be filled with the good things of your house.
       Holy is your temple, wonderful in righteousness.
   5   Hear us, O God our Saviour, the hope of all the ends of the earth,
       and [of those] in the sea far away,
   6   you who make the mountains ready by your strength,
       you who are clothed in power,
   7   you who agitate the depth of the sea,
       the sound of its waves.
       The nations shall be troubled.
   8   And those who inhabit the ends [of the earth]
       shall be fearful of your signs.
       You will give joy to east and west.
   9   You have visited the earth, and you have made it drunk,
       you have multiplied it to enrich it.
       God's river is filled with water;
       you have prepared their food, for this is how you have prepared it.
  10   Make earth's furrows drunk; multiply its produce.
       Earth shall rejoice in drops of water as it buds forth.
  11   You will bless the crown of the year with your goodness;
       and your plains shall be filled with fatness.
  12   The beautiful places of the wilderness shall be enriched,
       and the hills shall be clothed in gladness.
  13   The rams of the flock are clothed;
       and the valleys shall be filled with corn.
       They shall cry out; indeed they shall sing.

Psalm 66 (65)   **Thanksgiving to God**

To the end. A melody, accompanied on strings. Of resurrection.

66:1   Cry aloud to God, all the earth,
   2   sing a song to his name; give glory to his praise.
   3   Say to God, how awesome are your deeds;
       because of the might of your power,
       your enemies shall be false with you.

---

65   **Heading:** *A song of Jeremiah and Ezekiel, as a result of the business of the Exile, when they were about to go out:* This is an addition to the heading in the MT, and seems a bit vague about the history; probably we are to see this heading as inserted rather late in the process, and certainly not as evidence for the dating of the psalm.

65:7   *the sound of its waves:* this is what it must mean, and what

the Hebrew says; but in fact the Greek says 'of the sound of its waves', which makes less sense.

65:8   *east and west:* here the Greek translates the Hebrew over-literally as 'the exits of morning and evening'.

65:9   *this is how you have prepared it:* literally, 'for thus is your preparation'.

4 Let all the earth worship you, and let them sing a song to you,
sing a song to your name.

Interlude

5 Come and see God's works;
he is awesome in his plans for the children of Adam.

6 God is the one who turns the sea into dry land;
they shall go through the river on foot.
There shall we rejoice in him,

7 in the One who by his power is Lord of the age.
His eyes look upon the nations.
Let not those who rebel exalt themselves.

Interlude

8 You nations, bless our God,
and let the sound of his praise be heard,

9 him who restores my soul to life,
and does not allow my feet to be shaken.

10 For you tested us, O God;
you put us to the fire as silver is put to the fire.

11 You led us into the snare;
you placed oppression on our backs.

12 You made people tread on our heads;
we went through fire and through water,
but you led us into refreshment.

13 I shall go into your house with burnt offerings;
I shall repay my vows to you,

14 the vows which my lips uttered,
and my mouth spoke in my troubles.

15 I shall offer burnt offerings full of marrow,
with incense and rams;
I shall make [offerings] to you of bulls with he-goats.

Interlude

16 Come and hear, and I shall recount to all you who fear God
what great things he has done for my soul.

17 I cried out to him with my mouth,
and I exalted him under my tongue.

18 If I looked upon iniquity in my heart,
let not the Lord listen to me.

19 Therefore God has listened to me;
he has paid attention to the sound of my prayer.

20 Blessed be God, who did not turn away my prayer,
nor his mercy from me.

66:7 *those who rebel:* the Greek literally means 'those who provoke'; but this Greek word is quite often used in LXX to translate words for 'rebel'.

lord of the age: this could equally be translated 'rules for ever'. The ambiguity is in both the Hebrew and the Greek.

66:14 *which my lips uttered:* this is a 'no-nonsense' translation; but the verb in Greek means something like to 'separate' or 'distinguish', and the Hebrew verb means 'open wide'.

66:17 *under my tongue:* here LXX has literally translated the Hebrew, which presumably meant something like 'on my tongue'.

Psalm 67 (66) **Praising God for the harvest**

To the end; among the hymns. A melody on strings.

67:1 O God have pity on us, and bless us,
and make his face shine upon us.

Interlude

2 To know your way on earth,
your salvation among all the nations.

3 Let the peoples praise you, O God,
let all the people praise you.

4 Let the nations rejoice and exult,
for you will judge the peoples in righteousness,
and you will guide the nations on earth.

Interlude

5 Let the peoples praise you, O God,
let all the people praise you.

6 The earth has yielded its fruit;
let God, our God, bless us.

7 Let God bless us,
and let all the ends of the earth revere him.

Psalm 68 (67) **Celebrating the victories of God**

To the end; of David, a melody on strings

68:1 Let God arise, and let his enemies be scattered;
and let those who hate him flee from his presence.

2 As smoke disappears, so let them disappear;
as wax melts in the presence of fire,
so let sinners perish in the presence of God.

3 Let the just rejoice; let them exult in the presence of God;
let them delight with gladness.

4 Sing to God, play a tune to his name,
make a way for the one who rides on the West:
the Lord is his name.
Exult before him; they shall be disturbed at his presence,

5 who is the father of orphans and judge of widows:
God in his holy place.

6 God makes the lonely dwell in a house,
mightily leads out those who are in chains,
those who are rebellious, those who live in tombs.

7 O God, when you went forth in the presence of your people,
when you went through the desert . . .

Interlude

67:3 *let the peoples praise:* the word here translated as 'praise' can also mean 'thank' and 'confess', both in Hebrew and in Greek. (see also verse 5).

68 **Title**: *Celebrating the victories of God:* the Hebrew text of this psalm is so corrupt, that as the psalm goes on, it is not possible to be sure what it is really about.

68:6 *the lonely . . . those . . . in chains . . . rebellious, those who live in tombs:* Christians reading this will find an echo in the story of the Gerasene demoniac (Mark 5:1-20).

8   . . . the land was shaken, the heavens let drops fall,
at the presence of God, the God of Sinai,
at the presence of the God of Israel.

9   You will set apart a spontaneous rain, O God, for your inheritance;
it was sick, but you made it better.

10 Your animals live in it;
in your goodness, O God, you have prepared for the poor.

11 The Lord will give a word
to those who spread the good news, with great power:

12 'The king of the armies of the beloved . . . and for the beauty of the house
to divide the spoils',

13 if you lie down in the midst of the plots of land,
a dove's wings, overlaid with silver,
and her back with the yellowness of gold.

Interlude

14 When the Heavenly One sets kings apart on it,
they shall be snowed upon in Zalmon.

15 God's mountain is a rich mountain,
a mountain that has curdled, a rich mountain.

16 Why, O curdled mountains, do you suppose
the mountain where God was pleased to dwell?
For the Lord will pitch his tent there for ever.

17 God's chariotry is ten-thousandfold,
thousands of people who flourish,
the Lord is among them, in Sinai, in the holy place.

18 You have gone up on high;
you have taken captivity captive;
you have received gifts among humans;
for they were disobedient in pitching their tents.

19 Blessed be the Lord God.
Blessed be the Lord from day to day;
the God of our salvation will give prosperity.

Interlude

20 Our God is a God to save;
and to the Lord belong the ways out from Death.

21 But God shall crush the heads of his enemies,
the crest of hair of those who march on in their sins.

22 The Lord said, 'From Bashan I shall return them,
I shall return them through the depths of the sea,

23 that your foot may be dipped in blood,
and the tongues of your dogs in [the blood] of your enemies.'

24 Your processions, O God, have been seen,
the processions of my God, of the king who is in the sanctuary.

68:12- *The king . . . yellowness of gold:* this is what the Greek
13   says; but the translator is struggling with a very difficult
Hebrew text here.

68:18 *You have gone up on high; you have taken captivity captive;*
you have received gifts among humans: Ephesians 4:8 has a
slightly different version of this text.

68:19 *the Lord God . . . the Lord:* The LXX translates two
different Hebrew words as 'Lord' here: *YHWH* (the
sacred name of God) and *Adonai*, the word for God.

25 The rulers went first, next those who played on strings,
  in the midst of the girls who played the drums.
26 Bless God the Lord in the assemblies,
  from the streams of Israel.
27 There is Benjamin the younger, in astonishment,
  the rulers of Judah their leaders,
  the rulers of Zebulun, the rulers of Naphthali.
28 O God, command your power,
  strengthen, O God, that which you have wrought in us.
29 From your temple in Jerusalem kings shall bring gifts to you.
30 Rebuke the wild beasts of the reeds;
  the gathering of bulls is among the heifers of the peoples,
  so that they may not be not be excluded,
  those who have been tested with silver;
  scatter the nations that desire wars.
31 Ambassadors shall arrive out of Egypt;
  Ethiopia shall eagerly stretch out its hand to God.
32 Kingdoms of the earth, sing to God,
  play a tune for the Lord.

  Interlude

33 Play a tune for God who rides on the heaven of heaven, towards the East.
  Behold, he will utter a powerful noise with his voice.
34 Give glory to God; his majesty is over Israel,
  and his power is in the clouds.
35 God is wonderful in his sanctuary;
  the God of Israel – he it is who will give power and strength to his people.
  Blessed be God!

Psalm 69 (68)   A cry for help

  To the end; for those who will be changed. Of David.

69:1 Save me, O God, for the waters have reached my soul.
2 I am stuck fast in deep mud, and there is nowhere to stand;
  I have gone into the depths of the sea, and a storm has swamped me.
3 I am exhausted from crying out;
  my throat is sore;
  my eyes are worn out from [looking] expectantly for God.
4 Those who hated me for no reason
  are more numerous than the hairs of my head.
  My enemies who persecuted me unjustly have grown strong;
  then I paid for what I had not stolen!
5 O God, you know my folly; and my wrongdoings were not hidden from you.

68:27 *astonishment:* the Greek word here is often transcribed into English as 'ecstasy', which means 'standing outside oneself'. The Hebrew here means 'small/insignificant', and it is hard to see any connection.

69 **Heading:** *for those who will be changed:* see note on the heading of Psalm 45.

69:4 *Those who hated me:* the change of tense between verses 3 and 4 reflects the Greek translator's attempt to make sense of Hebrew tenses, never an easy task. The upshot is that it is not clear in the Greek whether we are talking of a present situation, or one that has happily passed.

⁶ Let those who wait for you, Lord, Lord of hosts,
   not be put to shame on my account.
   Let those who seek you, O God of Israel,
   not be humiliated because of me.

⁷ Because for your sake I have endured insult; humiliation has covered my face.

⁸ I was alienated from my brothers and sisters,
   a stranger to the children of my mother.

⁹ Because zeal for your house has eaten me up,
   and the insults of those who insult you have fallen upon me.

¹⁰ I bowed down my soul with fasting;
   and it became a reason to insult me.

¹¹ And I put on sackcloth as my clothing,
   and I became a proverb for them.

¹² Those who sit at the gate started gossiping about me,
   and the wine drinkers sang songs against me.

¹³ While I, by my prayer to You, O Lord –
   it is a time of your good pleasure, O God,
   in the abundance of your mercy,
   hear me in the truthfulness of your salvation.

¹⁴ Save me from the mud, that I may not be stuck fast in it;
   may I be delivered from those who hate me,
   and from the depth of the waters.

¹⁵ Let the storm of water not swamp me,
   nor the deep drink me down;
   do not let the pit close its mouth upon me.

¹⁶ Hear me, O Lord, for your mercy is kindly;
   in the abundance of your compassion, look upon me.

¹⁷ Do not turn your face away from your servant,
   for I am afflicted – hear me without delay.

¹⁸ Come near to my soul, and redeem it;
   because of my enemies deliver me.

¹⁹ For you know my insults, and my shame and disgrace;
   all those who afflict me are before you.

²⁰ My soul has expected insult and humiliation;
   and I waited for someone to grieve with me – and there was none;
   for comforters – and I did not find any.

²¹ And they gave me gall for my food,
   for my thirst they gave me vinegar.

²² Let their table be a snare before them,
   and a recompense and a stumbling block.

²³ Let their eyes be darkened, so that they see nothing,
   and make their backs bend down all the time.

69:6 *Lord, Lord:* once again (see note on 68:20 above) the translator uses a single word, repeated, to translate *YHWH* and *Adonai*.

69:9 *zeal . . . insults:* oddly the two lines of this verse are quoted at separate points in the NT. 'Zeal for your house' is used in reference to Jesus' cleansing of the Temple in John 2:17; and Paul uses the second line in Romans 15:3, where it is part of the case for the Christians in Rome to look out for each other. Interestingly, in both cases the author simply assumes that the quotation can be applied to Christ, without any defence or explanation.

69:10 *I bowed down:* this probably represents a misreading of two very similar Hebrew consonants in a verb meaning 'I wept', but the meaning is in the end not very different.

69:15 *the pit:* the Hebrew here uses a word that can mean 'well' or 'pit'; the Greek here really only means 'well'. I have opted to be guided by the Hebrew.

69:16 *hear me . . . look upon me:* in the Hebrew, this is quite a neat chiasmus (reversal); in the Greek, it is a bit more awkward, and this is reflected in the English.

24   Pour out your anger upon them,
     and let the fury of your anger take hold of them.

25   Let their dwelling place be laid waste,
     let there be no one living in their tents.

26   For the one whom you have struck,
     they have persecuted,
     and they have added to the pain of the wounds you [inflicted].

27   Add iniquity to their iniquity,
     and let them not enter into your justice.

28   Let them be blotted out of the book of the living;
     let them not be written down with the righteous.

29   I am poor and in pain;
     but the salvation of your presence, O God, has supported me.

30   I shall praise God's name with a song;
     I shall magnify him with praise;

31   and it will please God more than a young calf with horns and hooves.

32   Let the poor see and rejoice;
     seek God, and your soul shall live.

33   For the Lord has heard the poor,
     and has not disdained his captives.

34   Let the heavens praise him, and the earth,
     the sea and all that move along in them.

35   For God will save Sion, and the cities of Judah shall be built up;
     they shall dwell there, and inherit it.

36   And the offspring of his slaves shall possess it;
     those who love his name shall dwell in it.

Psalm 70 (69)   A prayer in distress

To the end; of David. For remembrance.

70:1   Be pleased, O Lord, to deliver me;
     give heed to help me.

2   May they be put to shame and embarrassed together,
     those who seek my life to destroy it;
     may they be turned backwards and put to shame, those who desire evil for me.

3   Let those who say, 'Bravo, bravo,' to me,
     immediately carry off shame as their prize.

4   Let all those who seek you rejoice and exult in you;
     let those who love your salvation always say,
     'May God be magnified.'

5   But I am poor and destitute; O God help me,
     you are my help and my rescuer, O Lord,
     do not delay.

69:26 *the wounds you [inflicted]:* literally, 'your wounded one'.

69:28 *Let them be blotted out:* many people find a certain discomfort at reading this sort of language in the Bible. The thing to do is recognise that each of us has been tempted to think in this way at times, and that we can bring it safely to God, who will (if we allow him) defuse our mean-mindedness.

69:30 *I shall praise God's name with a song:* suddenly, and for the rest of this psalm, the tone changes to one of great confidence, and the assurance of having been heard. This is very common in psalms of lament, and reminds us of the God who is always listening, even when things are at their very worst, always labouring to put things right.

70   **Heading:** *For remembrance:* see note on Psalm 38, Heading.

This psalm has already appeared as Psalm 40:13-17, with just a few minor textual variants.

Psalm 71 (70)   An old person's prayer

Of David, of the sons of Jonadab and of the first ones who were taken prisoner.

71:1   O God, I have hoped in you,
     let me not be put to shame for ever.
2   By your righteousness deliver me and rescue me;
     turn your ear to me and save me.
3   Be a God who shields me, and a fortress to save me,
     for you are my strength and my refuge.
4   My God, rescue me from the hands of the sinner,
     from the hand of the transgressor and the unjust.
5   For you are my hope, O Lord.
     The Lord is my trust from my youth.
6   I have been established on you since my birth;
     from my mother's womb you are my protector;
     my songs of praise are always of you.
7   I was like a portent to many,
     but you are my strong helper.
8   Let my mouth be filled with your praise,
     that I may sing your glory, and your majesty all the day long.
9   Do not reject me in the time of my old age;
     when my strength fails, do not abandon me.
10   For my enemies spoke about me,
     and those who keep watch on my life plotted together,
11   saying, 'God has abandoned him; hunt him down, and seize him,
     for there is no deliverer.'
12   O God, do not go far from me,
     my God come near to help me.
13   Let them be ashamed and come to an end,
     those who lay false accusations against my life;
     let them be clothed with shame and humiliation,
     those who seek evil against me.
14   But I shall hope always,
     and I shall praise you more and more.
15   My mouth shall proclaim your justice,
     your salvation all the day long,
     for I am unacquainted with learning.
16   I shall enter in the power of the Lord.
     O Lord, I shall tell of your justice, only yours.
17   You have taught me, O God, since my youth,
     and up to the present moment I shall declare your wonders,

71   **Heading**: *of the sons of Jonadab and of the first ones who were taken prisoner*: the Hebrew has no heading here. J[eh]onadab is a nephew of David, who played an unsavoury role in the Amnon incident (see 2 Samuel 13:3-5), but it is impossible to know what this Greek heading has in mind.

71:15 *I am unacquainted with learning*: there is a similar idea, though the words are different at Acts 4:13, where the Sanhedrin are surprised at the confidence of Peter and John, despite their lack of learning. The Hebrew here may imply no more than that God's works are past counting.

71:16 *I shall enter*: this is what both the Hebrew and the Greek say; English versions tend to omit or expand or emend, without telling us.

71:17 *I shall declare*: this is what the Greek says, but it conceals a Hebrew imperfect tense, and we must think of it as something like 'I have been proclaiming/declaring'.

18 even until my old age and advancing years.
  O God, do not abandon me,
  until I proclaim your arm to every coming generation,
  proclaim your power and your righteousness,

19 O God, to the highest,
  the mighty works that you have done.
  O God, who is like you?

20 How many evil afflictions you have shown me;
  yet you returned and gave me life;
  you led me up again from the depths of the earth.

21 You increased your greatness;
  you turned and comforted me,
  and you led me up again from the depths of the earth.

22 For I shall praise you, on a stringed instrument.
  I shall sing of your truth on the lyre, O God,
  on the harp, O Holy One of Israel.

23 My lips shall rejoice when I sing to you,
  and my life, which you have ransomed.

24 My tongue also shall meditate all day long on your righteousness,
  when those who seek evil against me are put to shame and humiliated.

Psalm 72 (71)   A prayer for the king

For Solomon

72:1 O God, give your judgement to the king,
  and your righteousness to the king's son,

2 to judge your people with righteousness,
  and the poor with justice.

3 Let the mountains lift up peace for your people,
  and the hills in righteousness.

4 He shall judge the poor of the people,
  and will save the children of the needy;
  he will humble those who make false accusations.

5 He will continue as long as the sun,
  and before the moon, for all generations.

6 He will come down like rain on a fleece,
  and like raindrops watering the earth.

7 Righteousness will spring up in his days,
  and abundance of peace until the moon is removed.

71:18 *old age and advancing years:* the Hebrew has 'old age and grey hair'; the Greek has gallantly tried to produce two separate words for the concept.

71:22 *a stringed instrument:* literally 'a pot of a psalm', the Greek literally translating the Hebrew, which is 'the vessel of the lyre'.

72 **Heading:** *For Solomon:* it is not out of the question that this psalm was sung at Solomon's coronation, of which a version is given at 1 Kings 1:39-40; or it might arise from reading 'king' and 'king's son' in verse 1 as referring to David and Solomon respectively.

72:4 *He shall judge the poor:* notice how the new king is given a none too veiled warning about the importance of defending the poor. The Old Testament God preferred the poor and needy.

those who make false accusations: the Greek word here is the one that gives us the English 'sycophant'. It has some connection with figs and fig trees, but the precise relationship is uncertain. 'Slanderer' is a possible meaning, and so, perhaps, is 'informer' or 'exploiter'.

72:5 *He will continue:* the Hebrew here has 'he will come down'. It is quite likely that the LXX has here read the text correctly.

72:6 *on a fleece:* the Hebrew here has a word that means 'mowing' (as most of the English versions have it, the mown grass in the royal meadows) or 'shearing', which would account for the 'fleece'. The translator might perhaps have in mind the story of Gideon's fleece at Judges 6:36-40.

8 And he will have dominion, from sea to sea,
and from the Nile to the ends of the world.
9 The Ethiopians shall fall before him;
his enemies shall lick the dust.
10 The kings of Tarsis and the islands shall bring gifts;
the kings of the Arabians and of Saba will offer presents.
11 All kings shall worship him;
all the nations shall be his slaves,
12 for he has delivered the poor from the hand of the oppressors,
and the needy who have no helper.
13 He will spare the poor and the destitute,
and will save the lives of the needy.
14 He shall redeem their souls from usury and injustice,
and their name is precious in his eyes.
15 And he shall live, and some of the gold of Arabia shall be given him;
and they shall pray for him continually;
all day long they shall bless him.
16 There shall be support on the earth on the tops of the mountains.
His fruit shall be exalted above Lebanon;
and they shall flourish from the city like the grass of the earth.
17 May his name be blessed for ever;
his name shall be blessed before the sun;
and all the tribes of the land shall be blessed in him;
all the nations shall call him blessed.
18 Blessed be the Lord, the God of Israel,
the one who alone does marvellous deeds
19 and blessed is the name of his glory for ever, and for ever and ever.
All the earth shall be filled with his glory.
Let it be; let it be.
20 The hymns of David son of Jesse are ended.

72:8 *the Nile:* the Greek, like the Hebrew, has 'the River'. In the latter case that normally refers to the Euphrates (though some scholars read it as the cosmic waters around the earth). For Egypt (where our text was very likely translated into Greek), there is only one 'River'.

72:9 *Ethiopians:* the MT here has 'inhabitants of the desert', possibly a scribal error for 'foes'. The Ethiopians would of course be neighbours in Egypt, and doubtless there were occasional tensions between the two races, which may account for this translation.

72:12 *he has delivered the poor:* notice, once again, this firm reminder to the king where his priorities must lie.

72:14 *redeem their souls from usury:* that is what the Greek says. The Hebrew has a word that means 'injury' or 'oppression', but which sounds very like the Greek word that LXX has used. Possibly we should think of it as 'injury' here.

their name is precious: here the Hebrew has 'their blood', which is different by just one consonant; but on the other hand the consonants are not such as to be easily mistaken for each other.

72:16 *support:* the Hebrew here has a rare word that does not appear elsewhere in the MT, which might mean 'fullness of wheat', or could be read as 'increase of grain'. The translator here was doing his best.

they shall flourish from the city: this is what the Hebrew also has, but it is possible to read, transposing just two consonants, 'may his stalks bloom', which fits a bit better in the context.

72:18- *Blessed be the Lord, the God of Israel:* this is the beginning
20 of a doxology, marking the end of Book Two of the Psalms. It comes quite naturally after the prayer for the blessing of the king, in verse 17.

72:19 *Let it be; let it be:* this accurately translates the Hebrew, which reads 'Amen and Amen'. This doxology ends Book Two of the Psalms, so it is not strictly part of the psalm itself. The reference in verse 20 to the 'hymns of David' is an editorial addition, found in both the Hebrew and the Greek.

BOOK THREE (Psalms 73–89)

Psalm 73 (72) Learning from personal experience

A psalm of Asaph

73:1 How good God is to Israel,
to the upright of heart!

2 My feet were almost shaken;
my steps nearly slipped.

3 For I was jealous of the lawless,
when I saw the tranquillity of sinners.

4 There is no refusal in their death;
they remain firm under the whip.

5 They do not share the troubles of others;
they will not be whipped like other mortals.

6 Therefore arrogance has mastered them;
they are clothed with their immorality and their godlessness.

7 Their immorality shall go forth as though from fatness;
they have done as they liked.

8 They have thought and uttered in wickedness;
they have uttered immorality against the Highest.

9 They have set their mouth against heaven;
and their tongue has gone through on earth.

10 Therefore my people shall return here;
and full days shall be found for them.

11 And they said, 'How does God know?',
and 'Is there knowledge in the Most High?'

12 Look! These are sinners,
and they are prosperous for ever, they have come to possess wealth.

13 And I said, 'So it was in vain that I kept my thoughts right,
and washed my hands in innocence.'

14 And I was scourged all day long,
and my rebuke lasted till the early morning.

15 If I said, 'I shall tell it in this way,'
see – I would have been faithless to the generation of your children.

16 And I thought about how to understand;
this was a labour in my eyes,

17 until I entered God's sanctuary,
and understood their end.

18 Because of their deceitfulness, you made a decree for them;
you flung them down when they were lifted up.

---

73 **Heading:** *A psalm of Asaph:* we have already seen this heading, at Psalm 50. Psalms 73–83 are all so headed. The 'sons of Asaph' were a Levitical guild, who traced their ancestry to David's chief musician (see 1 Chronicles 16:5).

73:4 *no refusal ... firm under the whip:* this seems to be what the Greek is saying here, although the point ought to be that the wicked don't seem to have the kind of suffering that we should expect, if God is really running the universe.

73:7 *fatness:* the idea here is that the wicked seem to do far better than you might expect, if God is just. Fatness in that society was a sign of God's favour rather than proof of an unhealthy life-style. The psalms have a gift for asking important questions, and this one is about the problem of undeserved fates.

they have done as they liked: literally, 'they have gone through to the disposition of their hearts'. Some translate the Greek here as 'they have fulfilled their intention'. The meaning of the Hebrew is not altogether clear.

73:10 *full days:* the Hebrew is rather difficult, but reads 'full waters', which is different by just one consonant. It is possible that the Greek has preserved the correct reading.

73:13 *washed my hands:* this is a regular way of demonstrating innocence. See Deuteronomy 21:6-9 and Psalm 26:6; and of course Pilate takes this action at Matthew 27:24, to demonstrate his conviction that Jesus is innocent.

19 How they have now turned to desolation!
Suddenly they have failed; they are destroyed for their iniquity.
20 Like the dream of someone waking up, O Lord;
in your city you will disdain their image.
21 For my heart was inflamed,
and my kidneys changed.
22 But I was set at naught and I did not realise;
I became like a beast in your presence.
23 Yet I am continually with you;
you held my right hand.
24 With your counsel you guided me;
you took me along in glory.
25 For what do I have in heaven?
And apart from you what do I want on earth?
26 My heart and flesh have failed, O God of my heart,
and my portion, O God, for ever.
27 For behold you will destroy those who remove themselves far from you;
you have utterly destroyed all those who go fornicating away from you.
28 But for me it is good to cling to God,
to place my hope in the Lord,
to proclaim all your praises at the gates of the daughter of Sion.

Psalm 74 (73)   The destruction of the Temple

[A song of instruction.] Of Asaph.

74:1 Why have you rejected [us], O God, for ever?
[Why] is your anger enraged at the sheep of your pasture?
2 Remember your congregation, which you acquired in the beginning;
you redeemed the rod of your inheritance,
this Mount Sion where you have pitched your tent.
3 Lift up your hands always against their arrogance;
what great evils the enemy has committed in your sanctuary!
4 And those who hate you have exulted in the middle of your festival;
they have set up their standards, their standards,
and they did not know,
5 as it were into the upper entrance,
6 as though in a thicket of trees, they cut down its doors with axes altogether,
with battleaxe and stonecutter's tool they broke it down.
7 They have burnt your sanctuary with fire, [razed it] to the ground;
they have profaned the dwelling place of your name.

73:19 *desolation:* Jesus uses this Greek word for the fate of Jerusalem at Luke 21:20.

73:20 *in your city:* this would be an accurate translation of the Hebrew consonants (except the letter indicating 'your' is missing); but with different vowels the Hebrew probably means something like 'when you arise'.

73:21 *my kidneys changed:* this is what the Greek says; the MT has 'my kidneys are sharpened'. The general idea is presumably that he was pretty cross with God for the fact that the wicked flourish.

73:25 *what do I have . . . what do I want on earth?:* the Hebrew here reads: 'what is there for me in heaven? And with you I desire nothing on earth', which is clear enough in its rough outline, but less precise when you come down to details.

74:4-5 *they did not know, as it were into the upper entrance:* the Hebrew here is corrupt, but even so it is hard to relate it to what we find in the Greek, which may have been dealing with a different text.

74:6 *cut down its doors . . . broke it down:* the 'it' here is feminine, and must refer to the 'upper entrance' to the Temple.

8 They said in their hearts, their kinsfolk together,
  'Come – let us utterly burn up all God's festivals from the earth.'

9 We have not seen our standards;
  and there is no prophet; and He will not know us any more.

10 How long, O God, shall the enemy revile us?
  Shall the adversary provoke your name for ever?

11 Why do you turn away your hand,
  and your right hand from the midst of your bosom for ever?

12 But God, our King from of old,
  has worked salvation in the midst of the earth.

13 You strengthened the sea by your power;
  you shattered the heads of the dragons on the water;

14 you crushed the heads of the dragon;
  you gave them as food to the peoples, to the Ethiopians.

15 For you broke open springs and wadis;
  you dried up the rivers of Ethan.

16 Yours is the day, and yours is the night;
  you have created the light and the sun.

17 You made all the boundaries of the earth;
  you fashioned summer and spring.

18 Remember this: an enemy has reviled the Lord,
  and a foolish people has provoked your name.

19 Do not hand over to the wild beasts the soul that praises you;
  do not forget for ever the souls of your poor ones.

20 Look upon your covenant,
  for the dark [places] of the earth are filled with the dwellings of the lawless.

21 Let not those who are humiliated and ashamed be turned away;
   the poor and the needy shall praise your name.

22 Arise, O God, and plead your cause;
  remember the reproaches that are directed at you by the fool, all day long.

23 Do not forget the voice of your suppliants;
  the arrogance of those who hate you has gone up continually to you.

74:8 *kinsfolk:* here the Hebrew probably means 'let us oppress them'; the translator has gone for another Hebrew root, which is possible, but makes less sense in the context.

74:12 *but God, our King:* as so often in the middle of a psalm of lament, the tone changes, and the psalmist now starts to recall what God has done in the past.

74:13 *you strengthened the sea:* this is what the Greek says, perhaps understanding this as a reference to the creation of the world. The Hebrew seems to mean something like 'you divided the sea', referring to the Exodus story of the crossing of the Red Sea (Exodus 14:23-31).

74:14 *Ethiopians:* here the Hebrew has a word that means 'jackals', or 'sharks'. It is possible that the Egyptians for whom this translation was made did not have a very high regard for their neighbours the Ethiopians.

74:15 *Ethan:* a wise man, mentioned in 1 Kings 5:11; but the Hebrew here can also mean 'ever-flowing', which is perhaps a bit more likely.

74:16 *the light:* probably to be understood as 'the moon', to judge by the reference in the previous line to 'day' and 'night'.

74:17 *summer and spring:* the Hebrew has the more expected 'summer and winter'.

74:18 *Remember this:* it is not clear to what 'this' (which is feminine in the Greek) refers in the translation. Some scholars suggest that it might be 'creation', implicitly referred to in the previous lines. The Greek word for creation is feminine, so that is certainly possible.

74:20 *dark [places]:* the Greek here translates the Hebrew precisely; although the word for 'places' is missing in the Greek, the gender of the Greek adjective makes it an almost certain guess.

74:22 *plead your cause:* the Greek has a phrase that means something like 'judge your judgement', translating a Hebrew idiom that is best rendered by something like 'defend your own case'.

74:23 *your suppliants:* so the Greek. The Hebrew here has 'adversaries', which makes better sense.

those who hate you: here the Hebrew has 'those who rise against you'.

has gone up: this is a possible reading of the Hebrew consonants, but the MT gives the word vowels that turn it into a present participle 'goes up'.

Psalm 75 (74) God judges the earth

To the end; 'Do not destroy'; A psalm of Asaph, of a song.

75:1 We shall give you thanks, O God, we shall give you thanks,
and we shall call upon your name

2 I shall recount all your wonders;
when I seize the opportunity, I shall judge with uprightness.

3 The earth melted, and all those who dwell in it;
I have strengthened its pillars.

Interlude

4 I said to the transgressors, 'Do not transgress,'
and to the sinners, 'Do not lift up [your] horn.

5 Do not raise your horn on high;
do not speak injustice against God.'

6 For neither from the East nor from the West,
nor from the barren mountains

7 for God is the judge:
this one he brings low, and that one he raises on high.

8 For there is a cup in the Lord's hand, full of unmixed wine poured out;
and he has turned it to this side and to that,
but the lees were not emptied out;
all the sinners of the earth shall drink them.

9 But as for me, I shall rejoice for ever;
I shall make a melody to the God of Jacob.

10 And I shall shatter the horns of sinners,
and the horns of the just shall be exalted.

Psalm 76 (75) Jerusalem's God, judge of the earth

To the end; among the hymns; a psalm of Asaph. A song for the Assyrian.

76:1 God is known in Judah; in Israel his name is great.

2 And his place has come to be in peace,
and his dwelling place in Sion.

3 There he broke the power of the bows,
the spear, and the sword, and the battle.

Interlude

4 You give light wonderfully from the eternal mountains.

75:2 *seize the opportunity:* the Hebrew really means something like 'when I take the appointed time', though the translations do not always manage to present that idea.

75:6 *barren mountains:* the reader will notice that there is neither verb nor subject in this verse. Some scholars want to read the Hebrew for 'mountains' as 'exaltation', which gives us at least a noun that might function as subject.

75:8 *unmixed wine:* in general in the Greek and Roman world, it was thought a very bad sign if people drank wine without diluting it with water.

poured out: this is the translation suggested by some scholars; the basic meaning of the word is 'of a mixture'.

76 **Heading:** *for the Assyrian:* this is not in the Hebrew, and it may come from an alternative, duplicated reading of the consonants that read 'for Asaph, a song'. Or it may simply be a matter of reading it back into the story of Sennacherib's invasion (2 Kings 18-19).

76:2 *in peace:* the Hebrew here could mean either 'in peace' or 'in Salem', an ancient name for Jerusalem; the latter is more probable, in view of 'Sion' in the second line.

76:3 *spear, and the sword, and the battle:* for 'spear' the Greek really means 'weapon', though it can be a spear; the Hebrew has 'shield'. 'Battle' is what the Hebrew actually says, though translations often surmise that it really means 'weapons of war'.

5 All the stupid of heart were disturbed; they have slept their sleep.
  And all the men of affluence found nothing with their hands.
6 Because of your rebuke, O God of Jacob,
  those who rode on horses grew drowsy.
7 You are awesome; who shall resist you,
  because of your anger?
8 From heaven you made [them] hear your verdict;
  earth was afraid, and kept its peace
9 when God arose for judgement,
  to save all the meek of the earth.

Interlude

10 For human thought shall praise you,
   and a remnant of thought shall celebrate you.
11 Make a vow; and repay it to the Lord your God;
   all those who are around [God] shall bring gifts,
12 to the Awesome One, the one who takes away the spirits of rulers,
   who is awesome among the kings of the earth.

Psalm 77 (76) Has God changed?

To the end. For Jeduthun. A Psalm of Asaph.

77:1 With my voice I cried to the Lord;
   with my voice to God, and he paid attention to me.
2 On the day of my affliction I sought for God;
  with my hands by night before him;
  and I was not disappointed.
  My soul refused to be comforted.
3 I remembered God, and I rejoiced;
  I complained, and my spirit was disheartened.

Interlude

4 My eyes stayed awake;
  I was disturbed, and did not speak.
5 I considered the days of old;
  and I recalled the eternal years – and I meditated
6 by night I complained in my heart,
  and my spirit probed,
7 'Will the Lord reject for ever?
  And will he not be pleased any more?
8 Or will he cut off his mercy for ever,
  from generation to generation?

76:5 *stupid of heart:* so the Greek, which possibly read a Hebrew word that differs by very little from the MT, which means 'valiant of heart'.

men of affluence . . . with their hands: the Hebrew text here has 'they found nothing, all the men of valour, their hands', whose meaning is not immediately clear.

76:6 *grew drowsy:* the Hebrew has them fast asleep.

76:7 *because of your anger:* here the Greek has translated the Hebrew ('from then') exactly as 'from that time is your anger'; scholars suggest a small change in the word for 'then', which would yield 'from the force of your anger'.

76:10 *human thought:* the Hebrew here has 'human anger', or, possibly, 'the wrath of Edom'.

a remnant of thought: the Hebrew probably means 'the survivors of your anger', or, possibly, 'the remnant of Hamath'.

77 **Heading**: *For Jeduthun:* see notes on the headings of Psalms 39 and 62.

77:4 *My eyes stayed awake:* literally, 'my eyes anticipated the watchers'. The Hebrew has 'you hold my eyelids open'.

9   Or will God forget to have compassion,
   or in anger will he close up his compassion?'

Interlude

10   And I said, 'Now I have begun:
   this change is of the right hand of the Most High'.

11   I remembered the works of the Lord;
   for I shall remember your wonders from the beginning.

12   And I shall meditate on all your works;
   and on your ways I shall speak.

13   O God, your way is in the sanctuary;
   what god is as great as our God?

14   You are the God who does wonders;
   you have made known your power among the peoples.

15   You redeemed your people with your arm,
   the children of Jacob and Joseph.

Interlude

16   The waters saw you, O God, the waters saw you and feared;
   the deeps were disturbed, the immensity of the roar of waters.

17   The clouds uttered their noise;
   for your arrows are passing through.

18   The noise of your thunder was in the whirlwind;
   your lightning-flashes appeared to the world;
   the earth was shaken and trembled.

19   Your way was in the sea, and your paths in many waters;
   and your footsteps will not be known.

20   You guided your people like sheep,
   by the hand of Moses and Aaron.

Psalm 78 (77)   Learning from the history of God's people

Of instruction. Of Asaph.

78:1   Pay attention, O my people, to my law;
   incline your ear to the words of my mouth.

2   I shall open my mouth in parables;
   I shall utter riddles from the beginning;

3   such things as we have heard and known,
   the things our ancestors have related to us.

4   They were not hidden from their children to the next generation,
   proclaiming the praises of the Lord,
   his mighty deeds, and the wonders he has done.

5   He set up a witness in Jacob, and placed a law in Israel,
   which he commanded our ancestors to make known to their offspring,

---

77:10 *I have begun:* the translator here seems to have read the Hebrew 'it is my grief' or 'it afflicts me' as a word coming from a slightly different root, which can mean (among many other things) 'to begin'.

this change: the translator reading this Hebrew word, 'change', for a very similar one that means 'years'.

77:13 *your way is in the sanctuary:* this is certainly a possible reading of the Hebrew, although most scholars translate the MT as 'your way is in holiness'.

77:18 *in the whirlwind:* literally 'in the wheel', translating a Hebrew word that can mean either.

and trembled: if it were not too archaic, you might render this as 'was all a-tremble'.

78:1 *Pay attention … to my law:* this is the beginning of the second longest psalm in the book (for the longest, see Psalm 119). Its aim is to reread the history of God's dealings with Israel, so that in the present day, Israel may gain in confidence, and return to God. That, of course, is why we in our turn read the psalms today.

6 so that the next generation might know it, the children yet to be born,
and they [in turn] will rise up and proclaim them to their children,

7 that they might place their hope in God, and not forget God's works,
that they might seek out his commandments,

8 that they may not be like their ancestors,
a crooked and provocative generation,
a generation that did not direct its heart aright,
whose spirit was not steadfast with God.

9 The Ephraimites, bending their bows and shooting with them,
were routed on the day of battle.

10 They did not keep God's covenant;
they would not walk in his Law.

11 They forgot God's good deeds,
and the wonders that he had shown them,

12 the wonders he had done before their ancestors,
in the land of Egypt, in the plain of Tanis.

13 He shattered the sea, and led them through [it];
he made the waters stand still like a wineskin.

14 He guided them with a cloud by day,
and all night long by the light of a fire.

15 He shattered a rock in the wilderness,
and made them drink as in a great deep;

16 and he brought water out of the rock,
and brought down water like rivers.

17 And they increased their sins against him;
they provoked the Most High in the desert.

18 They tempted God in their hearts,
by asking for food for their souls.

19 They spoke against God;
they said, 'Surely God can't prepare a table in the wilderness, can he?

20 For he struck the rock, and water flowed; wadis flowed abundantly.
He can't give us bread as well, can he? Or prepare a table for his people?'

21 Therefore the Lord heard, and was angry;
and a fire was kindled in Jacob; wrath went up against Israel,

22 because they had not trusted in God,
nor placed their hope in God's saving power.

23 He commanded the clouds from above,
and he opened the doors of heaven,

24 and showered down manna upon them;
he gave them bread from heaven.

78:8 *a crooked and provocative generation:* this line is quoted in Peter's Pentecost speech (Acts 2:40), where his hearers are being reminded of earlier infidelities.

78:12 *Tanis:* after about 1100 BC, this was the name given to the Egyptian royal city of Zoan, which is what the Hebrew reads. Interestingly this city is not mentioned in the Exodus story; so there is evidence here of an independent tradition.

78:13 *shattered* or 'split in two': in both Greek and Hebrew the verb is the same here and in verse 15: God can both prevent the water from drowning the Israelites and bring water out of the rock to give them water to drink and so save their lives.

like a wineskin: this is an alternative reading of the Hebrew word, which as it stands means 'like a dam' or possibly 'like a heap'.

78:21 *was angry:* this is probably what the Hebrew means. The Greek verb chosen by the translator means all sorts of different things according to its context, such as 'postpone', 'throw over (one's shoulder)', 'adjourn', and cannot easily be put into English here. Some scholars suggest 'threw up his hands', as in despair, which might catch it.

78:24 *bread from heaven:* the 'Bread of Life' discourse in John's Gospel meditates extensively on this idea. See, for example, John 6:31, where this line is quoted.

25 Human beings ate the bread of angels;
   God sent them provisions, as much as they could eat.
26 He took away the south wind from heaven;
   by his power, he brought up the south-west wind.
27 He rained flesh upon them like dust,
   and winged birds like the sand of the sea.
28 They fell into the middle of their camp,
   all around their tents.
29 They ate, and they were utterly sated;
   he gave them their desire.
30 They were not deprived of their desire;
   but while their food was still in their mouths,
31 the anger of God came up on them,
   and he slew some of their most well-fed;
   he hobbled the chosen of Israel.
32 In the midst of all this, they still sinned,
   and they did not trust in his wonders.
33 And their days died out in emptiness,
   and their years in dismay.
34 When he killed them, they went looking for him,
   and they came back, and rose up early to look for God.
35 Then they remembered that God was their help,
   and that God the Most High was their Redeemer.
36 But they deceived him with their mouth,
   and with their tongue, they lied to him.
37 Their hearts were not straight with him,
   nor were they faithful to his covenant.
38 But God is compassionate, and will pardon their sins, and not destroy them;
   he will frequently turn away his anger, and he will not kindle all his wrath.
39 And he remembered that they are merely flesh,
   a breath that passes and does not return.
40 How often they provoked him in the desert,
   and enraged him in the barren land!
41 And they turned and tempted God,
   and provoked the Holy One of Israel.
42 They did not remember his hand,
   the day when he redeemed them from the hand of those who oppressed them.
43 When he set his signs in Egypt,
   and his portents in the field of Tanis,
44 and changed their rivers into blood,
   and their rainwater, so that they could not drink it.
45 He sent the dog-fly against them, and it devoured them;
   and the frog, and it destroyed them.

78:25 *angels:* the Hebrew here has a word which is often translated 'strong' or 'powerful', but can also mean 'angels'. The term 'bread of angels' (Latin *panis angelicus*) is often used in Catholic Eucharistic devotion.

78:33 *in dismay:* this is what the Hebrew word means, which the Greek is certainly aiming to translate. The Greek word is more often translated 'at speed' or 'in haste' (see Luke 1:39), but it can also mean 'with difficulty' or even 'concern'.

78:34 *rose up early to look:* unusually, both the Hebrew and the Greek words here carry both senses, to 'rise early' and to 'seek'.

78:41 *turned and tempted:* here the Greek has literally translated a Hebrew phrase that really means 'they kept on tempting'.

⁴⁶ He gave their fruit up to mildew,
and their labours to the locust.
⁴⁷ He killed their vines with hail,
and their sycamores with frost.
⁴⁸ He handed over their cattle to hail,
and their possessions to fire.
⁴⁹ He sent the fury of his rage upon them,
his rage and fury and affliction,
a message [sent] through wicked angels.
⁵⁰ He cleared a path for his anger;
he did not spare their souls from death;
he consigned their cattle to death.
⁵¹ He struck all the first-born in Egypt,
the first fruits of their labours in the tents of Ham.
⁵² Then he took away his people like sheep,
and led them like a flock in the desert.
⁵³ He guided them in hope – and they were not afraid;
the sea covered their enemies.
⁵⁴ He led them into the territory of his sanctuary,
this mountain which his right hand had acquired.
⁵⁵ He expelled the nations before them,
gave them an inheritance by the measure of their inheritance;
and he made the tribes of Israel dwell in their tents.
⁵⁶ And they tempted and provoked God the Most High,
and they did not keep his testimonies.
⁵⁷ And they lapsed and became faithless, just like their ancestors,
and they changed into a crooked bow.
⁵⁸ And they enraged him with their high places;
and with their graven images they made him jealous.
⁵⁹ God heard, and disregarded [them], and utterly disdained Israel.
⁶⁰ And he rejected the tent at Shiloh, his tent where he dwelt among mortals.
⁶¹ He gave their might into captivity,
and their splendour into the hands of the enemy.
⁶² He consigned his people to the sword,
and disregarded his inheritance.
⁶³ Their young men were devoured by fire;
and their young women did not mourn.

78:55 *by the measure of their inheritance:* literally, 'by the rope of their inheritance'. The Hebrew word for a 'plot' (or allotment of land) can also mean a 'rope'.

made the tribes . . . dwell: literally, 'camp in their camps', which we can't do in English.

78:57 *changed into a crooked bow:* this is a powerful metaphor, the idea that suddenly Israel is an artillery weapon that could shoot off in any direction, regardless of where God points it.

78:58 *high places . . . graven images . . . made him jealous:* these are important concepts, as, in the light of the Exile to Babylon, Israel reflects on its fate. God alone is God, and therefore it is both sensible and proper to worship only the one God. Putting anything else at the centre of our lives is invariably disastrous, and results in exile.

78:59 *disregarded:* there are two identical but different Hebrew words here. One means to 'overlook' (among many other meanings), and the other has to do with 'anger'. Most translators adopt the latter meaning; the Greek translator has opted for the former.

78:60 *tent . . . tent:* the Greek here uses two different but related words. The Hebrew uses two different words, one referring to the 'tabernacle', the other meaning precisely 'tent'. The phrase translated as 'he dwelt among mortals' is very similar to the phrase used in John's Gospel of the Incarnate Word (John 1:14).

64 Their priests fell by the sword;
and their widows shall not weep.

65 The Lord awoke like a sleeper,
like a powerful man hung-over from wine.

66 He struck their enemies on the backside;
he gave them eternal disgrace.

67 He rejected Joseph's tent;
he did not choose the tribe of Ephraim.

68 But he chose the tribe of Judah,
Mount Sion, which he loved.

69 He built his sanctuary like the place of unicorns;
he founded it on the earth for ever.

70 He chose David his servant, and took him from the flocks of sheep,

71 from following the ewes in lamb, he took him to be shepherd of his people
Jacob, and Israel his inheritance.

72 He was their shepherd in the innocence of his heart;
he guided them by the skill of his hands.

Psalm 79 (78) The Gentiles are in the Temple!

A psalm of Asaph

79:1 O God, the Gentiles have come into your inheritance;
they have defiled your holy temple,
they have made Jerusalem an orchard-keeper's hut.

2 They have placed the carcasses of your servants
as food for the birds of heaven,
the flesh of your holy ones for the beasts of the earth.

3 They have poured out their blood like water around Jerusalem,
and there was no one to bury them.

4 We have become an object of reproach to our neighbours,
contempt and mockery to those around us.

5 How long, O Lord? Will you be angry for ever?
Will your jealousy burn like fire?

6 Pour out your anger on the Gentiles who do not know you,
and on kingdoms that have not called upon your name,

7 for they have devoured Jacob, and laid waste his dwelling place.

8 Do not remember our ancient transgressions;
let your compassion quickly overtake us,
for we have become very poor.

78:64 *widows shall not weep:* the Greek here has 'widows shall not be wept for', but the Hebrew has it as 'shall not weep', which is clearly intended, from the parallelism with the previous line. At this stage in the poem, the Greek translator appears a little bit over-literal.

78:65 *a powerful man hung-over from wine:* this is a rather daring comparison. The people of Israel were very 'at home' with their God.

78:69 *the place of unicorns:* this rather startling translation may reflect an alternative reading of a Hebrew word that means something like 'high heavens' or 'high hills'.

on the earth: the MT has 'like the earth', which would be a difference of only one (very similar) consonant in Hebrew. It is possible that LXX has here preserved the correct reading.

79:1 *have made Jerusalem an orchard-keeper's hut:* this is what the Greek says, although clearly the sense demands that Jerusalem be turned into 'ruins', which is what the Hebrew says.

79:2 *carcasses of your servants . . . flesh of your holy ones:* this was what happened in the ancient world when a city was conquered. In that culture the failure to bury corpses was an appalling outrage. Our translator, though presumably not the original Hebrew poet, may have known Sophocles' play *Antigone,* where the drama depends precisely on this issue of unburied corpses.

79:8 *we have become very poor:* the Hebrew here has a variety of meanings, such as 'scanty', 'low', 'poor', even 'helpless', 'powerless', or 'insignificant'. Of these meanings, the Greek translator has opted for 'poor'; English versions tend to go for 'brought low'.

9 Help us, O God, our Saviour, for the sake of the glory of your name;
   O Lord, deliver us and forgive us our sins, for the sake of your name,
10 lest the nations should say, 'Where is their God?'
   And let the avenging of the blood of your servants that has been poured out
   be made known among the nations, before their very eyes.
11 Let the groans of those who are in chains come before you,
   in accordance with the greatness of your arm,
   to preserve the children of those who have been slain.
12 Repay our neighbours seven times over, to their very bosom,
   the reproach with which they have reproached you, O Lord.
13 But we your people, and the sheep of your pasture,
   we will give you thanks for ever;
   from generation to generation we shall proclaim your praise.

Psalm 80 (79) **The restoration of God's vineyard**

To the end. Of those who will be changed. A testimony of Asaph. For the Assyrian.

80:1 O Shepherd of Israel, you who guide Joseph like sheep;
   you who sit upon the cherubim, show yourself,
2 before Ephraim and Benjamin and Manasseh;
   stir up your power and come to save us.
3 Restore us, O God, and show your face;
   and we shall be saved.
4 O Lord, God of hosts, how long will you be angry at your servant's prayer?
5 You will feed us with the bread of tears;
   you will give us drink, tears in full measure.
6 You have made us a contradiction to our neighbours;
   and our enemies have mocked us.
7 Lord, God of hosts, restore us, and show your face;
   and we shall be saved.

Interlude

8 You removed a vine from Egypt;
   you cast out the nations and planted it.
9 You prepared a way for it;
   you planted its roots, and the land was filled [with it].
10 Its shadow covered the mountains,
   and its tree-climbers covered the cedars of God.
11 It stretched out its branches as far as the sea,
   and its shoots as far as the Nile.
12 Why did you destroy its protecting wall,
   [so that] all those who pass by the way pick [grapes] off it?
13 The boar from the oak-coppice has ravaged it,
   the solitary wild beast has made it his pasture.

79:11 *children of those who have been slain:* this is what the Greek says. Scholars are not agreed about the meaning of the Hebrew: 'those who are going to die', 'those under the sentence of death', even 'those who have been set free'.

79:12 *to their very bosom:* this is what both the Greek and Hebrew say, but modern translations tend to be coy about so translating it.

80 **Heading:** *Of those who will be changed:* see note on the heading of Psalm 45.

80:4 *Lord, God of hosts:* for Greek 'Lord, God of powers', translating MT 'YHWH, God of Sabaoth'.

80:6 *a contradiction:* this translation is borrowed from the early Syriac version. The Greek is struggling to render a Hebrew word that means something like 'strife' or 'contention', and has produced 'contradiction'.

80:10 *tree-climbers:* this slightly awkward rendering is intended to reproduce the idea of *vitis arbustiva*, that kind of vine that depends on trees for its support.

14 God of hosts turn, then; look down from heaven and see,
visit this vine,

15 and restore the vine that your right hand planted;
visit the Son of Man whom you made strong for yourself.

16 It is burnt with fire, and dug up;
they shall perish at the rebuke of your face.

17 Let your hand come upon the man of your right hand,
and upon the Son of Man whom you made strong for yourself.

18 Then we shall never depart from you;
you will give us life, and we shall call upon your name.

19 Lord, God of hosts, restore us, and show your face;
and we shall be saved.

Psalm 81 (80)   **A song for the harvest festival**

To the end. On the winepresses. A psalm for Asaph.

81:1 Exult in God our helper, shout aloud to the God of Jacob.

2 Take up a psalm, and sound the drum,
the lovely lyre, and the harp.

3 Play the trumpet at the new moon,
on the auspicious day of our festival.

4 For this is a command for Israel,
and a judgement of the God of Jacob;

5 he placed it as a testimony in Joseph,
when he came out of the land of Egypt.
He heard a tongue that he did not know:

6 He removed his back from burdens;
his hands worked like slaves at the basket.

7 You called on me in distress;
I heard you in the secret place of the storm;
I tested you at the water of Contradiction.

Interlude

8 Hear, my people, as I give my evidence,
Israel, if [only] you would hear me.

9 There shall be no new gods among you;
nor shall you worship a foreign god.

10 For I am the Lord your God, who led you up out of the land of Egypt;
open wide your mouth, and I shall fill it.

11 My people did not listen to my voice;
Israel paid no attention to me.

80:15 *Son of Man:* there are several possible references here. The Hebrew has 'the son whom you made strong for yourself', which has perhaps come in from verse 17. It could also, however, refer to the king. Or, given that the LXX was preserved in Christian circles, it could be an explicit reference to Jesus.

80:17 *man . . . Son of Man:* this translation does not represent an abandonment of our policy of inclusive language. It is simply very difficult otherwise to capture what is almost certainly a reference to the king.

81 **Heading**: *On the winepresses:* see note on Psalm 8, Heading.

81:2 *take up . . . sound:* the Greek here follows the Hebrew exactly ('take . . . give'), so we have gone for the meaning that the psalmist evidently intended.

81:3 *the auspicious day:* the Greek here has a word that means something like 'conspicuous' or 'well-omened'. The Hebrew has no adjective, but we might think of something like 'The Day'.

81:7 *water of Contradiction:* the Hebrew here reads 'the waters of Meribah', which could be translated as 'strife' or 'contradiction'.

12 I sent them out, in accordance with the ways of their own hearts;
they will go their own ways.
13 If my people had listened to me,
if Israel had walked in my ways,
14 in no time at all I should have humiliated their enemies,
and I should have laid my hand on those who oppressed them.
15 The Lord's enemies lied to him;
and their doom shall be for ever.
16 He fed them with the best part of the wheat;
satisfied them with honey from the rock.

Psalm 82 (81) Lesser gods rebuked

A psalm of Asaph.

82:1 God stands in the assembly of the gods;
in the midst [of them] he will give judgement:
2 'How long will you judge unjustly,
and favour the cause of the wicked?'

Interlude

3 Give the verdict [in favour of] the orphan and the poor;
acquit the lowly and the destitute.
4 Rescue the destitute;
and deliver the poor from the power of the sinner.
5 They did not know, nor did they understand.
They pass through in darkness;
all the foundations of the earth shall be shaken.
6 I have said, 'You are gods,
and all sons of the Most High.'
7 But you die like mortals;
you fall just like one of the princes.
8 Arise, O God, judge the earth,
for you shall make your inheritance among all the nations.

Psalm 83 (82) Israel's enemies are gathering

A song of a psalm of Asaph.

83:1 O God, who shall be like you?
Do not be silent nor appeased, O God;
2 for behold, your enemies have made a noise,
and those who hate you have lifted up their head.
3 They have laid crafty plans against your people;
they have plotted against your holy ones.
4 They said, 'Come, let us utterly eliminate them from being a people;
let the name of Israel never be remembered any more!'
5 For they plotted together with one accord;
they made a covenant against you,

81:12 *ways:* the Hebrew here uses two words; the first means 'stubbornness', and the second means 'counsels' or 'devices' or (in that sense) 'ways'. LXX only uses a single word, which is closer to the latter.

81:15 *their doom:* both the Greek and the Hebrew here mean 'time', but the Hebrew word can occasionally refer to times of judgement, and hence 'doom'.

82:6 *I have said, 'You are gods, and all sons of the Most High':* this is cited by Jesus at John 10:34, to defend himself against the charge of blasphemy for describing himself as Son of God. However in its original context, the psalm clearly reaches back to a time when Israel's God was just one among many gods (see verse 1), though undoubtedly the most powerful.

6 the tents of the Edomites, and the Ishmaelites, Moab and the Hagarites;
7 Gebal and Ammon, Amalek and the foreigners,
along with the inhabitants of Tyre.
8 Indeed Assyria has come together with them,
they have come to the assistance of the children of Lot.

Interlude

9 Deal with them as with Midian and Sisera,
like Jabin at the Wadi Kishon.
10 They were utterly destroyed at Endor,
they became like dung for the earth.
11 Make their rulers like Oreb and Zeeb, like Zebah and Zalmunna,
12 who said, 'Let us make God's sanctuary our possession.'
13 My God, make them like a wheel,
like stubble before the face of the wind,
14 like fire which will burn up an oak thicket,
a flame to burn up the mountains;
15 so you will hunt them down with your storm,
and with your anger you will trouble them.
16 Fill their faces with dishonour,
and they shall seek your name, O Lord;
17 let them be embarrassed and be troubled for evermore,
let them be ashamed and destroyed.
18 And let them know that your name is 'Lord';
you alone are the Most High over all the earth.

Psalm 84 (83)   A pilgrim song

To the end. On the winepresses. A psalm for the sons of Korah.

84:1 How lovely are your tents, O Lord of hosts!
2 My soul is longing and fainting for the courts of the Lord;
my heart and my flesh rejoice in the living God.
3 For the sparrow has found a home for himself,
and the turtle-dove a nest for herself, where she will put her nestlings,
your altars, O Lord of hosts, my King and my God.
4 Blessed are those who dwell in your house;
for evermore they shall praise you.

Interlude

5 Blessed are those whose help comes from you, O Lord;
they have placed ascents in their heart,
6 in the Valley of Weeping, to the place which [God] has appointed;
for the Lawgiver will grant blessings.

83:6 *Hagarites:* these people are mentioned at 1 Chronicles 5:10, 19-21. It is possible that like the Ishmaelites of the same line they claim descent from Hagar.

83:13 *like a wheel:* this is one possible meaning of the Hebrew word. Other possibilities include 'tumbleweed' or 'thistledown'. I have gone for 'wheel' here since it is the only possible meaning of the Greek.

84:5 *ascents:* here is a place where the Greek has almost certainly preserved the correct reading. MT has 'paths' or 'highways'; but the word for 'ascent' (to Jerusalem) is different by only one consonant in Hebrew.

84:6 *Valley of Weeping:* the Hebrew text is corrupt in this verse, and the translator is doing his best.

the place which [God] has appointed: for the same emphasis on God's choice of Jerusalem as the place of divine worship, compare Deuteronomy 12:5, 11, 14, 18, 21, 26.

7 They shall go from strength to strength;
the God of gods shall be seen in Sion.

8 Lord, God of hosts, listen to my prayer,
turn your ear, O God of Jacob.

Interlude

9 See, O God, our shield, and look upon the face of your Anointed.

10 For a single day in your courts is better than thousands;
I have chosen to be thrown aside in God's house
rather than dwell in the tents of sinners.

11 For the Lord God loves mercy and truth;
the Lord will give grace and glory;
those who walk in integrity he will not deprive of good things.

12 Lord of hosts, happy are those who hope in you!

Psalm 85 (84) **Praying for God's blessing**

To the end. For the sons of Korah. A psalm.

85:1 Lord, you found pleasure in your land;
you turned away the captivity of Jacob.

2 You have forgiven your people for their iniquities;
you have covered all their sins.

Interlude

3 You put an end to all your anger;
you turned away all the anger of your rage.

4 Bring us back, O God of our salvation, and turn away your rage from us.

5 Do not be angry with us for ever;
do not continue your anger from generation to generation.

6 O God, you will turn, and give us life;
and your people will rejoice in you.

7 O Lord, show us your mercy,
and grant us your salvation.

8 I shall hear what the Lord will say about me;
for he will speak peace to his people and to his holy ones,
and to those who turn their heart towards him.

9 However his salvation is near to those who revere him,
that glory may dwell in our land.

10 Mercy and truth have met;
justice and peace have embraced.

11 Truth has risen up from the earth,
and justice looked down from heaven.

12 For the Lord will give kindness,
and our earth shall yield its fruit.

13 Justice shall go before him,
and he shall place his steps on the way.

84:9 *your Anointed:* the Greek here could equally be translated
'your Messiah'; it actually says, 'your Christ'.

Psalm 86 (85)   Asking for help

A prayer of David

86:1 O Lord, turn your ear and hear me,
for I am poor and needy.

2 Preserve my life, for I am holy;
save your servant, O God, the one who hopes in you.

3 Have mercy on me, Lord, for I cried to you all day long.

4 Give joy to the soul of your servant;
for to you, O Lord, have I lifted up my soul.

5 For you, O Lord, are kind and gentle,
rich in mercy to all who call upon you.

6 O Lord, give ear to my prayer;
and pay attention to the sound of my pleading.

7 On my day of distress I cried to you;
for you heard me.

8 There is none like you among the gods, O Lord;
and there are no [deeds] like your deeds.

9 All the nations whom you have made will come and adore before you, O Lord;
they will glorify your name.

10 For you are great, and you perform wonders;
you are the only God, the Great One.

11 Guide me, Lord, in your way,
and I shall walk in your truth;
let my heart rejoice, that I may revere your name.

12 I shall give you thanks, Lord my God, with all my heart;
and I shall glorify your name for ever.

13 For your mercy is great;
and you have delivered my life from the depths of Hades.

14 O God, transgressors have risen up against me;
and the assembly of the mighty have sought my life;
they did not place you before them.

15 But you, Lord God, are compassionate and merciful,
long-suffering and rich in mercy, and true.

16 Look upon me and have mercy on me;
give your strength to your servant, and save the child of your slave-girl.

17 Show me a sign for good;
and let those who hate me see it and be ashamed;
for you, O Lord, have helped me and comforted me.

Psalm 87 (86)   A song of Sion

For the sons of Korah. A Psalm of a song

87:1 His foundations are in the holy mountains;

2 the Lord loves the gates of Sion more than all the tents of Jacob.

3 Glorious things are spoken of you, O city of God.

Interlude

87:1 *His foundations are in the holy mountains:* this unintelligible opening to the psalm is in both the Hebrew and the Greek, though you would not guess as much from the modern versions. Indeed many scholars regard the whole psalm as practically impossible to understand. What we have done here is simply to record how the Greek has translated it.

87:3 *Glorious things:* both MT and LXX read 'glorified things' here.

4 I shall make mention of Rahab and Babylon to those who remember me;
and behold, foreigners and Tyre, and the people of the Ethiopians;
these were born there.

5 'Mother Sion,' someone will say,
'for I came into existence in her.'
The Most High himself founded her.

6 The Lord will tell of it in the writing of the peoples,
and of these rulers who were born in her.

Interlude

7 The dwelling of all who are glad is in you.

Psalm 88 (87)   A bleak lament

A song of a psalm for the sons of Korah. To the end. Over Mahalath, to reply.
Of instruction. Of Heman the Israelite.

88:1 Lord God of my salvation, I cried to you by day,
and in the night before you.

2 Let my prayer come before you;
bend your ear to my petition, O Lord.

3 For my soul is filled with evils; my life has drawn near to Hades.

4 I have been reckoned with those who go down to the Pit,
I have become like a person without help,
free among the dead,

5 like the dead, those cast out, those who sleep in the tomb,
those whom you remember no more;
they have been rejected from your hand.

6 They have placed me in the lowest pit,
in dark places, and in the shadow of death.

7 Your anger was fixed on me,
and you brought all your waves upon me.

Interlude

8 You distanced my friends from me;
they have regarded me as an abomination;
I was handed over – I could not get out.

9 My eyes became feeble because of poverty;
and I cried out to you, O Lord, all day long;
I opened my hands to you.

10 You surely will not work your wonders for the dead, will you?
Will doctors rise and praise you?

11 Will anyone in the tomb declare your mercy,
and your truth in annihilation?

---

88 **Title:** *A bleak lament:* This is one of the bleakest of the psalms. Unusually for a lament, there is no glimmer of hope whatever. Perhaps the thing to notice is that the poet is still able to pray in the midst of his sufferings.

Over Mahalath: see note on Psalm 53, Heading.

Heman the Israelite: (the Hebrew calls him an Ezrahite). A wise man, according to 1 Kings 5:11, a singer in 1 Chronicles 6:18; according to 1 Chronicles 2:6, his father was Zerah.

88:4 *free:* this is what the Hebrew means (rather bafflingly – and the versions tend to ignore it).

88:5 *like the dead:* literally 'the wounded', but this word is often used to translate a word that means 'slain'. Here the Hebrew word simply means 'among the dead'. The letter that means 'among' can easily be confused with that which is translated 'like'.

88:10 *Will doctors rise:* this is not so much a slur on the medical profession as an alternative reading of the Hebrew noun here, which is more likely to mean 'the shades of the dead' or 'dead spirits' than 'healers', though it could be either.

12 Will your wonders be known in the darkness,
   or your righteousness in a forgotten land?
13 But I have cried out to you, O Lord,
   and in the morning my prayer shall come before you.
14 Why, O Lord, do you reject my life,
   and turn away your face from me?
15 I am poor and in difficulties since my youth;
   I was raised on high and then brought low; and I was in despair.
16 Your anger passed over me;
   and your terrors agitated me.
17 They surrounded me like water, all the day long;
   they encompassed me from all sides.
18 You distanced my friend and my neighbour from me,
   and my acquaintances from [my] wretchedness.

Psalm 89 (88) God made a covenant with David

Of instruction; for Ethan the Israelite.

89:1 I shall sing your mercies, O Lord for ever;
    from generation to generation I shall proclaim your truth with my mouth.
2 For you said, Mercy shall be built up for ever;
   your truth shall be prepared in the heavens.
3 'I made a covenant with my chosen ones;
   I swore to David my servant,
4 "I shall establish your offspring for ever,
   and I shall build up your throne from generation to generation."'

Interlude

5 The heavens shall confess your wonders, O Lord,
   and your truth in the assembly of the saints.
6 For who in the clouds shall be the Lord's equal?
   And who among the children of God shall be likened to the Lord?
7 God is glorified in the council of the holy ones;
   and awesome to those who surround him.
8 Lord, God of hosts, who is like you?
   You are powerful, O Lord, and your truth surrounds you.
9 You are master of the sea,
   and you calm the surge of its waves.
10 You brought down the arrogant, like those that are slain;
   with the arm of your power you scattered your enemies.
11 Yours are the heavens, and yours is the earth;
   you founded the earth and all that fills it.
12 You created the north and the south;
   Tabor and Hermon shall rejoice in your name.
13 Yours is the arm with power; may your hand be strengthened,
   your right hand be exalted.

89 **Heading**: *Ethan the Israelite:* the Hebrew calls him an Ezrahite (cf. Psalm 88, Heading). Like Heman he is a wise man in 1 Kings 5:11; and see also 1 Chronicles 2:6.

89:9 *You are master of the sea:* the Israelites were not, on the whole, very good with the sea, which therefore functioned for them as a terrifying symbol of unpredictable chaos. They could conceive nothing more telling than to call God its 'master'. This is what gives edge to the awestruck question of Jesus' disciples, 'who is this that even the winds and the sea obey him?' (Mark 4:41).

89:12 *the south:* the Greek here has 'the seas', which is different by only one letter from the word for 'right hand' or 'south'.

14 Righteousness and judgement are the foundation of your throne;
   mercy and truth shall go before your face.

15 Happy is the people that knows the joyful cry;
   they shall walk, O Lord, in the light of your countenance.

16 They shall rejoice all day long in your name;
   by your righteousness they shall be exalted.

17 For you are the glory of their power;
   it is by your good pleasure that our horn shall be exalted.

18 For our help is from the Lord,
   and from the Holy One of Israel, our King.

19 Then you spoke in a vision to your holy ones,
   and you said, 'I placed help on a mighty one;
   I have exalted one chosen from my people.

20 I found David my servant;
   I anointed him with my holy oil.

21 For my hand will come to his assistance,
   and my arm will give him strength.

22 The enemy shall have no advantage against him;
   the wicked shall no longer damage him.

23 I shall cut his enemies to pieces before his face,
   I shall rout those who hate him.

24 My truth and my mercy shall be with him;
   his horn shall be exalted in my name.

25 I shall place his hand on the sea;
   and his right hand on the rivers.

26 He shall call on me, "My Father, you are my God,
   and the protector of my salvation."

27 I shall make him [my] first-born, higher than the kings of the earth.

28 For ever I shall keep my mercy for him,
   and my covenant will be reliable for him.

29 I shall establish his offspring for ever and ever,
   and his throne as the days of heaven.

30 If his offspring abandon my law, and do not walk in my judgements,

31 if they defile my statutes, and if they do not keep my commandments,

32 I shall visit their iniquities with a stick,
   and their sins with whips;

33 but I shall not take my mercy from him and scatter it;
   nor shall I betray my own truthfulness.

34 I shall not violate my covenant,
   nor abrogate the words that come from my lips.

35 Once [and for all] I have sworn by my holiness;
   never shall I lie to David.

89:19 *help on a mighty one . . . one chosen from my people:* the one 'chosen from my people' is almost certainly David. The Hebrew text may be corrupt here, and scholars suggest 'crown' or 'youth' instead of 'help'. There may be an echo of Nathan's oracle to David in 2 Samuel 7.

89:22 *the wicked:* literally, in both Greek and Hebrew, 'the son of lawlessness'.

89:25 *sea . . . rivers:* this could either be an assertion of the Davidic king's rule, from Mesopotamia to the Mediterranean, or a declaration that he will be victorious over the forces of chaos (represented by the waters).

89:26 *the protector:* the Hebrew here has 'the rock of my salvation', which expresses the same idea rather differently.

89:27 *I shall make him [my] first-born:* the relationship of God and the king is similarly expressed as 'Father and Son' in Psalm 2:7 and 2 Samuel 7:14.

89:29 *his offspring . . . his throne:* the psalmist is presumably here meditating on 2 Samuel 7:16.

36 His offspring shall remain for ever,
   and his throne like the sun before me.
37 And they shall be like the moon established for ever,
   and like the faithful witness in heaven.'

Interlude

38 But you have repelled and scorned,
   you have rejected your anointed one.
39 You have overturned your servant's covenant;
   you have defiled his sanctuary into the dust.
40 You have torn down all his walls;
   you have turned his fortresses into cowardice.
41 All those who pass by the way have plundered him;
   he has become a reproach to his neighbours.
42 You have exalted the right hand of his enemies;
   you have made his enemies rejoice.
43 You have turned away the help of his sword;
   and you did not help him in war.
44 You have deprived him of his purification,
   and you have broken his throne down to the ground.
45 You have cut short the days of his time;
   you have poured shame over him.

Interlude

46 How long, O Lord? Will you turn away for ever?
   Will your anger be kindled like fire?
47 Remember what my being is;
   surely you did not create all human beings in vain?
48 Who is there who can live and not see death?
   Will they rescue their life from the hand of Hades?

Interlude

49 Where are your ancient mercies, O Lord,
   which you swore to David by your truth?
50 O Lord, remember the reproach of your servants,
   which I have borne in my bosom, [the reproach] of many nations,
51 with which your enemies have reproached me, O Lord,
   with which they reviled the footsteps of your anointed one.
52 Blessed be the Lord for ever. May it be; may it be.

89:38 *anointed one:* or, of course, 'Messiah' or 'Christ'.

89:40 *cowardice:* the Hebrew word here can mean either 'terror' or 'ruins'; the latter is more likely here.

89:43 *help of his sword:* the Hebrew here has (though you would not guess it from the English versions) 'the rock of his sword', which some scholars think of as referring to the sword's sharpness.

89:44 *of his purification:* this is what we find in both Greek and Hebrew. English translations tend to emend (without telling you) to 'his sceptre', which is what the parallelism of the verse demands.

89:51 *the footsteps:* this is what the Hebrew has. LXX has read a word meaning 'reward', which has the same consonants, but different vowels in Hebrew.

89:52 *Blessed be the Lord . . . may it be:* this verse is not part of the psalm, but the editors' way of noting the end of the end of the Third 'Book' of the Psalms.

BOOK FOUR (Psalms 90–106)

Psalm 90 (89)   The shortness of human life

A prayer of Moses, the man of God

90:1   O Lord, you were our refuge in all generations.
 2   Before the mountains came to be,
  and [before] the earth and the world were fashioned,
  from age to age you are.
 3   Do not turn us back into humiliation;
  and you said, ' Turn back, you mortals.'
 4   For a thousand years in your eyes are like the yesterday which has passed,
  and like a watch in the night.
 5   Years will be their vanities;
  in the early morning let it pass away like grass.
 6   In the early morning let it flower;
  in the evening let it fall away;
  let it wither and dry up.
 7   For we have perished in your anger;
  and in your rage we have been troubled.
 8   You have placed our transgressions before you,
  and our age in the light of our countenance.
 9   For all our days have perished, and in your anger we have perished;
  I meditated our years like a spider's web.
 10   The days of our years – in them there are seventy years;
  and if people are on top form, eighty years.
  And most of them are toil and labour,
  for weakness comes upon us, and we shall be chastened.
 11   Who knows the power of your anger, or your wrath, from the fear of you?
 12   Teach us so to reckon your right hand,
  and those who are instructed in their heart in wisdom.
 13   Return, O Lord, how long?
  And relent with regard to your servants.
 14   We were filled in the morning with your mercy,
  and we rejoiced and exulted all our days.
 15   We rejoiced in compensation for the days when you humiliated us,
  for the years when we saw evil.
 16   And now, look upon your servants, and upon your works,
  and guide their children.

90:2 *came to be . . . were fashioned:* the Hebrew here uses imagery about birth, which the Greek translator seems deliberately to have avoided.

90:3 *Do not turn us back:* the Hebrew here reads 'you turn us back', which perhaps makes more sense.

90:4 *a thousand years:* this finds a NT echo in 2 Peter 3:8.

90:5, *it . . . it . . . it:* the translator here is following the
6 Hebrew, which wobbles, a shade uncertainly, between singular and plural. This goes back to verse 4, where 'a thousand years' is singular in form, but obviously plural in meaning.

90:9 *I meditated our years like a spider's web:* this could equally mean 'they meditated'. The Hebrew means something like 'our years have come to an end like a groan'. The 'spider's web' is a vivid metaphor for the insubstantiality of human life, but it is hard to reconstruct the Hebrew that our translator had in front of him.

90:12 *right hand:* this is an alternative reading of the Hebrew word for 'our days'.

those who are instructed: the Greek here actually reads 'those who are chained', but this might represent a mishearing of the Greek word for 'instructed', and 'instructed' is in turn a possible reading of the Hebrew, which might come from one of two verbs, one meaning 'instruct', and the other meaning 'bring in'. It is a good example of the difficulties faced by translators!

90:13 *relent:* the Greek literally means something like 'be comforted', though the verb has a number of possible meanings. The Hebrew may have this meaning, but in this form perhaps means 'to be sorry'.

90:16 *guide:* this is a possible alternative reading of the Hebrew text.

¹⁷ And let the radiance of the Lord our God be upon us;
and direct the works of our hands upon us.

Psalm 91 (90)   Confidence in God's protection

A song of praise, of David

91:1 The one who dwells in the help of the Most High,
will lodge in the protection of the God of Heaven,

² will say to the Lord, 'You are my protector and my refuge,
my God – I shall hope in him,

³ for he will deliver me from the hunter's snare,
and from the word that spells trouble.'

⁴ He will overshadow you with the broad of his back;
under his wings you will find hope;
his truth will encircle you with a shield.

⁵ You will not fear the nocturnal terror,
nor the arrow that flies by day,

⁶ nor the thing that passes through the darkness,
nor mishap nor the noonday devil.

⁷ A thousand shall fall at your side,
and ten thousand at your right hand;
it shall not approach you.

⁸ But with your eyes you will understand;
and you will see the reward of sinners.

⁹ For you, O Lord, are my hope;
you have made the Most High your refuge.

¹⁰ Evils shall not approach you,
nor the scourge draw near to your tent.

¹¹ For he will command his angels concerning you,
to keep you in all your ways.

¹² On their hands they shall raise you up,
lest you strike your foot against a stone.

¹³ You will tread on the asp and the basilisk;
and you will trample on lion and dragon.

¹⁴ For he has hoped in me, so I shall rescue him;
I shall protect him for he has known my name.

¹⁵ He will call upon me, and I shall listen to him;
I am with him in affliction, and I shall glorify him.

¹⁶ With length of days I shall satisfy him;
and I shall show him my salvation.

Psalm 92 (91)   Thanks for God's faithfulness

A psalm of a song for the Sabbath day

92:1 It is good to sing praise to the Lord,
and to sing a psalm to your name, O Most High,

91:11-12 *he will command his angels . . . foot against a stone:* these verses are quoted, though not completely, by the devil, when he tempts Jesus, in Luke 4:10-11, and, slightly less fully, in the parallel passage Matthew 4:6.

91:13 *asp . . . basilisk . . . dragon:* a similar notion of the immunity of God's holy ones is to be found in Isaiah 11:6-8, and Daniel 6:22. It is perhaps echoed in Jesus' words to the returning 72 disciples at Luke 10:19.

91:15 *He will call upon me, . . . I shall glorify him:* early Christian readers of the LXX will inevitably have thought of John 12:27-28, and John 17:1-2.

2 to announce your mercy in the morning,
   and your truth by night,
3 on a ten-stringed lyre, with a song on the harp.
4 For you delighted me, O Lord, with your work;
   and at the deeds of your hands I shall rejoice.
5 How your deeds have been made great, O Lord;
   your thoughts are very deep.
6 The foolish person does not know this;
   the unintelligent will not understand.
7 When sinners rise up like grass,
   and all those who do iniquity peep out,
   may they be destroyed for ever and ever.
8 But you, the Most High, are for ever, O Lord.
9 For behold your enemies will perish,
   and all those who do iniquity will be scattered.
10 My horn shall be exalted like the unicorn,
   my old age with rich oil.
11 And my eye looked upon my enemies;
   my ear shall hear the evil who rise up against me.
12 The just shall flourish like a palm tree,
   like a cedar in Lebanon they shall be multiplied.
13 Planted in the Lord's house,
   in the courts of our God they shall flourish.
14 They shall be multiplied with well-fed old age;
   and they will prosper,
15 so as to proclaim that the Lord God is upright;
   and there is no immorality in him.

Psalm 93 (92)   The Lord is King

For the day before the Sabbath, when the land was inhabited.
A praise-song of David.

93:1 The Lord has become King; he is clothed with dignity.
   The Lord is clothed and has girded himself with power,
   for he has established the world,
   which shall not be shaken.
2 Your throne is ready since then;
   from all time you are.
3 The rivers have lifted up, O Lord,
   the rivers have lifted up their voices,
4 from the voices of many waters.
   Wonderful are the billows of the sea,
   wonderful on high is the Lord.
5 Your testimonies have been confirmed in abundance;
   holiness is fitting to your house,
   O Lord, for [all] the length of days.

92:4 *work:* the Hebrew word here means 'deed'; but the Greek word is the origin of the English word 'poem'.

92:10 *old age:* reading a Hebrew word very close to the present one, which means 'I have made a mixture'.

92:12 *just shall flourish like a palm tree:* the notion of the tree as a metaphor for God's chosen ones is also to be found, of course, at Psalm 1:3; compare also Jeremiah 17:8; Ezekiel 17:5-8.

93 **Heading:** *the day before the Sabbath, when the land was inhabited:* The Hebrew has no heading here. The reference is to Genesis 1:24-31, the last day of Creation according to the first chapter of the Bible.

Psalm 94 (93)   **God avenges the righteous**

A psalm of David, for the fourth day of the week

94:1   A God of vengeance is the Lord,
the God of vengeance has spoken boldly.

2   Be exalted, you who judge the earth;
repay a reward to the arrogant.

3   How long shall sinners, O Lord,
how long shall sinners boast?

4   They shall utter and speak immorality,
all those who do iniquity.

5   They have humbled your people, O Lord,
and afflicted your inheritance.

6   They have killed the widow and the stranger;
and they have slaughtered orphans.

7   And they said, 'The Lord shall not see;
nor shall the God of Jacob understand.'

8   Understand now, fools among the people;
and idiots, when will you understand?

9   The one who planted the ear, does he not hear?
The one who fashioned the eye, does he not perceive?

10   The one who disciplines the Gentiles, will he not chastise,
the one who teaches humanity knowledge?

11   The Lord knows the thoughts of human beings,
that they are empty.

12   Happy is anyone whom you discipline, O Lord,
and whom you teach from your Law,

13   to give them rest from evil days,
until a pit is dug for the sinner.

14   For the Lord will not reject his people,
and will not abandon his inheritance,

15   until righteousness returns to judgement,
and all the upright of heart cling to it.

Interlude

16   Who will rise up for me against those who do evil?
Who will stand at my side against those who work iniquity?

17   If the Lord had not helped me,
my soul would all but have sojourned in Hades.

18   If I said, 'My foot has been shaken,'
your mercy, O Lord, helps me,

19   O Lord, in accordance with the multitude of the pains in my heart,
your comforts loved my soul.

20   Shall the throne of iniquity have fellowship with you,
those who shape trouble with their decrees?

---

94   **Heading**: *A psalm of David, for the fourth day of the week:* there is no heading in the Hebrew. Presumably the day refers to some practice within the Jewish community, but this heading is not evidence for the original use of this psalm.

94:1   *has spoken boldly:* this is a possible reading of the Hebrew, which is normally read as an imperative, telling God to 'shine forth'.

94:6   *stranger:* the Greek word here is the one that gives us 'proselyte'. This simply means 'one who has drawn near', but is a regular translation in LXX of the word for 'stranger' or 'resident alien', a category of the marginalised who in the Old Testament are privileged and marked out for God's special attention.

21 They will chase after the life of the righteous;
    they will condemn innocent blood.
22 And the Lord became a refuge for me;
    my God became the helper in whom I hoped.
23 God will repay them for their iniquity;
    in accordance with their wickedness our God shall destroy them.

Psalm 95 (94) An invitation to praise

A song of praise for David

95:1 Come, let us sing joyfully to the Lord;
     let us cry aloud to God our Saviour.
  2 Let us come before his face with thanksgiving;
     and with psalms let us cry aloud to him.
  3 For the Lord is a great God,
     and a great king over all the gods;
  4 For in his hands are the ends of the earth,
     and the heights of the mountains are his.
  5 For the sea is his – he made it;
     and his hands fashioned the dry land.
  6 Come, let us worship and fall down before him;
     and let us weep before the Lord who made us.
  7 For he is our God, and we the people of his pasture,
     and the sheep of his hand.
     Today if you would hear his voice,
  8 do not harden your hearts as at the Rebellion,
     as on the Day of Temptation in the desert,
  9 when your ancestors put me to the test
     (and they had seen my works!).
  10 For forty years I was angry with that generation, and I said,
     'They are always astray in their heart;
     they did not know my ways.'
  11 So I swore in my wrath,
     'Never shall they enter my rest.'

Psalm 96 (95) A new song to the Lord

When the House was being built, after the Captivity. A song of David.

96:1 Sing a new song to the Lord,
     sing to the Lord, all the earth.
  2 Sing to the Lord, bless his name,
     spread the good news of his salvation, day after day.

---

95 **Title:** *An invitation to praise:* that is certainly an accurate description, but we should notice how the psalm ends, reflecting edgily on the history of Israel under God's leadership. The letter to the Hebrews meditates carefully on this psalm (Hebrews 3:7–4:11), using the fact that the word for Joshua and for Jesus are the same in Greek.

95:8 *Rebellion:* the Greek here means 'Provocation' or 'Embitterment', but is clearly translating 'Meribah' which is best understood as 'Rebellion' here.

95:9 *your ancestors put me to the test:* this picks up Numbers 14:22, an episode on which Paul reflects at 1 Corinthians 10:9, when trying to sort out the question of eating food offered to idols.

96 **Heading:** *When the House was being built, after the Captivity:* this title is not in the Hebrew, but it is perhaps evidence for the original setting of the psalm.

A song of David: since David was dead long before the Captivity, clearly 'song of David' does not mean that David wrote a particular psalm, in the editor's view.

3 Proclaim God's glory among the nations,
his wonders among all the peoples.
4 For the Lord is great, and much to be praised;
he is terrible above all the gods.
5 For all the gods of the Gentiles are demons;
but the Lord made the heavens.
6 Thanksgiving and beauty are before him,
holiness and majesty are in his sanctuary.
7 Bring to the Lord, families of the peoples,
bring to the Lord glory and honour.
8 Bring to the Lord glory to his name,
lift up sacrificial offerings,
and enter his courts.
9 Worship the Lord in his holy court,
let all the earth be shaken before his face.
10 Say among the nations,
'The Lord has become King – for he established the world
which shall not be shaken.
He will judge the peoples with uprightness.'
11 Let the heavens rejoice and the earth be glad;
let the sea be shaken, and all that fills it.
12 The plains shall rejoice, and all that is in them;
then all the trees of the wood shall exult,
13 before the Lord's face,
for he comes, for he comes to judge the earth;
he will judge the world with righteousness, and the peoples with his truth.

Psalm 97 (96)   The glory of God's reign

Of David, when his land is established

97:1 The Lord has become King,
let the earth exult, and many islands be glad.
2 Cloud and darkness surround him,
righteousness and judgement direct his throne.
3 Fire shall go before him,
and shall consume his enemies round about.
4 His lightnings shone over the world;
the earth beheld, and was shaken.
5 The mountains melted like wax because of the Lord's presence,
because of the presence of the Lord of all the earth.
6 The heavens proclaimed his justice;
and all the peoples saw his glory.
7 Let all those who worship graven images be ashamed,
those who boast of their idols.
Worship God, all you his angels.
8 Sion heard, and rejoiced,
and the daughters of Judea exulted,
because of your judgements, O Lord.

97:7 *all you his angels:* the Hebrew here reads 'all you gods';
but this is the version quoted in the Letter to the
Hebrews (Hebrews 1:6).

9   For you are the Lord, the Most High over all the earth;
     you are greatly exalted above all the gods.
10   You who love the Lord, hate evil;
     the Lord guards the souls of his holy ones;
     from the hand of sinners he shall deliver them.
11   Light dawns for the righteous;
     and joy for the upright of heart.
12   Rejoice, you just, in the Lord,
     and give thanks for the remembrance of his holiness.

Psalm 98 (97)   The Lord is coming

A Psalm of David

98:1 Sing a new song to the Lord, for the Lord has done wonders;
      his right hand and his holy arm have brought him salvation.
2   The Lord has made known his salvation;
      in the sight of the nations, he has revealed his righteousness.
3   He has remembered his mercy for Jacob,
      and his truth for the house of Israel;
      all the ends of the earth have seen the saving power of our God.
4   Cry out to God, all the earth;
      sing and exult and utter a psalm.
5   Utter a psalm to the Lord on the harp,
      on the harp and with the sound of a psalm.
6   With brazen trumpets, and the sound of a trumpet of horn,
      cry aloud before the Lord, the King.
7   Let the sea be shaken and that which fills it,
      the world and those who dwell in it.
8   The rivers shall clap their hands together;
      the mountains shall exult.
9   For he comes to judge the earth;
      he will judge the world with righteousness,
      and the peoples with uprightness.

Psalm 99 (98)   The Lord will judge the earth

A Psalm of David

99:1 The Lord has become King;
      let the peoples rage;
      [God] dwells on the cherubim – let the earth be shaken.
2   The Lord is great in Sion, and high above all the peoples.
3   Let them give thanks to your great name;
      for it is terrible and holy.

97:10 *hate evil:* this is perhaps echoed at Romans 12:9, although there is no evidence of verbal parallel.

98:1 *have brought him salvation:* this is a very literal translation of the Hebrew. Obviously neither poet nor translator thought that God was in need of salvation.

98:3 *for Jacob:* this is not in the MT. Or it may have dropped out of the Hebrew original; it may have been inserted into the Greek in order to make the two lines parallel.

98:6 *brazen trumpets:* the word that I have translated as 'brazen' really means 'metal', and it is not in the Hebrew. The point is presumably to distinguish this kind of wind instrument from one made of horn.

4   And the King's honour loves judgement;
      you have prepared uprightness;
      and you have done judgement and justice in Jacob.
5   Exalt the Lord our God,
      and worship at his footstool;
      for he is holy.
6   Moses and Aaron were among his priests,
      and Samuel among those that call upon his name.
      They called upon the Lord and he heard them.
7   In a pillar of cloud he would speak to them;
      they kept his testimonies, and the decrees which he gave them.
8   O Lord, our God, you heard them;
      O God, you were merciful to them,
      but you took vengeance on all their practices.
9   Exalt the Lord our God, and worship at his holy mountain,
      for the Lord our God is holy.

Psalm 100 (99)   Seven reasons to praise God

A Psalm for Thanksgiving

100:1   Cry out with joy to the Lord, all the earth.
2   Serve the Lord with gladness,
      come before him with exultation.
3   Know that the Lord is God;
      he made us, and not we ourselves.
      We are his people, and the sheep of his pasture.
4   Enter his gates with thanksgiving, his courts with hymns;
      give him thanks, praise his name.
5   For the Lord is good, his mercy is for ever,
      and his truth [endures] from generation to generation.

Psalm 101 (100)   The king prays to his God

A psalm of David

101:1   I shall sing to you, O Lord, of mercy and judgement,
2   I shall sing a psalm and I shall understand the way that is blameless.
      When will you come to me?
      I walked in the innocence of my heart, in the midst of my house;
3   I have not set before my eyes any unlawful thing;
      I hated those who commit transgressions.
4   A crooked heart did not cling to me;
      when the evil turned away from me, I did not recognise [them].
5   I would chase away those who slander their neighbour in secret;
      I would not eat with persons of arrogant expression and insatiable heart.

99:4   *King's honour:* the Hebrew here means 'the King's strength'.

uprightness: the Greek here follows the Hebrew in making the noun plural; but we cannot do that in English.

100   **Title**: *Seven reasons to praise God:* this short psalm, filled with language connected with God's covenant, has seven imperative verbs to encourage a correct response to what God has done. Count them as you read.

100:3   *not we ourselves:* here the Greek exactly follows the Hebrew, but it is quite likely that the original read 'we are his', which would sound much the same in Hebrew.

6 My eyes shall be on the faithful of the land,
for them to sit with me.
The one who walked in the way that is blameless,
is the one who ministered to me.
7 They did not dwell in the midst of my house,
those who act arrogantly;
those who speak injustice did not prosper in my sight.
8 In the early morning I would kill all the sinners in the land,
to root out from the city of the Lord all those who work iniquity.

Psalm 102 (101)   The fifth 'Penitential Psalm'

A prayer for the poor, when they are weary, and pour out their prayer before the Lord.

102:1 Hear my prayer, O Lord, and let my cry come to you.
2 Do not turn your face away from me;
on the day when I am afflicted, turn your ear to me.
On the day when I call upon you, hear me quickly.
3 For my days have vanished like smoke,
and my bones burnt up like firewood.
4 My heart is smitten like grass, and dried up;
I have forgotten to eat my bread.
5 Because of the sound of my groaning,
my bone has stuck to my flesh.
6 I have become like a desert pelican,
like a night raven in a building site.
7 I could not sleep; I became like a sparrow,
living alone on a rooftop.
8 All day long my enemies reproached me,
those who praised me made an oath against me.
9 I ate ashes like bread;
and I mixed my drink with weeping,
10 because of the presence of your anger and you wrath;
for you lifted me up and then dashed me down.
11 My days faded like a shadow,
I am dried up like grass.
12 But you, O Lord, remain for ever,
and your remembrance is from generation to generation.
13 You will arise and have pity on Sion,
for it is time to have pity on her, for the time has come.
14 For your servants delighted in her stones;
and they will have pity on her dust.
15 The nations shall hold the Lord's name in awe,
and all the kings of the earth your glory.
16 For the Lord will build up Sion,
and he will appear in his glory.
17 He has looked upon the prayer of the lowly,
and has not despised their entreaty.

102:6 *night raven:* or 'long-eared owl'. Our grasp of Hebrew and Greek ornithology is somewhat tenuous.

102:8 *those who praised me:* rather confusingly, the Hebrew word that is being translated here can mean either 'curse' or 'praise'. The Greek translator has opted for the latter.

18 Let this entreaty be written down for a later generation;
and the people that is being created shall praise the Lord.
19 For the Lord peeped down from his holy height,
from heaven he looked down on the earth,
20 to hear the groaning of prisoners,
the children of those who have been put to death,
21 to proclaim the Lord's name in Sion,
and his praise in Jerusalem,
22 when the peoples gather together,
and kingdoms, to serve the Lord.
23 He answered him in the way of his strength;
tell me of the brevity of my days.
24 Do not lead me up with my days half-run;
your years are from generation to generation.
25 In the beginning, O Lord, you founded the earth,
and the heavens are the work of your hands.
26 They shall perish; but you will remain;
they shall all grow old like a garment,
and like a cloak you will change them, and they shall be changed.
27 But you are the same;
and your years shall not fail.
28 The children of your servants shall pitch their tents,
and their offspring shall prosper for ever.

Psalm 103 (102)   Praising God's goodness

Of David

103:1 Bless the Lord, my soul;
and let all that is within me [bless] his holy name.
2 Bless the Lord, my soul, and do not forget all his rewards,
3 the one who is merciful on all your iniquities,
who heals all your diseases,
4 who redeems your life from destruction,
who crowns you with mercy and compassion,
5 who satisfies your desire with good things;
your youth will be renewed like an eagle's.
6 The Lord who performs acts of mercy,
and judgement for all those who suffer injustice,
7 he made his ways known to Moses,
his will to the children of Israel.
8 The Lord is compassionate and merciful,
slow to anger, and rich in mercy.
9 He will not be angry to the end,
nor will he cherish his wrath for ever.

102:23 *answered him in the way of his strength:* the Hebrew could be read in this way, but the verb meaning 'answered' could, with different vowels, be read as 'he humbled in the way of his [or 'my'] strength. Either way, it is not particularly easy to understand.

102:25 *In the beginning . . . work of your hands:* the psalmist is here clearly musing on God's creation of the world, though neither in Hebrew nor in Greek is there any echo of Genesis 1.

103:1 *Bless the Lord, my soul:* this psalm and the one that follows it are closely related, not just because they start identically, and finish in the same way.

103:2 *all his rewards:* some Greek manuscripts have 'all his praises', but this reading is to be preferred, and is closer to the Hebrew. The idea is gratitude for all that God has done.

10 He did not deal with us in accordance with our iniquities;
  nor did he repay us in accordance with our sins.

11 For as far as the heaven is high above the earth,
  [so] the Lord increased his mercy on those who fear him.

12 As far as the East is from the West,
  [so] he has removed our iniquities far from us.

13 As a father has compassion on his children,
  so the Lord has compassion on those who fear him.

14 For he knows how we are formed;
  remember that we are dust.

15 Human beings' days are like grass,
  as the flower of the field,
  so shall they flourish.

16 For the wind passes through it, and it shall not be;
  and it shall know its place no more.

17 But the Lord's mercy is from generation to generation
  upon those who fear him;
  and his righteousness upon children's children

18 for those who keep his covenant,
  and who remember his commandments, to perform them.

19 The Lord has prepared his throne in heaven,
  and his sovereignty rules over all.

20 Bless the Lord, all his angels, mighty in strength,
  those who do his word, to listen to the sound of his words.

21 Bless the Lord, all you his powers,
  his ministers who do his will.

22 Bless the Lord, all his works,
  in every place of his dominion.
  My soul, bless the Lord.

Psalm 104 (103) In praise of God's creation

Of David

104:1 Bless the Lord, my soul,
  O Lord my God, you have been greatly magnified;
  you are clothed with thanksgiving and honour.

2 robed in light as with a garment,
  stretching out the heaven like a curtain,

3 he who roofs his upper chamber with waters,
  who lays down clouds as his footsteps,
  who walks on the wings of the winds,

4 who makes winds his messengers,
  and flaming fire his servants.

5 He founded the earth on its stable footing;
  it shall never tip over.

103:14 *remember:* the Greek is an imperative; the Hebrew could be in almost any mood, but is often translated as 'God remembers'.

103:15 *days are like grass:* for the idea of grass as a symbol of mortality and transience, see Isaiah 40:6, and James 1:10-11.

104 **Heading:** *Of David:* this heading is not in the Hebrew. The psalm is one of the loveliest in the Psalter.

104:4 *winds his messengers . . . flaming fire his servants:* this passage is quoted at Hebrews 1:7, as a way of demonstrating the superiority of 'the Son' to the angels.

104:5 *on its stable footing:* literally, 'on its truth'. The Hebrew simply means 'on its fixed place'.

6   The deep, like a garment, is his covering;
    the waters shall stand above the mountains.

7   At your rebuke they will flee;
    at the sound of your thunder they shall panic.

8   Mountains ascend, and plains descend,
    to the place that you established for them.

9   You set a boundary which the [waters] shall not pass;
    nor shall they return to cover the earth.

10 [It is God who] sends out springs in ravines;
    the waters shall run between the mountains;

11 they shall give drink to all the beasts of the field;
    wild donkeys will receive them for their thirst.

12 Upon them the birds of the heaven shall dwell,
    from the midst of the rocks they shall utter their song.

13 [It is God who] waters the mountains from his upper chamber;
    the earth shall be filled with the fruit of your works.

14 [It is God who] makes grass grow for the cattle,
    and greenery for the service of human beings,
    so that they bring bread out of the earth;

15 and wine gladdens the human heart,
    to make their faces cheerful with olive oil;
    and bread strengthens the human heart.

16 The trees of the plain shall be sated,
    and the cedars of Lebanon which he planted.

17 There the sparrows shall make a nest;
    the house of the heron leads them.

18 The high mountains are for deer,
    the rock is a refuge for cony rabbits.

19 God made the moon for the seasons;
    the sun knows its time for setting.

20 You made the darkness – and it was night;
    all the beasts of the forest will go through it,

21 lion cubs roaring for prey, to seek food for themselves from God.

22 The sun rose, and they gathered;
    and they shall sleep in their dens.

23 Human beings shall go out to their work,
    and to their labour until evening.

24 How great are your works, O Lord!
    You have made them all with wisdom;
    the earth is full of your creation.

25 This is the sea, great and wide;
    there are creepy-crawlies there beyond numbers,
    small animals and large.

26 There the ships go through,
    and the dragon, which you made to play with.

104:9 *nor shall they return to cover the earth:* the reference here is clearly to the aftermath of the Flood (Genesis 9:12-17). The Israelites could hardly imagine a greater instance of God's power than his ability to control the waters.

104:26 *the dragon, which you made to play with:* this is a rather charming notion. The Hebrew could mean that it is the dragon who plays in the sea, but the gender of the Greek pronoun means that it has to be God playing with the dragon (presumably a whale, or something along those lines).

27   They all look expectantly to you,
     to give them their food at the right time.
28   When you give it to them, they gather;
     when you open your hand, they shall all be filled with goodness.
29   When you turn away your face, they shall be dismayed;
     you will take their breath away; they shall fall faint,
     and they shall return to their dust.
30   You will send out your spirit, and they shall be created;
     and you will renew the face of the earth.
31   Let the glory of the Lord be for ever;
     the Lord shall rejoice in his works,
32   the Lord who looks on the earth and makes it tremble,
     who touches the mountains and they smoke.
33   I shall sing to the Lord all my life;
     I shall play a tune for my God while I exist.
34   May my meditation be pleasing to him;
     as for me, I shall rejoice in the Lord.
35   Let sinners disappear from the earth, and the lawless,
     so that they exist no more.
     My soul, bless the Lord.

Psalm 105 (104)   God is faithful

105:1   Alleluia! Give thanks to the Lord, and call upon his name;
     proclaim his works among the nations.
2   Sing to him, and play a melody;
     recount all his wonders.
3   Sing praise in his holy name;
     let the hearts of those who seek the Lord rejoice.
4   Seek the Lord, and be strengthened;
     seek his face always.
5   Remember his wonders that he has done,
     his portents that he performed, and the judgements of his mouth.
6   You offspring of Abraham, his servants,
     children of Jacob, his chosen ones.
7   He is the Lord our God;
     his judgements are in all the earth.
8   He has remembered his covenant for ever,
     the word which he commanded for a thousand generations,
9   which he established as his covenant with Abraham,
     and his oath to Isaac.
10   He established it for Jacob as a commandment,
     an eternal covenant for Israel,
11   saying, 'I shall give you the land of Canaan,
     your allotted inheritance,'
12   when they were little in number,
     a tiny group, and strangers in the land.
13   They passed through from nation to nation,
     from one kingdom to another people.

---

105   **Title:** *God is faithful*: listen to the note of astonishment as the poet invites his fellow Israelites to review what God has done in their history. Is this something that we can do today?

14 He did not let anyone oppress them,
   and for their sakes he rebuked kings,
15 'Do not touch my anointed ones,
   and do no evil among my prophets.'
16 And he called a famine upon the land,
   and broke all provision of bread in pieces.
17 He sent a man before them;
   Joseph was sold for a slave.
18 They humiliated his feet with fetters,
   his soul entered the iron,
19 until his word came to pass,
   and the Lord's saying tried him by fire.
20 The king sent and freed him,
   the prince of the peoples let him go free.
21 He made him lord over his house, and ruler of all his creation,
22 to educate his princes like himself,
   and to teach wisdom to his elders.
23 And Israel entered into Egypt,
   Jacob sojourned in the land of Ham.
24 [God] made his people increase greatly,
   and made them stronger than their enemies.
25 He changed [the Egyptians'] hearts, to hate his people,
   and to deal deceitfully with his people.
26 He sent out Moses his servant,
   Aaron whom he had chosen.
27 He established the words of his signs among them,
   and of his portents in the land of Ham.
28 He sent darkness and made it dark,
   and they rebelled against his words.
29 He changed their waters into blood, and killed their fish.
30 Their land swarmed with frogs,
   in the chambers of their kings.
31 He spoke, and the dog-fly came,
   and gnats in all their frontiers.
32 He made their showers into hail,
   and burning fire in their land.
33 And he struck their vines and their fig trees,
   and shattered every tree of their land.
34 He spoke, and the locust came,
   and young locusts beyond counting.
35 And they devoured all the grass in their land,
   and devoured the fruit of their land.
36 He struck every first-born in their land,
   the first-fruits of all their labour.
37 He led them out with silver and gold,
   and there was no one sick among their tribes.
38 Egypt rejoiced at their departure,
   for the fear of [the Israelites] had fallen upon them.

105:18 *soul entered the iron:* this is what the Greek says, and it is a possible translation of the Hebrew. However it is normally understood as expressing the effect of captivity on Joseph: 'the iron had entered his soul'.

105:38 *departure:* the Greek word here is 'exodus', the same word used at Luke 9:31, when Moses and Elijah speak of what will happen to Jesus in Jerusalem.

39 He spread out a cloud to cover them,
and fire to give them light at night.

40 They asked, and the quail came;
and he satisfied them with the bread of heaven.

41 He split the rock, and waters flowed,
rivers ran in waterless places.

42 For he remembered his holy word to Abraham his servant.

43 And he led his people out with exultation,
and his chosen ones with gladness.

44 He gave them the lands of the nations,
and they inherited the labours of the peoples,

45 that they might keep his decrees,
and might seek out his Law.

Psalm 106 (105) God's goodness and Israel's sins

106:1 Alleluia! Give thanks to the Lord, for he is good, for his mercy is for ever.

2 Who shall tell the mighty deeds of the Lord?
Who shall make all his praises heard?

3 Happy are those who keep judgement,
and who do righteousness at all times.

4 Remember us, O Lord, with the pleasure that you take in your people;
visit us with your saving power,

5 that we may look upon the prosperity of your chosen ones,
that we may rejoice with the joy of your people,
to sing praise with your inheritance.

6 We have sinned, along with our fathers,
we have acted lawlessly and unjustly.

7 Our fathers in Egypt did not understand your wonders;
they did not remember the abundance of your mercy;
and they rebelled as they went up by the Red Sea.

8 But he rescued them for the sake of his name,
to make known his mighty power.

9 He rebuked the Red Sea and it dried up;
and he led them through the deep as though through a desert.

10 He rescued them from the hand of those who hated them,
and redeemed them from the hand of the enemy.

11 The water covered their oppressors;
not one of them was left.

12 They believed in his words,
and they sang his praise.

13 They quickly forgot his works;
they did not wait for his counsel.

14 They gave way to their desires in the desert;
they put God to the test in the dry country.

15 He gave them what they asked for;
he sent abundance into their lives.

105:40 *quail:* technically, not quail at all, but a bird, possibly the 'landrail', that migrates with quail.

106:7 *by the Red Sea:* the Hebrew here has a slightly awkward 'at the sea, in the Sea of Reeds', and the Greek translator has tried to capture some of this, while smoothing the awkwardness.

16 They provoked Moses to anger in the camp,
   and Aaron, the holy one of the Lord.
17 The earth opened and swallowed up Dathan,
   and covered Abiram's synagogue.
18 And fire flamed out in their synagogue;
   flame burnt up sinners.
19 They made a calf at Horeb,
   and worshipped a graven image.
20 They exchanged their glory for the likeness of a calf that eats grass!
21 They forgot the God who saved them,
   who had done great things in Egypt,
22 wonderful things in the land of Ham,
   terrible things at the Red Sea.
23 And he said that he would have destroyed them,
   if Moses, his chosen one, had not stood in the breach before him,
   to turn away his anger, to prevent it destroying them.
24 And they despised the land they had desired;
   they did not trust his word.
25 And they complained in their tents;
   they did not listen to the voice of the Lord.
26 He lifted up his hand against them,
   to destroy them in the desert,
27 and to destroy their offspring among the Gentiles,
   and to scatter them among the lands.
28 they were initiated into [the rites of] Baal-Peor,
   and ate the sacrifices of the dead.
29 And they provoked him with their practices,
   and destruction was multiplied among them.
30 And Phinehas arose and made atonement;
   and the slaughter ceased.
31 And it was reckoned to him as righteousness,
   from generation to generation for ever.
32 They also provoked him at the waters of Meribah,
   and Moses was maltreated on their account.
33 For they provoked his spirit, and he tore into them with his lips.
34 They did not destroy the nations which the Lord had told them to [destroy].
35 But they mingled with the nations,
   and learnt to do what they did.
36 They served graven images,
   and it became a snare to them.
37 They sacrificed their sons and their daughters to the demons.

106:17 *Dathan . . . Abiram:* the story of their rebellion and consequent punishment is told in Numbers 16:12-14, 25-34.

synagogue: this is what the Greek says, although it is not clear when synagogues can be said to have started in Judaism, and the word could equally be translated 'gathering' or 'congregation'.

106:28 *Baal-Peor:* we do not know where this is, but clearly it was a place where pagan rites were celebrated. The Greek has 'Baal-Phegor', which will be the nearest they could get to transcribing a guttural consonant in the middle of the second word. The episode that is alluded to here and in the next two verses is to be found at Numbers 25:1-13.

106:32 *Meribah:* the translator has here rendered the original literally, as 'contradiction'. It seemed reasonable to opt for the more familiar version.

106:33 *he tore into them:* the Hebrew here has 'he spoke rashly'. Perhaps the translator did not want Moses to 'speak rashly'.

38 They shed innocent blood,
    the blood of their sons and their daughters,
    whom they sacrificed to the idols of Canaan,
    and the land was defiled with slaughter,
39 and was polluted by their deeds;
    and they committed fornication by their actions.
40 So the Lord was utterly enraged against his people,
    and the Lord loathed his inheritance.
41 He handed them over into the hands of the nations,
    and those who hated them ruled over them.
42 Their enemies oppressed them,
    and they were humiliated at their hands.
43 Again and again he delivered them;
    but they provoked him by their [evil] intentions;
    they were humiliated by their [own] iniquities.
44 And the Lord looked upon them when they were being oppressed,
    when he listened to their entreaty.
45 He remembered his covenant, and repented,
    according to his rich mercy.
46 He gave them over to compassion in the sight of all those who held them captive.
47 Save us, Lord our God, and gather us from the nations
    to give thanks to your holy name,
    and to glory in your praise.
48 Blessed be the Lord, the God of Israel, for ever and for ever;
    and all the people shall say, 'Amen, Amen'.

BOOK FIVE (Psalms 107–151)

Psalm 107 (106)   God saves the distressed

107:1 Alleluia! Give thanks to the Lord for he is good,
       for his mercy is for ever.
2 Let those redeemed by the Lord say it,
   those whom he has redeemed from the hands of the enemy,
3 and gathered from the lands,
   from east and west, north and south.
4 They had wandered in the desert, in the place of no water;
   they did not find a way to a city they could dwell in.
5 They were hungry and thirsty;
   their soul fainted within them.
6 Then they cried out to the Lord in their affliction;
   and he rescued them from their distress.

106:45 *repented:* the idea of God 'repenting' seems odd to us, who have grown up with the idea that God cannot change, but that is the meaning of the word in both Hebrew and Greek. Love and mercy are more important for the Israelite understanding of God than divine impassibility.

106:48 *Blessed be the Lord:* so begins the doxology that marks the end of the fourth 'book' into which the psalms are divided.

107:3 *south:* Greek and Hebrew here have 'Sea', which would presumably mean 'west'; it is best to assume that a syllable has dropped out in Hebrew and to read 'south', which is clearly required.

107:6 *Then they cried out to the Lord:* this refrain appears four times, with slight variations (verses 6, 13, 19, 28), and with the other refrain (see note on verse 8 below) divides this charming psalm according to four groups of people who have reasons for thanking God: those lost in the desert, those stuck in prison, those afflicted with sickness, and those unwise enough to do serious commercial sailing. In the psalmist's view, they all have themselves to blame.

7 He guided them onto a direct path,
    to journey to a city they could dwell in.

8 Let them give thanks to the Lord for his mercies,
    and his wonders for the children of Adam.

9 For he has satisfied the empty soul;
    and the hungry he has filled with good things,

10 those who sit in darkness and in the shadow of death,
    chained in poverty and iron,

11 for they had rebelled against God's words,
    and provoked the counsel of the Most High.

12 Their heart was troubled with hard labour; they became weak, and there
    was no one who was their helper.

13 Then they cried out to the Lord in their affliction;
    and he saved them from their distress.

14 He led them out of darkness and out of the shadow of death;
    and he broke their chains.

15 Let them give thanks to the Lord for his mercies,
    and his wonders for the children of Adam.

16 For he shattered the doors of bronze,
    and broke the iron bars.

17 He helped them from their way of lawlessness;
    for because of their lawlessness they were brought low.

18 Their soul loathed all food;
    and they came near to the gates of death.

19 Then they cried out to Lord in their affliction;
    and he saved them from their distress.

20 He sent forth his word and healed them,
    and rescued them from their destruction.

21 Let them give thanks to the Lord for his mercies,
    and his wonders for the children of Adam.

22 And let them sacrifice a sacrifice of praise;
    and let them proclaim his works with rejoicing.

23 Those who go down to the sea in boats,
    doing business on the great ocean,

24 they saw the Lord's works, and his wonders in the deep.

25 He spoke: and the stormy wind arose;
    and its waves were lifted up.

26 They go up to the heavens, and down to the depths;
    their soul melted because of their troubles.

27 They were troubled and staggered like drunkards,
    and all their skill was swallowed up.

28 Then they cried out to Lord in their affliction;
    and he led them out from their distress.

29 He commanded the storm and it stood still, turned into a breeze;
    and its waves were silenced.

30 They were delighted because they were quiet,
    and he led them to the harbour they longed for.

107:8 *Let them give thanks:* this is the other refrain, which appears again in verses 15, 21, 31.

107:9 *the hungry he has filled with good things:* this is echoed in Mary's Magnificat (Luke 1:53).

107:29 *He commanded the storm and it stood still:* readers of the Synoptic gospels are meant to recall this verse when they hear Mark 4:39 ('he rebuked the wind, and said to the sea, "Silence! Be muzzled."') and its parallels (Mt 8:26, Luke 8:24).

31 Let them give thanks to the Lord for his mercies,
   and his wonders for the children of Adam.
32 Let them exalt him in the congregation of the people;
   let them praise him in the seat of the elders.
33 He turns rivers into a desert, and streams of water into thirsty land,
34 fruitful land into a salt waste,
   because of the wickedness of its inhabitants.
35 But he turned desert into lakes of water,
   waterless land into streams of water;
36 and he made the hungry dwell there;
   they established a city to dwell in.
37 They sowed fields and planted vineyards;
   and they produced the fruit of the harvest.
38 God blessed them, and they multiplied greatly,
   and he did not diminish the number of their cattle.
39 Then they became few in number and were afflicted,
   because of the oppression of evil and pain.
40 Contempt was poured out on their rulers,
   and he led them astray in inaccessible and trackless [places].
41 And he helped the poor out of poverty,
   and made their families [as numerous] as sheep.
42 The upright shall see and shall rejoice
   and all lawlessness shall stop its mouth.
43 Who is wise, and will keep these things?
   And who will understand the Lord's mercies?

Psalm 108 (107)   God will rescue his people

A song; a psalm of David

108:1 My heart is ready, O God, my heart is ready.
   I shall sing and I shall play in my glory.
2 Awake, lyre and harp;
   I shall awake at dawn.
3 I shall praise you among the peoples, O Lord;
   I shall play on the harp for you among the Gentiles.
4 For your mercy is great above the heavens;
   and your truth reaches to the clouds.
5 Be exalted as far as the heavens, O God,
   and may your glory be over all the earth,
6 so that your beloved may be rescued;
   save them with your right hand, and listen to me.
7 God has spoken in his holy place,
   'I shall be exalted, and I shall divide up Shechem,
   and I shall measure out the Valley of Tents.
8 Mine is Gilead, and mine is Manasseh;
   and Ephraim is the strength of my head. Judah is my king.

107:40 *inaccessible and trackless [places]:* this is what the Greek means, trying to translate a Hebrew line that means 'in formlessness and No Way'. Our translator is clearly doing his best.

108 **Title:** *God will rescue his people:* This psalm is 'composite' in the sense that, with only minor differences it combines two laments (57:7-11 and 60:6-13), but in a rather unusual way, in that what we have here is the song of confidence in which most psalms of lament end, so the tone here is entirely cheerful. It is an interesting example of the way in which liturgical texts can be recycled to praise the same God in very different circumstances.

9 Moab is the cauldron of my hope;
  over Edom I shall stretch out my sandal;
  the foreigners have been subjected to me.'
10 Who will lead me into the fortified city?
  Who will guide me into the land of Edom?
11 Is it not you, O God, who has rejected us?
  And will you not go forth, O God, with our armies?
12 Give us help in our time of trouble;
  for human deliverance is useless.
13 In God we shall do mighty deeds,
  and God will bring our enemies to nothing.

Psalm 109 (108)   Praying against one's accusers

To the end; a psalm of David

109:1 O God, do not pass over my praise in silence,
2 for the mouth of the sinner and the mouth of the deceitful
  have opened against me;
  they spoke against me with a deceitful tongue.
3 They have surrounded me with words of hatred;
  they waged war upon me with no reason.
4 Instead of loving me, they made false accusations against me;
  but I was praying.
5 They gave me evil for good, and hatred in place of my love:
6 'Set up a sinner against him, and let a slanderer stand at his right side.
7 When he is put on trial, let him emerge condemned;
  let his prayer be counted as sin.
8 Let his days be few, and let someone else take his position.
9 Let his children be orphans, and his wife a widow.
10 Let his children be shaken and become emigrants,
  let them be beggars, and expelled from their homesteads.
11 Let his creditor seize all his assets,
  let foreigners plunder all this labours.
12 Let him have no one to protect him,
  let there be no one to show compassion to his orphans.
13 Let his children be given over to destruction;
  in a single generation, let his name be wiped out.
14 Let the iniquity of his ancestors be remembered before the Lord;
  let his mother's sin not be wiped away;
15 let them be continually before the Lord,
  and let their memory be destroyed from the earth.
16 Because he did not remember to do acts of compassion,
  but hunted down the needy and the poor,
  to put those pierced in heart to their death.
17 He loved to curse; and it shall come upon him also;
  he did not wish for blessing – and it shall be removed from him!

109:6 *slanderer:* the Greek word could equally be translated as 'devil'. The most likely reading of verses 6-19 is that it is a collection of quotations from the poet's enemies. They are cursing him, and his prayer is for the curse to fall back upon them.

109:8 *let someone else take his position:* interestingly, Peter quotes this line in his speech in Acts 1:20, where it refers to finding a replacement among the Twelve for Judas Iscariot after his death.

18   He put on cursing like a garment,
     and it has entered his bowels like water,
     and like oil into his bones.

19   May it be like a garment to him, which he puts on,
     and like a girdle with which he is always girded.'

20   May this be the Lord's dealing with those who slander me,
     and those who speak evil against my life.

21   But you, Lord, Lord, deal mercifully with me, for the sake of your name,
     for your mercy is good.

22   Rescue me, for I am poor and destitute,
     and my heart is disturbed within me.

23   I am removed like a shadow as [the day] goes to bed;
     I am expelled as locusts are.

24   My knees are weak from fasting,
     and my flesh is altered from lack of oil.

25   I became a reproach to them;
     they saw me, they shook their heads.

26   Help me, Lord my God,
     save me, in accordance with your mercy.

27   Let them know that this is your hand;
     and you, O Lord, have done it.

28   They shall curse, but you will bless,
     let those who rise up against me be put to shame,
     and let your servant rejoice.

29   Let those who slander me put on humiliation as a garment;
     let them wear [their] shame like a wraparound cloak.

30   I shall give great thanks to the Lord with my mouth;
     and in the midst of many I shall praise him.

31   For he stood at the right of the poor,
     to save them from those who persecute my life.

Psalm 110 (109)   A priest like Melchisedek

A psalm of David

110:1   The Lord said to my Lord, 'Sit at my right hand,
        until I make your enemies your footstool.'

2   The Lord shall send forth a staff of your power from Sion:
    'Rule in the midst of your enemies'.

3   'With you there is rule in the day of your power, in the splendour of the saints;
    from the womb before the morning star I have begotten you.'

4   The Lord has sworn, and will not change his mind,
    'You are a priest for ever, according to the order of Melchisedek.'

109:23 *[the day]*: this is not in the Greek, but there is a feminine pronoun, which might imply 'day' or 'shadow'. For this version, compare, perhaps, the remark of Cleophas and his companion to Jesus at Emmaus, Luke 24:29 'the day has already gone to bed'.

109:31 *he stood at the right of the poor*: this is the Lord's answer to the threats of the opponents in verses 6-7 to have someone quite different 'on the right'.

110:2 *Rule in the midst of your enemies*: I have set this in speech-marks, to indicate that 'rule' here is a verb, in the imperative mood. That is what God is telling the king, to

whom the psalm is sung, to do. Early Christians, of course, applied this song to Jesus.

110:3 *in the day of your power*: this is what both the Greek and the Hebrew say, but if you look at modern English versions, you will see that some talk of 'the day of your birth', which is different by only two (quite similar) letters in Hebrew.

110:4 *a priest for ever, according to the order of Melchisedek*: this slightly enigmatic phrase is taken up in the letter to the Hebrews, in its presentation of Jesus as 'the real thing' (Hebrews 5:6; 7:15-17). For the Melchisedek story, so far as it goes, see Genesis 14:18-20).

5 The Lord at your right hand
   has crushed kings in pieces on the day of his wrath.
6 He will judge among the nations;
   he shall fill up those [who have] fallen;
   he will crush the heads of many on earth.
7 He shall drink from the stream by the way,
   therefore he shall lift up his head.

Psalm 111 (110)   The Lord's wonderful works

111:1 Alleluia! I shall give you thanks, O Lord, with all my heart,
       in the council of the upright, and in the congregation.
2 Great are the works of the Lord,
   sought out for all that he desires.
3 His work is thanksgiving and majesty,
   and his righteousness remains for ever and ever.
4 He has given a reminder of his wonders;
   merciful and compassionate is the Lord.
5 He has given food to those who fear him;
   he will remember his covenant for ever.
6 He has proclaimed to his people the power of his works,
   to give them the inheritance of the nations.
7 The works of his hands are truth and justice;
   all his commands are to be trusted,
8 fixed for ever and ever in truth and uprightness.
9 He sent forth redemption to the people;
   he commanded his covenant for ever;
   holy and terrible his name.
10 The fear of the Lord is the beginning of wisdom;
    there is a good understanding for all who perform [wisdom].
    His praise lasts for ever and ever.

Psalm 112 (111)   How the just behave

112:1 Alleluia! Happy are those who fear the Lord;
       they will delight greatly in his commandments.
2 Their offspring shall be mighty in the land;
   a generation of the upright shall be blessed.
3 Glory and wealth shall be in their house,
   and their righteousness remains for ever and ever.
4 Light has risen in darkness for the upright;
   they are merciful, compassionate and righteous.
5 They are kindly who take pity and lend;
   they shall conduct their affairs with right judgement.
6 For they shall not be shaken, ever;
   the just shall be remembered for ever.

111:1 *Alleluia:* this lovely psalm is alphabetical (as is its successor), in that each half-line begins with a new letter of the Hebrew alphabet. The Greek translators never tried to reproduce that in Greek, and we have followed this sensible example. So don't think of Alleluia as representing the first letter of the alphabet: the word actually begins with 'h' in Hebrew! Think of this poem as a teaching device, telling the young what God is like.

111:10 *The fear of the Lord is the beginning of wisdom:* this is a common enough theme in the Wisdom literature. See, for example, Proverbs 1:7; 9:10.

7 They shall not be afraid of an evil report,
  their hearts ready to hope in the Lord.
8 Their hearts are set firm;
  they shall not be afraid until they look on their enemies.
9 They scatter and give to the poor;
  their righteousness endures for evermore;
  their horn shall be exalted in glory.
10 Sinners shall look on and be angry;
  they shall grind their teeth and melt away;
  The desires of the wicked shall perish.

Psalm 113 (112) God looks after those in need

113:1 Alleluia! Praise the Lord, O [you his] servants,
   praise the name of the Lord.
2 May the name of the Lord be blessed, now and for evermore.
3 From the rising of the sun to its setting,
  praise the name of the Lord.
4 High above all nations is the Lord;
  above the heavens is his glory.
5 Who is like the Lord our God,
  the one who dwells in the high places,
6 who looks upon lowly things, in heaven and on earth,
7 who raises up the poor from the earth,
  and lifts up the needy from the dungheap,
8 to set him with the rulers, with the rulers of his people,
9 who makes the barren woman dwell in a house,
  a mother who rejoices in her children?

Psalm 114 (113:1-8) God's wonders at the Exodus

114:1 Alleluia! At Israel's exodus from Egypt,
   and Jacob's from a barbarian people,
2 Judah became his sanctuary, and Israel his dominion.
3 The sea saw and fled; Jordan turned back.
4 The mountains leapt like rams, and the hills like lambs.
5 What was up with you, O sea, that you fled?
  What was up with you, Jordan, that you went backwards?
6 Or, you mountains, that you leapt like rams, and you hills, like sheep?

112:8 *until they look on their enemies:* this may seem a bit odd, since it is just when you look upon your enemies that you don't want to be afraid. But it is what both the Greek and the Hebrew say. If you look at modern translations they tend to say things like 'look upon their foes in triumph', which solves the problem, but is not what the text actually says!

112:9 *They scatter:* this is the reading of both the Hebrew and the Greek, which puzzles us, because it sounds as though it means throwing good money after bad. Modern translations tend to avoid the problem by offering 'give generously'. Interestingly, Paul quotes this verse when he is trying to persuade his Corinthians to be generous in giving to the collection for poor Christians in Jerusalem (2 Corinthians 9:9).

112:10 *grind their teeth:* in Luke's Gospel, Jesus ascribes a similarly ungenerous reaction to his opponents, 'when you see Abraham and Isaac and Jacob and all the prophets inside the Kingdom of Heaven, and you lot flung outside' (Luke 13:28).

113:1 *Alleluia! Praise:* it is these verbs that give Psalms 113-118 the name of the 'Lesser Hallel' in Jewish tradition. (The 'Greater Hallel' is variously understood as Psalm 136, or 135-136, or 120-136, thus including the 'psalms of ascent'; in some traditions this name is even given, and for similar reasons, to Psalms 146-150).

114 **Title:** *113:1-8:* the LXX combines psalms 114 and 115, probably incorrectly, as they look like different psalms.

7　The earth was shaken at the presence of the Lord,
　　at the presence of the God of Jacob,
8　who turned the rock into lakes of water,
　　and the flint into springs of water.

Psalm 115 (113:9-26)　　The glories of God

115:1　Not to us, Lord, not to us, but to your name give the glory,
　　because of your mercy and your truth.
2　Otherwise the Gentiles may say, 'Where is their God?'
3　Our God is in heaven above;
　　in the heavens and on earth, he does whatever he wants.
4　The idols of the Gentiles are silver and gold,
　　the products of human hands.
5　They have a mouth – but they will not speak.
　　They have eyes – but they will not see.
6　They have ears – but they will not hear.
　　They have noses – but they will not smell.
7　They have hands – but they will not touch.
　　They have feet – but they will not go anywhere.
　　They will not make sounds with their throat.
8　May their makers become like them,
　　and all those who place their trust in them.
9　The house of Israel has hoped in the Lord;
　　he is their help and their shield.
10　The house of Aaron has hoped in the Lord;
　　he is their help and their shield.
11　Those who fear the Lord have hoped in the Lord;
　　he is their help and their shield.
12　The Lord has remembered us and blessed us;
　　he blessed the house of Israel;
　　he blessed the house of Aaron.
13　He blessed those who fear the Lord,
　　the little along with the great.
14　May the Lord give you increase,
　　you and your children.
15　May you be blessed by the Lord,
　　who made heaven and earth.
16　The heaven of the heaven belongs to the Lord;
　　but the earth he has given to the children of Adam.
17　It is not the dead who will praise you, Lord,
　　nor all those who go down to Hades.
18　No – it is we who live who shall bless the Lord,
　　now and for evermore.

115　**Title**: *113:9-26*: a separate psalm in MT, but not in the LXX.

115:3　*Our God in heaven . . . whatever he wants*: these words are perhaps echoed, though in a rather different sense, in Matthew's version of the Lord's Prayer: Matthew 6:9-10.

115:4-8　*The idols of the Gentiles*: some readers occasionally feel discomfort at the jeering tone of this polemic against the images of the pagan gods, and their inability to do anything, though we must set this in the context of the apparent power of the pagan cultures that surrounded Israel, and Israel's certainty that their God was the real God. For the theme, compare Psalm 135:15-18; Isaiah 44:9-20 and Wisdom 15:15.

Psalm 116 (114-115) An individual psalm of thanks

116:1 Alleluia! I loved [the Lord] because he will hear the sound of my entreaty,

2 because he has inclined his ear to me,
   and in my days I shall call [upon him].

3 The pangs of death encircled me;
   the dangers of Hades found me;
   I found affliction and pain.

4 I called upon the name of the Lord:
   'O Lord, deliver my life.'

5 The Lord is merciful and just;
   our God has compassion.

6 The Lord preserves the simple;
   I was brought low, but he saved me.

7 My soul, come back to your rest,
   for the Lord has shown goodness to you.

8 For he delivered my soul from death,
   my eyes from tears, and my feet from slipping.

9 I shall be pleasing before the Lord, in the land of the living.

10 Alleluia. I trusted and therefore I spoke;
   but I was brought very low.

11 I said in my astonishment: 'All human beings are liars.'

12 What shall I repay the Lord
   for all that he has repaid me?

13 I shall take the cup of salvation,
   and I shall call upon the Lord's name.

14 [ ]

15 Precious before the Lord is the death of his holy ones.

16 O Lord, I am your servant;
   I am your servant, and the son of your slave girl,
   you have broken my bonds,

17 I shall offer you a sacrifice of praise.

18 I shall repay my vows to the Lord,
   before all his people,

19 in the courts of the house of the Lord,
   in your midst, O Jerusalem.

---

116 **Title**: *(114–115):* LXX, followed by Vulgate, divides this psalm after verse 9. There is no particular reason to see a division here; it is perhaps part of a prevailing uncertainty about the divisions of the psalms at this part of the book, which presumably reflects different ways in which the Hallel was prayed.

116:2 *in my days I shall call:* here, LXX translates the Hebrew text quite literally, to a point where we have to add 'upon him', in order to make sense in English.

116:3 *pangs of death:* this is a common LXX translation for a Hebrew expression that means something like the 'ropes' or 'cords' of death.

116:9 *I shall be pleasing:* the Hebrew here has 'I shall walk'.

116:10 *Alleluia:* this is LXX's way of indicating the beginning of the new psalm. It is taken from the last line of the psalm, where MT has it, and LXX does not.

I trusted and therefore I spoke: Paul quotes this in 2 Corinthians 4:13, where he is defending his ministry, against some people who had been rather disparaging of his apostolate.

116:11 *astonishment:* or 'ecstasy'. The Hebrew word here means 'terror'.

116:14 this line is not in the LXX.

Psalm 117 (116)   An invitation to praise

117:1 Alleluia! Praise the Lord, all you nations,
       praise him all you peoples.
   2   For his mercy has been strong upon us,
       and the Lord's truth lasts for ever.

Psalm 118 (117)   Celebrating God in the Temple

118:1 Alleluia! Give thanks to the Lord, for he is good,
       for his mercy is for ever.
   2   Let the house of Israel now say 'He is good, for his mercy is for ever.'
   3   Let the house of Aaron now say, 'He is good, for his mercy is for ever.'
   4   Let all those who fear the Lord now say, 'He is good, for his mercy is for ever.'
   5   In trouble I called on the Lord,
       and he heard me [and brought me] into a broad place.
   6   The Lord is my help; I shall not fear.
       What can human beings do to me?
   7   The Lord is my help; and I shall look upon my enemies.
   8   It is better to trust in the Lord than to trust in human beings.
   9   It is better to hope in the Lord than to hope in rulers.
  10   All the nations surrounded me;
       in the Lord's name I defended myself against them.
  11   They surrounded me, surrounded me;
       but in the Lord's name I defended myself against them.
  12   They surrounded me like bees round a honeycomb;
       and they blazed out like a fire among thorns;
       but in the Lord's name I defended myself against them.
  13   I was thrust down and overthrown, ready to fall;
       but the Lord came to my help.
  14   The Lord is my strength and my song;
       and he became my salvation.
  15   The sound of rejoicing and of salvation is in the tents of the righteous.
       The Lord's right hand has worked a miracle.
  16   The Lord's right hand lifted me up;
       the Lord's right hand has worked a miracle.
  17   I shall not die – no, I shall live;
       and I shall recount the Lord's works.
  18   The Lord disciplined me; he disciplined me indeed;
       but he did not hand me over to death.
  19   Open to me the gates of righteousness;
       I shall go in them and I shall give thanks to the Lord.
  20   The is the Lord's gate;
       the righteous shall enter through it.

---

117 **Title: *invitation to praise:*** This tiny psalm ends the Lesser Hallel; it is an enchanting little summary of Israel's understanding of their relationship to God, and God's relationship to all humanity.

117:1 *Praise the Lord, all you nations, praise him all you peoples:* Paul quotes this at Romans 15:11, when he wants to emphasise to the Roman church that the gospel is for both Jews and Gentiles.

118:5 *into a broad place:* this is how the Greek has translated the Hebrew, quite correctly. Oddly enough, however, he has missed the metaphor at the other end of the verse where the Greek word translated by 'trouble' really means something like being in a 'tight place'.

21 I shall give thanks to you, for you heard me,
and you became my salvation.

22 The stone which the builders rejected,
this is the one that has become the cornerstone.

23 This came from the Lord, a marvel in our eyes.

24 This is the day which the Lord made;
let us rejoice and be glad in it.

25 O Lord, save [us] now, O Lord, give [us] prosperity!

26 Blessed is the one who comes in the name of the Lord;
we have blessed you from the house of the Lord.

27 God is the Lord, and has shone upon us.
Celebrate the festival with thick [garlands], up to the horns of the altar.

28 You are my God, and I shall give you thanks;
you are my God and I shall exalt you;
I shall give you thanks, because you heard me,
and you became my salvation.

29 Give thanks to the Lord for he is good,
for his mercy is for ever.

Psalm 119 (118)   The Law as God's precious gift

119:1 Alleluia.

{1. Aleph}

1 Happy are those whose way is blameless,
who walk in the Law of the Lord.

2 Happy are those who search out his decrees;
with all their hearts they will seek him.

3 For those who work iniquity have not walked in his ways.

4 You have commanded us to keep your commandments carefully.

5 O that my ways were directed to keep your ordinances!

118:22 *The stone which the builders rejected . . . the cornerstone:* this text is taken up in several places in the NT and applied to Jesus. See Mark 12:10, and the parallels at Matthew 21:42; Luke 20:17. It is also used at Acts 4:11; Romans 9:33 and 1 Peter 2:7.

118:23 *This:* the word is feminine in Greek, imitating the Hebrew. Possibly it goes back to the 'cornerstone', which is feminine in Greek.

118:25 *save [us] now:* In Hebrew this is 'Hosanna', and it was of course the psalm that they sang when Jesus made his impressive entry into Jerusalem (Matthew 21:9; Mark 11:9-10; John 12:13). The same is true of 'Blessed is the one who comes in the name of the Lord' in the following line, which is quoted in Luke 19:38.

118:27 *Celebrate the festival with thick [garlands]:* very likely a reference to the feast of Tabernacles, when palm branches were waved. And compare, of course, the Gospel accounts of Jesus' entry into Jerusalem: Mark 11:8; Matthew 21:8; John 12:13.

119:1 *1. Aleph:* This lovely psalm is the longest in the book, and it is an alphabetical psalm. There are 22 stanzas of 8 lines each. In Hebrew, each of them begins with a new letter. So stanza one begins with Aleph. The Greek translator has not attempted to follow that technique, and neither shall we. However they have listed the stanzas by number and (Hebrew) letter, so it seems appropriate for us to do the same: 1. Aleph; 2. Beth, etc . . . .

Law of the Lord: one of the ways this psalm treats the Law is to use a number of different words for it. Law is one of them; we shall notice the others as we come to them. 'Walking in the way', in the present verse, is one way of describing one who observes the Law. The culminating effect of all this is to make it impossible to sustain the view that Jewish people found the Law an impossible burden: the author of this poem loves the Law as God's great gift to the people.

119:2 *decrees:* this word, which could also be translated as 'testimonies', is the second of the words that the poet uses for God's Law.

119:3 *those who work iniquity:* this is a frequent phrase in the psalms, of course. The Greek word here means 'lawlessness', i.e. the opposite of keeping God's Law. The Hebrew word is a bit less precise, meaning something in the general area of 'badness', 'malice', 'injustice'.

119:4 *commanded . . . commandments:* this set of terms is the third that the poem employs.

keep: this is a common word in connection with 'Law'; we have met it frequently in the psalms. In both Hebrew and Greek, it has the sense of 'keep guard over'.

119:5 *directed:* this idea is very common in the psalms, as a way of indicating responsiveness to God. The Hebrew here has more of a sense of 'established'.

ordinances: this, obviously, is the fourth word that the poet uses for 'Law'.

6   I shall not be ashamed when I look upon all your commandments.
7   I shall give you thanks, O Lord, in uprightness of heart,
      when I have learnt the judgements of your justice.
8   I shall keep your ordinances; do not leave me utterly alone.

{2. Beth}

9   How shall the young direct their way?
      By keeping your words.
10 With all my heart I have sought you;
      do not reject me from your commandments.
11 I hid your oracles in my heart,
      lest I should sin against you.
12 Blessed are you, Lord, teach me your ordinances.
13 With my lips I have proclaimed all the judgements of your mouth.
14 I delighted in the way of your testimonies,
      as much as in all riches.
15 I shall muse on your precepts,
      and I shall consider your ways.
16 I shall meditate on your ordinances;
      then I shall not forget your words.

{3. Gimel}

17 Repay your servant, and I shall live,
      and I shall keep your words.
18 Uncover my eyes, and I shall understand your wonders out of your law.
19 I am a sojourner in the land;
      do not hide your commandments from me.
20 My soul longed for you, yearning for your judgements always.
21 You rebuked the arrogant;
      cursed are those who turn aside from your commandments.
22 Remove abuse and contempt from me,
      for I have sought for your testimonies.
23 For rulers sat in judgement and condemned me;
      but your servant was musing on your ordinances.
24 For your testimonies are my meditation,
      and your ordinances are my counsels.

{4. Daleth}

25 My soul clung to the ground;
      give me life according to your word.
26 I proclaimed my ways, and you heard me;
      teach me your ordinances.
27 Make me understand your ways, and I shall muse on your wonders.
28 My soul dripped tears of exhaustion;
      strengthen me with your words.

119:7 *judgements:* this is the fifth set of words for Law. 'Justice' is not etymologically connected, in Greek or Hebrew, but obviously has to do with keeping God's Law.

119:9 *words:* this is the sixth of the terms for Law in this psalm.

119:10 *do not reject me:* this (or 'do not thrust me aside from your commandments') is what the Greek means. The Hebrew has 'do not let me stray' or 'do not lead me astray'. Both of them have the sense that God is utterly in charge, and the notion that to be separated from God's Law is a disaster.

119:11 *oracles:* this is the seventh term that the poet uses for God's Law. The basic idea, in both Greek and Hebrew is that of God's 'speech' to us.

119:15 *precepts:* this is in fact the eighth term for 'law', but the Greek has used the word for 'commandments'. I have opted to preserve the richness of the original here.

29 Remove the way of unrighteousness from me,
and by your law have mercy on me.
30 I have chosen the way of truth;
and I have not forgotten your judgements.
31 I have clung to your testimonies, O Lord,
do not put me to shame.
32 I have run the way of your commandments,
when you enlarged my heart.

{5. He}

33 Teach me, O Lord, your Law, the way of your ordinances,
and I shall seek it always.
34 Instruct me, and I shall seek out your Law,
and I shall keep it with all my heart.
35 Guide me in the path of your commandments;
for I have delighted in it.
36 Incline my heart to your testimonies,
and not to greed.
37 Turn my eyes from seeing what is worthless,
give me life on your way.
38 Fulfil your oracle to your servant,
that I may fear you.
39 Take away my reproach which made me fearful,
for your judgements are good.
40 Look, I have desired your commandments,
give me life with your righteousness.

{6. Waw}

41 And let your mercy come upon me, O Lord,
and your salvation, according to your oracle.
42 And I shall answer a word to those who reproach me,
for I have hoped in your words.
43 And do not utterly take away the word of truth from my mouth,
for I have hoped in your judgements.
44 And I shall keep your Law continually for ever and for ever and ever.
45 And I used to walk in freedom,
for I sought your commandments.
46 And I spoke of your testimonies before kings,
and I was not ashamed.
47 And I meditated on your commandments,
which I greatly loved.
48 And I lifted up my hands to your commandments which I loved,
and I mused on your ordinances.

{7. Zayin}

49 Remember your word to your servant,
by which you have buoyed me up with hope.
50 This comforted me in my humiliation,
that your oracle gave me life.

119:29 *by your law have mercy on me*: or, staying a bit closer to the Hebrew, 'give me the gracious gift of your Law'.

119:50 *This*: the pronoun is feminine in both Hebrew and Greek; it is not clear what it refers to.

51 The arrogant have utterly transgressed;
   but I have not deviated from your Law.
52 I remembered your judgements from of old, O Lord, and I was comforted.
53 Despondency seized me, because of the sinners who abandon your Law.
54 Your ordinances were my melodies in the place of my sojourning.
55 I remembered your name in the night-time, O Lord,
   and I kept your Law.
56 This was mine, because I sought out your ordinances.

{8. Heth}

57 My portion, O Lord, I promised to keep your Law.
58 I begged for your presence with all my heart,
   have mercy on me, in accordance with your oracle.
59 I considered your ways, and I turned my feet towards your testimonies.
60 I was ready, and I was not troubled,
   to keep your commandments.
61 The snares of sinners entangled me;
   and I did not forget your Law.
62 In the middle of the night I rose to thank you,
   for the judgements of your justice.
63 I am a companion of all those who fear you,
   and of those who keep your commandments.
64 O Lord, the earth is full of your mercy;
   teach me your ordinances.

{9. Teth}

65 You have dealt kindly with your servant, O Lord,
   in accordance with your word.
66 Teach me kindness and discipline and knowledge,
   for I trust your commandments.
67 Before my humiliation I sinned,
   therefore I have kept your oracle.
68 You are kind, O Lord;
   in your kindness teach me your ordinances.
69 The immorality of the arrogant multiplied against me,
   but with my whole heart I will search out your commandments.
70 Their heart has curdled like milk,
   but I have meditated on your Law.
71 It is good for me that you brought me low,
   that I might learn your ordinances.
72 The Law of your mouth is better for me
   than thousands of gold and silver coins.

{10. Yodh}

73 Your hands have made me and shaped me;
   instruct me, and I shall learn your commandments.

119:51 *transgressed:* the Greek translation has here imported the notion of 'law', where the Hebrew had 'scorned me'.

119:53 *Despondency:* the Hebrew here has something like 'rage'.

119:69 *multiplied:* the Hebrew here means 'soil' or 'abuse'. It is a metaphor from painting.

119:70 *curdled like milk:* the Hebrew poet, perhaps running out of words that begin with ṭ, has reached for a very rare word here, which can mean something like 'become stupid', 'be fat/unfeeling/insensitive'. The Greek translator has made a perfectly sensible suggestion here.

74 Those who fear you will see me and rejoice,
    for I was buoyed up by hope in your words.
75 O Lord, I know that your judgements are righteousness,
    and in your truth you brought me low.
76 Let your mercy be my consolation,
    in accordance with your oracle to your servant.
77 Let your compassion come to me, and I shall live,
    for your Law is my meditation.
78 Let the arrogant be ashamed, for they transgressed unjustly against me;
    but I shall muse on your commandments.
79 Let those who fear you, and who know your testimonies,
    turn to me.
80 Let my heart be blameless in your ordinances,
    that I may not be put to shame.

{11. Kaph}

81 My soul is languishing for your salvation;
    and I have placed my hope in your word.
82 My eyes failed [from looking for] your oracle,
    saying, 'When will you comfort me?'
83 For I was like a bottle in the frost;
    I did not forget your ordinances.
84 How many are the days of your servant?
    When will you serve judgement on those who hunt me down?
85 The lawless recounted idle tales to me, but not like your Law, O Lord.
86 All your commandments are truth;
    [the lawless] hunted me down unjustly.
    Help me, O Lord.
87 They almost finished me off on earth;
    but I did not abandon your commandments.
88 In accordance with your mercy, give me life;
    and I shall keep the testimonies of your mouth.

{12. Lamedh}

89 Your word, O Lord, abides for ever in heaven.
90 For ever and ever is your truth;
    you founded the earth, and it endures.
91 The day endures by your judgement,
    for all things are your servants.
92 If not for the fact that your Law is my meditation,
    then I should have perished when I was brought low.
93 I shall never, ever, forget your ordinances,
    for with them you have given me life, O Lord.

119:83 *a bottle in the frost:* the idea here is presumably that it cracks and fails to contain the wine, though the connection with that and remembering God's ordinances is not, it has to be said, crystal clear. The Hebrew as it stands means 'thick smoke' or 'fog'; but some scholars have suggested a similar-sounding, and rather rare, word, which means 'ice'; and if that is the case, then the Greek text (and, incidentally, the Syriac also) has preserved the original reading.

119:85 *lawless recounted idle tales:* the Hebrew has 'have dug pits'. 'Lawless' is another example of a reference to 'law' being introduced by the translator (cf. note on 119:51 above).

119:91 *judgement:* the Greek word here is not one of the eight words for Law, but the Hebrew is, so we have translated it accordingly. It seemed important at this point to pick up what the Hebrew was trying to do.

94 I am yours, save me,
for I have sought for your precepts.
95 Sinners waited for me to destroy me,
but I understood your testimonies.
96 I have seen the limit of all perfection;
your commandment is very broad.

{13. Mem}

97 How I have loved your Law, O Lord;
it is my meditation all day long.
98 You have made me wiser than my enemies with your commandment,
for it is mine for ever.
99 I have understood more than all those who teach me,
for your testimonies are my meditation.
100 I have more understanding than the elderly,
for I have sought out your precepts.
101 I have kept my feet from every wicked way,
that I may keep your words.
102 I have not deviated from your judgements,
for you have taught me your Law.
103 How sweet for my throat are your oracles,
better than honey and the honeycomb for my mouth!
104 Through your precepts I have gained understanding;
therefore I have hated every way of unrighteousness.

{14. Nun}

105 Your word is a lamp to my feet, and a light to my paths.
106 I swore, and I confirmed my oath,
to keep your righteous judgements.
107 I was brought very low;
O Lord, give me life in accordance with your word.
108 Be pleased, O Lord, with the freewill offering of my mouth,
and teach me your judgements.
109 My soul is continually in my hands,
and I have not forgotten your Law.
110 Sinners spread a snare for me,
but I did not wander from your commandments.
111 I have inherited your testimonies for ever,
for they are the joy of my heart.
112 I inclined my heart to perform your ordinances for ever, as an exchange.

{15. Samekh}

113 I have hated the lawless, and loved your Law.

119:94 *precepts:* the Greek word here is the one that we have tended to translate 'ordinances', though the Greek translation varies, but the Hebrew word is the one translated 'precepts'. Once again, we are following the Hebrew here.

119:102 *taught me your Law:* the Greek word here has rather adroitly picked up the fact that the Hebrew word carries connotations of both 'teach' and 'Law'.

119:109 *My soul is continually in my hands:* we should expect 'in *your* hands' here, but this is what both the Greek and Hebrew have. It is not quite clear what it means; NAB suggests 'my life is always at risk', but this is an intelligent guess.

119:113 *the lawless:* once again, as at verses 51, 85 above, the translator has introduced the notion of 'law'; the Hebrew here has a word meaning 'divided', and hence 'common' or 'contemptible' instead of lawless.

114 You are my helper and my protector;
     I have hoped in your word.
115 Turn aside from me, all you who do evil,
     and I shall search out the commands of God.
116 Uphold me according to your oracle, and I shall live,
     do not put me to shame because of my expectation.
117 Help me, and I shall be saved,
     and I shall meditate continually on your ordinances.
118 You have brought to nothing all those who fall away from your ordinances,
     for their thoughts are unrighteous.
119 I have reckoned all the sinners on earth as transgressors
     therefore I have loved your testimonies all the time.
120 Penetrate my flesh with the fear of you,
     for I was afraid of your judgements.

     {16. Ayin}

121 I have done judgement and righteousness;
     do not hand me over to those who treat me unjustly.
122 Accept your servant for good;
     let not the arrogant slander me.
123 My eyes have wasted away [looking] for your salvation,
     and for the oracle of your righteousness.
124 Deal with your servant according to your mercy;
     and teach me your ordinances.
125 I am your servant; instruct me,
     and I shall know your testimonies.
126 It is time for the Lord to act;
     they have torn up your Law.
127 Therefore I loved your commandments,
     more than gold or topaz.
128 Therefore I went straight, in accordance with all your commandments;
     I loathed every immoral way.

     {17. Pe}

129 How wonderful are your testimonies,
     therefore my soul sought them out.
130 The revelation of your words will bring light,
     and will instruct the simple.
131 I opened my mouth and drew breath,
     for I longed for your commandments.
132 Look at me and have mercy on me,
     according to the judgement of those who love your name.
133 Direct my steps according to your oracle,
     and let not any lawlessness exercise dominion over me.
134 Redeem me from human calumny,
     and I shall keep your commandments.

119:114 *helper . . . protector:* the Hebrew here has 'refuge . . . shield'.

119:119 *all the time:* this is not in all the Greek manuscripts, nor in MT, but it may well be a correct reading.

119:126 *torn up:* the Greek here has 'scattered', presumably after it has been appropriately reduced to little pieces. The Hebrew means 'cause to split'.

119:134 *calumny:* the Hebrew word is closer to 'oppression'.

135 Show your face to your servant,
and teach me your ordinances.
136 My eyes have come down [in] streams of water,
because they did not keep your Law.

{18. Sadhe}

137 You are just, O Lord, and your judgement is upright.
138 You commanded righteousness and all truth as your testimonies.
139 Zeal for your house has made me melt away,
for my enemies have forgotten your words.
140 Your oracle has been utterly tried by fire,
and your servant has loved it.
141 I am young and despised;
but I have not forgotten your precepts.
142 Your righteousness is righteousness for ever,
and your Law is truth.
143 Trouble and distress found me;
your commands were my meditation.
144 Your testimonies are righteousness for ever;
instruct me and I shall live.

{19. Qoph}

145 I cried out with all my heart,
'Hear me, O Lord; I shall seek out your ordinances.'
146 I cried out to you, 'Save me, and I shall keep your testimonies.'
147 I was there at an ungodly hour, and cried out;
I hoped in your words.
148 My eyes were there before dawn,
to meditate on your oracles.
149 Hear my voice, O Lord, according to your mercy;
according to your judgement, give me life.
150 Those who hunt me down lawlessly drew near;
they have gone far from your Law.
151 You are near, O Lord,
and all your commands are true.
152 In the beginning I knew from your testimonies,
that you founded them for ever.

{20. Resh}

153 See my humiliation, and rescue me,
for I have not forgotten your Law.
154 Plead my case, and redeem me;
because of your word, give me life.
155 Salvation is far from sinners,
for they have not sought out your ordinances.
156 Your mercies are many, O Lord;
according to your judgement give me life.
157 They are many who hunt me down and oppress me;
I have not deviated from your testimonies.

119:139 *Zeal for your house:* quoted at John 2:17, in defence of Jesus' cleansing of the Temple, and cf. Psalm 69:9

119:150 *lawlessly:* once again, the translator has introduced the idea here. The Hebrew has 'those who hunt down wickedness'.

158   I saw people acting faithlessly, and I pined away,
     for they did not keep your oracles.

159   See: I loved your commandments, O Lord;
     in your mercy, give me life.

160   The beginning of your words is truth;
     and all the judgements of your justice are for ever.

{21. Shin}

161   Rulers hunted me down for no reason,
     and my heart was afraid, because of your words.

162   I shall rejoice over your oracles,
     as one who discovers much booty.

163   I hated injustice and loathed it;
     I loved your Law.

164   Seven times a day I praised you,
     because of your righteous judgements.

165   There is much peace for those who love your Law,
     and they have nothing to make them stumble.

166   I looked out for your salvation, O Lord,
     and I loved your commandments.

167   My soul kept your testimonies, and loved them very much.

168   I kept your precepts and your testimonies,
     for all my ways are before you, O Lord.

{22. Taw}

169   Let my entreaty come near before you, O Lord;
     instruct me according to your oracle.

170   May my petition come in before you;
     according to your oracle, rescue me.

171   Let my lips utter a hymn, when you teach me your ordinances.

172   May my tongue speak your oracle,
     because all your commands are righteous.

173   May your hand be present to save me,
     because I have chosen your commandments.

174   I have longed for your salvation, O Lord,
     and your Law is my meditation.

175   My spirit shall live and shall praise you,
     and your judgements will help me.

176   I wandered like a lost sheep;
     seek for your servant, for I have not forgotten your commandments.

119:165 *much peace for those who love your Law:* we sometimes tend to assume that the psalmist's life is trouble as far as the eye can see, so this line (admittedly from a Wisdom psalm, something very different indeed from the rest of the hymn book) corrects the balance. We might recall here Paul's prayer for peace for the Philippians, once they stop fighting (Philippians 4:7).

119:169 *oracle:* this is what the Greek word means, though it might also be translated 'word', which is what the Greek has.

119:176 *I wandered like a lost sheep; seek for your servant, for I have not forgotten your commandments:* the psalmist is no stranger to sin, but shares that sense of failure and lostness that can come to all who try to serve God (for the psalmist's profound awareness of human fallibility, see verses 5, 27, 29, 134, 136).

Psalm 120 (119) An exile returns

A song of ascents

120:1 I cried to the Lord in my affliction, and he heard me.
   2 O Lord, rescue my life from unjust lips,
      and from a treacherous tongue.
   3 What should be given to you, and what should be added to you,
      against a treacherous tongue?
   4 The warrior's sharpened arrows,
      along with the coals of the desert.
   5 Woe is me, that my sojourn was extended;
      I have pitched my tent with the tents of Kedar;
   6 my soul has sojourned too long.
   7 With those who hate peace I was for peace;
      when I spoke to them, they made war on me for no reason.

Psalm 121 (120) God is Israel's protector

A song of ascents

121:1 I lifted up my eyes to the mountains;
      from where shall my help come?
   2 My help is from the Lord,
      who made heaven and earth.
   3 Do not allow your foot to be shaken,
      nor let your Guardian slumber.
   4 Look, he does not slumber nor sleep,
      the Guardian of Israel.
   5 The Lord will guard you,
      the Lord is your shelter, at your right hand.
   6 By day the sun shall not burn you up,
      nor the moon by night.
   7 The Lord will guard you from evil;
      he will guard your soul.
   8 The Lord will guard your going in and your coming out,
      from now on and for ever.

Psalm 122 (121) A pilgrim's prayer for Jerusalem

A song of ascents

122:1 I rejoiced over those who said to me, 'We shall go into the house of the Lord'.
   2 Our feet were standing in your courts, O Jerusalem.

---

120 **Heading**: *A song of ascents:* This is the heading given to Psalms 120-134. Many explanations have been given, of which scholars think the most likely is that they were sung as pilgrims went up to Jerusalem, perhaps on the final stage, as they processed to the shrine in the Temple. They are all very charming psalms, whatever the explanation for the heading.

120:4 *coals of the desert:* this is what the Greek says, and it might be what the Hebrew means, but scholars are divided about what is going on here.

120:5 *my sojourn was extended:* the Hebrew here has 'I was a stranger/sojourner in Meshech', which is thought to be somewhere in the far north, while Kedar refers to the Bedouin tribes of the Arabian desert. Probably the general idea is that the psalmist is living among unsympathetic Gentiles, who do not understand his way of life.

121:6 *the sun shall not burn you up:* there may be an echo of this verse in Revelation 7:16, although Isaiah 49:10 may also have fed into it.

121:8 *your going in and your coming out:* this is a standard Hebrew expression for every aspect of our existence under God.

3 Jerusalem is built as a city, whose fellowship is complete.
4 For there the tribes went up, the tribes of the Lord,
a testimony for Israel, to give thanks to the Lord's name.
5 For there were placed thrones for judgement,
thrones for the house of David.
6 Ask then for the things that make for peace for Jerusalem,
and [let there be] prosperity for those who love you.
7 Let there be peace in your power,
and prosperity in your citadels.
8 For the sake of my brethren and my neighbours,
I spoke peace about you.
9 For the sake of the house of the Lord our God,
I sought carefully for good things for you.

Psalm 123 (122)   Paying careful attention to God

A song of ascents

123:1 To you I lifted up my eyes,
you who dwell in heaven.
2 See – as the eyes of slaves are on the hands of their lords,
as the eyes of a slave-girl are on the hands of her lady,
so our eyes are on the Lord our God,
until he takes pity on us.
3 Have mercy on us, Lord, have mercy,
for we are very full of contempt.
4 Our soul has been filled very full;
reproach upon those who are prosperous,
and contempt upon the arrogant.

Psalm 124 (123)   Thanksgiving for deliverance

A song of ascents

124:1 'If the Lord had not been among us.' Let Israel say,
2 'If the Lord had not been among us,
when people rose against us,
3 then they would have gobbled us up alive,
when their anger was kindled against us;
4 then the water would have drowned us,
our soul would have gone through the torrent;
5 then our soul would have gone through the overwhelming water.
6 Blessed be the Lord, who did not give us as a prey to their teeth!
7 Our soul was rescued, like a sparrow from the snare of the hunters;
the snare was shattered, and we were rescued.

122:3 *fellowship is complete:* that is a possible translation of the Greek, which could also be read, perhaps a bit woodenly, as 'whose sharing is to the same'. The Hebrew probably means 'which is linked to itself altogether'; the word has a sense of 'community', 'alliance', 'joined together'. Here the idea seems to be that the city walls of Jerusalem are impressively constructed.

122:7 *peace in your power:* this is what the Greek says, but the Hebrew word could also mean 'wall' or 'rampart', as well as 'power', and that is how modern versions tend to read it.

123:4 *Our soul . . . contempt upon the arrogant:* it must be confessed that this is not very clear, although we may get the general gist. The translator is doing his best with the Hebrew, which reads something like 'Our soul has been excessively filled with the mockery of those who are at ease, the contempt of the proud.'

124:4 *torrent:* the Greek word means 'winter-flowing', and can refer to a 'wadi', a stream that is dry in the summer, but can be a fearsome source of flash floods when there has been rain.

8 Our help is in the name of the Lord,
who made heaven and earth.'

Psalm 125 (124) Trust in the Lord

A song of ascents

125:1 Those who trust in the Lord [are] like Mount Sion;
those who dwell in Jerusalem shall never be shaken.
2 The mountains are around her,
so the Lord is around his people, from now on and for ever.
3 For the Lord will not permit the staff of sinners
[to be] upon the inheritance of the just;
otherwise the just might stretch out their hands to iniquity.
4 Do good, O Lord, to those who are good,
and to the upright of heart;
5 but those who turn aside to [get tied up in] knots,
the Lord will lead away, along with those who work iniquity.
Peace upon Israel!

Psalm 126 (125) The return from exile

A song of ascents

126:1 When the Lord turned Sion's captivity,
we became like those who have been comforted.
2 Then our mouth was filled with joy,
and our tongue with exultation.
Then they shall say among the Gentiles,
'The Lord has done great things with them.'
3 The Lord has done great things with us;
we were overjoyed.
4 Turn, O Lord, our captivity,
like winter streams in the south.
5 Those who sow in tears will reap in joy.
6 When they went out, they went out weeping, carrying their seeds;
and when they come in, they shall come in rejoicing, carrying their sheaves.

125:2 *her:* clearly Jerusalem. The MT has the name 'Jerusalem' in verse 2; in LXX it is at the end of verse 1.

125:3 *inheritance:* in both Hebrew and Greek the word means 'lot', but in the sense of the land that God has allotted to the chosen people.

125:5 *who turn aside to [get tied up in] knots:* the Hebrew has 'twisting roads', which is a different metaphor for the same thing.

126:1 *like those who have been comforted:* the Hebrew here has 'like those who dream'.

126:2 *has done great things with them:* literally (both in Hebrew and in Greek) 'the Lord has made great to act with them'.

126:3 *The Lord has done great things with us:* this is echoed, of course, in Mary's Magnificat (Luke 1:49).

126:4 *winter streams in the south:* 'winter streams' are the wadis that are dry except when the rain comes, when they can be very dangerous. The 'south' is an accurate translation of the Hebrew word 'Negev', which means both 'south', and the desert that lies to the south of the Holy Land.

Psalm 127 (126)   Only God can bless our efforts

A song of ascents, of Solomon.

127:1   Unless the Lord build the house,
those who build it labour in vain;
unless the Lord guard the city,
those who guard it keep watch in vain.

2   In vain it is for you to rise early in the morning after resting,
you who eat the bread of pain,
when he gives sleep to his beloved ones.

3   See – the Lord's inheritance:
children, the reward of the fruit of the womb.

4   Just like arrows in the hand of a mighty man,
so are the children of those who have been shaken off.

5   Happy are those who will satisfy their desire with them;
they shall not be put to shame when they speak to their enemies in the gateway.

Psalm 128 (127)   God blesses our work and family

A song of ascents

128:1   Happy are all those who fear the Lord,
those who walk in his ways.

2   You will eat the work of your hands;
happy are you, and it shall be well with you.

3   Your wife [shall be] like a flourishing vine in the sides of your house,
your children like newly planted olives around your table.

4   See – so shall they be blessed, those who fear the Lord.

5   May the Lord bless you from Sion,
and may you see the prosperity of Jerusalem, all the days of your life.

6   May you see your children's children.
Peace upon Israel!

Psalm 129 (128)   Triumph over Israel's enemies

A song of ascents

129:1   'Many times have they made war on me since my youth.' Now let Israel say,

2   'Many times have they made war on me since my youth
– and yet they did not prevail over me.

3   The sinners made schemes on my back;
they prolonged their iniquity.

---

127   **Heading:** *of Solomon:* possibly attributed to Solomon on the grounds that there is a reference to the building of the Temple. Compare the heading to Psalm 72, where 'of Solomon' may reflect that the opening verse refers to 'the king . . . the king's son', which was understood as David and Solomon.

127:4   *children of those who have been shaken off:* this is an alternative reading of a Hebrew phrase that more probably means 'children of one's youth'.

127:5   *satisfy their desire:* the human desire to have children. The Hebrew here has 'fill their quiver with them', continuing the arrow metaphor from the previous verse.

gateway: the standard place for conducting a lawsuit in the OT. See Deuteronomy 21:19; 25:7; Ruth 4:1; Amos 5:12.

128:2   *the work of your hands:* so the Hebrew. The Greek here reads 'the labours of your fruits', possibly misreading 'your hands' as 'your fruits', which is fairly similar in Hebrew.

129:3   *made schemes on my back:* the Hebrew here has a word that means 'ploughed' or 'engraved'. This is a metaphor, presumably, for corporal punishment. The Greek has taken the metaphor slightly differently, and used a word that can describe the work of an artisan, to 'wreak' (as in 'wrought iron', for example) or 'contrive'.

139

4 The righteous Lord has cut the necks of sinners asunder.
5 Let them be put to shame and routed,
all those who hate Sion.
6 Let them be like grass on the house-tops,
which is withered before it is plucked up,
7 with which the reapers have not filled their hands,
nor the sheaf-binder filled their laps.
8 And those who pass by did not say,
"The blessing of the Lord be upon you;
we have blessed you in the Lord's name."'

Psalm 130 (129) De profundis

A song of ascents

130:1 Out of the depths I cried out to you, O Lord.
2 Lord, listen to my voice;
let your ears be attentive to the voice of my entreaty.
3 If you, O Lord, would mark iniquity,
Lord who shall stand?
4 For with you is forgiveness;
for the sake of your Law I waited for you, O Lord;
my soul waited for your word.
5 My soul hoped in the Lord, from the early watch until night-time;
from the early watch let Israel hope in the Lord.
6 For with the Lord is mercy,
and with him generous redemption.
7 And he will redeem Israel from all their iniquities.

Psalm 131 (130) Humble trust in the Lord

A song of ascents. Of David

131:1 O Lord, my heart is not lifted up high,
nor have my eyes been raised up;
nor have I occupied myself with things too great or too wonderful for me.
2 If I was not humble in my thinking,
but exalted my soul,
like the weaned child to his mother,
so is the reward for my soul.
3 Let Israel hope in the Lord,
from now and for evermore.

131:1 *occupied myself:* literally 'journeyed' (Greek) or 'walked' (Hebrew).

131:2 *If I was not humble . . . reward for my soul:* this is an awkward, and on the face of it, ungrammatical sentence.

The translator is doing his best with a Hebrew expression that literally means 'If not . . . ' , which here signifies something like 'see if I have not'. It is hard to know what to do with it in English.

Psalm 132 (131)   The Lord has chosen Sion

A song of ascents

132:1 Remember David, O Lord, and all his humility,
2 how he swore to the Lord,
and made a vow to the God of Jacob:
3 'I shall not go into the tent of my house;
I shall not go up to the couch of my bedding,
4 I shall not give sleep to my eyes,
nor slumber to my eyelids,
nor rest to my temples,
5 until I find a place for the Lord,
a pavilion for the God of Jacob.'
6 See – we heard of it in Ephratha;
we found it in the plains of the forest.
7 We shall enter into his tents;
we shall worship in the place where his feet stood.
8 Arise, Lord, into your rest,
you and the ark of your holiness!
9 Your priests shall put on righteousness as their clothing,
and your holy ones shall exult.
10 For the sake of David your servant,
do not turn away the face of your Anointed One.
11 The Lord swore a true oath to David; and he will not go back on it:
'From the fruit of your body,
I shall place one upon your throne.
12 If your children will keep my covenant,
and my testimonies which I shall teach them,
their children shall sit on your throne for ever.'
13 For the Lord has chosen Sion,
has elected her as his dwelling place.
14 'This is my resting place for ever,
here shall I dwell, for I have elected her.
15 I shall indeed bless her provision,
and I shall satisfy her poor with bread.
16 I shall clothe her priests with salvation,
and her holy ones shall exult mightily.
17 There I shall raise up the horn of David;
I have prepared a lamp for my Anointed One.
18 I shall clothe his enemies with shame,
but on him shall my holiness blossom.'

132:1 *all his humility:* the Greek word here is connected with the word for 'meek' or 'gentle' in the beatitudes (Matthew 5:5); the Hebrew word has connotations of oppression or being brought low. Either way, humility is probably the best translation.

132:4 *nor rest to my temples:* this is not in the Hebrew, though obviously it continues the same idea.

132:5 *a pavilion for the God of Jacob:* the Hebrew here has 'the strong one of Jacob'. The word for 'pavilion' means 'tent' or 'dwelling place' in both languages, and this slightly out-of-the-way word is intended to capture both ideas.

132:7 *the place where his feet stood:* the Hebrew here speaks of

God's 'footstool'. It is possible that the translator did not care for so anthropomorphic an image.

132:8 *ark of your holiness:* the Hebrew here has 'ark of your might'.

132:10 *your Anointed One:* the Greek here has 'your Christ' (translating the Hebrew 'your Messiah'), and although this is an inevitable translation, a Christian reader could not fail to read it as referring to Jesus.

132:12 *children . . . children:* we are using inclusive language here. The Hebrew and the Greek inevitably speak of 'sons', who alone could sit on the throne.

132:17 *raise up the horn of David:* this is echoed in Zachariah's song at Luke 1:69.

Psalm 133 (132) **Living in unity**

A song of Ascents. Of David

133:1 See: what could be more lovely or delightful
than for brethren to dwell together?
2 It is like ointment which goes down on the beard,
upon the beard of Aaron,
which goes down onto the collar of his garment.
3 It is like the dew of Hermon,
which comes down upon the mountains of Sion;
for there the Lord commanded the blessing,
and life for ever.

Psalm 134 (133) **An evening blessing**

A song of ascents

134:1 See: bless the Lord, all you servants of the Lord,
you who stand in the house of the Lord,
in the courts of the house of our God.
2 In the night-time, lift up your hands to the holy places,
and bless the Lord.
3 The Lord, who made heaven and earth,
will bless you from Sion.

Psalm 135 (134) **A hymn of praise**

135:1 Alleluia! Praise the name of the Lord,
servants of the Lord, praise the Lord.
2 You who stand in the house of the Lord,
in the courts of the house of our God.
3 Praise the Lord, for the Lord is good;
sing a psalm to his name, for it is delightful.
4 For the Lord has chosen Jacob for himself,
Israel for his treasure.
5 For I know that the Lord is great,
and our Lord is above all the gods.
6 All that the Lord willed, he has done,
in heaven and on earth and in the seas and in all the deeps.
7 He brings up clouds from the end of the earth;
he has created lightnings for the rain;
he brings out winds from his treasury.
8 He struck the first-born of Egypt,
human and beast alike.
9 He sent signs and portents in your midst, O Egypt,
upon Pharaoh and all his servants.
10 He struck many nations,
and killed mighty kings,
11 Sihon, king of the Amorites, and Og the king of Bashan,
and all the kingdoms of Canaan.

134:1 *in the courts of the house of our God:* here the Hebrew has
'in the night-time'. The Greek has the same elements in a
slightly different order.

12 He gave their land as an inheritance,
    an inheritance for Israel his people.
13 O Lord, your name is for ever,
    your remembrance from generation to generation.
14 For the Lord will judge his people,
    and will have compassion on his servants.
15 The Gentiles' idols are silver and gold,
    the work of human hands;
16 they have a mouth, and they will not speak;
    they have eyes, and they will not see;
17 they have ears and they will not listen;
    they have noses and they will not smell;
    they have hands, and they will not touch;
    they have feet and they will not go on a journey;
    they will not talk with their throats,
    for there is no breath in their mouths.
18 Let those who make them become like them;
    and all those who have placed their trust in them.
19 House of Israel, bless the Lord;
    house of Aaron, bless the Lord.
20 House of Levi, bless the Lord;
    you who fear the Lord, bless the Lord.
21 May the Lord be blessed from Sion,
    the Lord who dwells in Jerusalem.

Psalm 136 (135) Praise for what God has done

136:1 Alleluia! Give thanks to the Lord, for he is good,
    for his mercy is for ever.
2 Give thanks to the God of gods,
    for his mercy is for ever.
3 Give thanks to the Lord of lords,
    for his mercy is for ever.
4 To [God] who has worked wonders,
    for his mercy is for ever.
5 To the one who made the heavens with intelligence,
    for his mercy is for ever.
6 To the one who set the earth firm on the waters,
    for his mercy is for ever.
7 To the one who alone made the great lights,
    for his mercy is for ever.
8 The sun to rule over the day;
    for his mercy is for ever.
9 The moon and the stars to rule over the night,
    for his mercy is for ever.

135:14 *will have compassion:* here the translator, trying to imitate the aspect of the Hebrew verb, has produced a Greek word that means 'will be comforted', but I have opted for the translation he was clearly aiming at.

135: *The Gentiles' idols . . . placed their trust in them:* for the
15-18 polemic against idols, see Psalm 115:4-8, Wisdom 15:15, and, of course, Isaiah 44:9-20.

135:20 *you who fear the Lord:* these may well be 'God fearers', non-Jews who have shown an interest in converting to Judaism.

10 To the one who struck Egypt and their first-born,
   for his mercy is for ever.
11 And who led Israel out of their midst,
   for his mercy is for ever.
12 With a mighty hand and a lofty arm,
   for his mercy is for ever.
13 To the one who divided the Red Sea into divisions,
   for his mercy is for ever.
14 To the one who led Israel through the midst of the sea,
   for his mercy is for ever.
15 And who shook off Pharaoh and his army into the Red Sea,
   for his mercy is for ever.
16 To the one who led his people in the desert,
   for his mercy is for ever.
   To the one who drew the water from the sharp rock,
   for his mercy is for ever.
17 To the one who struck great kings,
   for his mercy is for ever.
18 And who killed powerful kings,
   for his mercy is for ever.
19 And Sihon, king of the Amorites,
   for his mercy is for ever.
20 And Og, the king of Bashan,
   for his mercy is for ever.
21 And who gave their land as an inheritance,
   for his mercy is for ever.
22 An inheritance to Israel his servant,
   for his mercy is for ever.
23 For the Lord remembered us in our lowliness,
   for his mercy is for ever.
24 And redeemed us from our enemies,
   for his mercy is for ever.
25 Who gives food to all flesh,
   for his mercy is for ever.
26 Give thanks to the God of heaven,
   for his mercy is for ever.
   Give thanks to the Lord of lords,
   for his mercy is for ever.

Psalm 137 (136) An exile's song

Of David

137:1 By the rivers of Babylon, there we sat down and we wept,
   when we remembered Sion.
2 On the willows in her midst we hung up our harps.

136:16 *To the one who drew . . . is for ever:* these two lines are not in all manuscripts of the Greek. They do not appear in the Hebrew.

136:26 *Give thanks to the Lord of lords, for his mercy is for ever:* these two lines, likewise, are not in the Hebrew, and not in all manuscripts of the Greek.

137 **Title:** *An exile's song:* this is, so far as I am aware, the only psalm that has made it into the pop charts. The Hebrew is late, and, not surprisingly, it is thought to be written after the Exile.

3   Because our captors asked us for the words of a song,
     and those who had taken us off asked for a hymn:
     'Sing for us, one of the songs of Sion.'

4   How shall we sing the Lord's song in a foreign land?

5   If I forget you, Jerusalem, may my right hand forget.

6   May my tongue stick to my throat, if I do not remember you,
     if I do not prefer Jerusalem as the beginning of my joy.

7   Remember, Lord, the children of Edom,
     the day of Jerusalem, the day of those who said,
     'Empty her out, empty her out, down to the foundation within her.'

8   O wretched Daughter of Babylon,
     happy are those who repay you as you repaid us.

9   Happy are those who will take hold of your infants
     and dash them to the ground against the rock.

Psalm 138 (137)   Gratitude to God

Of David

138:1   I shall give you thanks, O Lord, with all my heart,
     for you have heard the words of my mouth;
     before the angels I shall sing to you.

2   I shall bow down towards your holy Temple,
     and I shall give thanks to your holy name, and to your truth;
     for you have made your word greater than all other names.

3   Hear me speedily, on whatever day I shall call upon you;
     you will care for me in my soul with your power.

4   O Lord, let all the kings of the earth give thanks to you;
     for they have heard all the words of your mouth.

5   And let them sing in the Lord's ways,
     for great is the glory of the Lord.

6   For the Lord is high, and he looks upon the lowly;
     and he knows high things from far away.

7   If I walk in the midst of affliction, you will give me life;
     you stretched out your hands against the anger of my enemies,
     and your right hand has saved me.

8   The Lord will repay on my behalf;
     O Lord, your mercy is for ever;
     do not disregard the works of your hands.

Psalm 139 (138)   God knows me through and through

To the end. A psalm of David

139:1   O Lord, you have tested me and known me.

2   You know my sitting down and my rising up;
     you understand my thoughts from afar.

137:5 *may my right hand forget:* the Hebrew here, in this poignant song, has a word which in one form means something like to 'wilt' or 'wither', or to sink low (unless, scholars point out, the Hebrew text is wrong).

137:8- *Daughter of Babylon . . . dash them to the ground against*
9   *the rock:* these verses are never read in church, presumably because of the violence of their sentiments; but perhaps we should not be too coy about recognising that the psalms embrace all possible human responses.

138:2 *your word:* this is the reading of the Hebrew and some Greek mss; other manuscripts have 'your name'.

3 You have searched out my path and the miles I have travelled;
   you know all my ways.
4 For there is no word upon my tongue;
5 see, Lord, you knew it all, endings and beginnings;
   you fashioned me, and laid your hand upon me.
6 Your knowledge is wonderful;
   it is too much for me; I cannot reach it.
7 Where am I to go from your Spirit?
   And where am I to flee from your face?
8 If I go up to heaven, you are there;
   if I go down to Hades, you are present.
9 If I were to take up my wings at dawn,
   and pitch my tent at the ends of the sea . . .
10 . . . for even there your hand will guide me,
   your right hand will hold me.
11 And I said, 'Then night will trample me down;
   even night is light in my luxury.'
12 For darkness will not be darkened with you;
   and night will be lit up like the day;
   as its darkness, so shall its light be.
13 For you, O Lord, have possessed my kidneys;
    you helped me from my mother's womb.
14 I shall give you thanks, for I have been marvellously, fearfully made;
   marvellous are your works, and my soul knows this very well.
15 My bones, which you made in secret, are not secret from you;
   nor my substance in the lowest parts of the earth.
16 Your eyes saw my unformed being;
   and all shall be written in your book.
   They shall be fashioned by day – and there is no one in them.
17 But your friends, O God, have been greatly honoured by me;
   their beginnings were greatly strengthened.
18 I shall count them, and they shall be multiplied, more than the sand.
   I awoke, and I am still with you.
19 If you would only kill sinners, O God;
   men of violence, keep away from me!
20 For you will say, with regard to [their] intention;
   they shall take your cities in vain.
21 Have I not hated them, O Lord, who hate you?
   Did I not pine away because of your enemies?

139:3 *miles I have travelled:* the word for 'miles' actually means a rope, and might refer to an ancient measuring device, and this would make sense. But it might also refer to a bed, which is one possible translation of the Hebrew. We have to admit that we do not really know what the Hebrew means.

139:4 *no word upon my tongue:* some Greek manuscripts here have 'no *unjust* word', which might make more sense; but this is not in the Hebrew, and not in all mss.

139:13 *kidneys:* this is what both the Hebrew and the Greek say. Translators tend to be a little bashful, and talk of 'my inmost being'.

139:16 *my unformed being:* so the Greek; the Hebrew has 'my embryo'.

and there is no one in them: this is a literal translation into Greek of the Hebrew.

139:17 *your friends:* this is certainly a possible reading of the Hebrew, but the modern versions of it are probably correct in understanding it as 'your thoughts'.

139:19 *If you would only kill sinners, O God:* this bloodthirsty sentiment is not often read out in church.

139:20 *they shall take your cities in vain:* this is what the Greek says, and it may be the meaning of the Hebrew, but the text seems corrupt here, and the Greek translation is a gallant attempt to make sense of it.

22 With a perfect hatred I hated them,
   they became my enemies.
23 Test me, O God, and know my heart;
   examine me, and know my paths.
24 And see if there is any way of iniquity in me;
   guide me in the everlasting way.

Psalm 140 (139)   Deliverance from the enemy

To the end. A psalm of David

140:1 Deliver me, O Lord from the wicked,
      from the evil rescue me,
   2 those who planned injustice in their hearts;
      all day long they were preparing wars.
   3 They sharpened their tongue like the serpent,
      the venom of asps under their lips.

   Interlude

   4 Keep me, O Lord, from the hand of sinners;
      rescue me from the unjust, who planned to trip up my steps.
   5 The arrogant have hidden a snare for me;
      they have stretched out ropes with snares for my feet;
      they placed a stumbling block for me in the path.

   Interlude

   6 I said to the Lord, 'You are my God; listen to the voice of my entreaty.'
   7 O Lord, Lord, the power of my salvation,
      you shade my head in the day of war.
   8 O Lord, do not hand me over to the sinner, against my desire;
      they have plotted against me.
      Do not abandon me, lest they be exalted.

   Interlude

   9 The head of those who surround me,
      the labour of their lips shall cover them.
   10 Coals of fire shall fall upon them,
      you will cast them down in their wretchedness;
      no way will they survive.
   11 The man who is a babbler will not prosper on the earth;
      evils shall chase the unjust, to their destruction.
   12 I know that the Lord will bring about his judgement for the destitute,
      and the verdict for the poor.
   13 But the righteous shall give thanks to your name,
      and the upright shall live in your presence.

Psalm 141 (140)   Praying for protection against evil

A psalm of David

141:1 O Lord, I cried out to you, give ear to me;
      pay attention to the sound of my entreaty,
      when I cry to you.

2 Let my prayer be directed before you like incense,
the lifting up of my hands like an evening sacrifice.
3 O Lord, place a guard on my mouth,
and a secure door around my lips.
4 Do not incline my heart to words of wickedness,
to offer empty pretexts for sins,
with those who perform iniquity;
may I never be joined with their chosen ones.
5 The righteous shall chastise me with mercy, and reprove me;
but let not the oil of a sinner anoint my head,
for still my prayer shall be in their friendship.
6 Their judges have been swallowed down;
they shall hear my words, because they prevailed.
7 As a thick lump of earth is broken up on the ground,
our bones have been scattered before Hades.
8 For on you, O Lord, Lord, are my eyes;
in you I have hoped; do not take away my life.
9 Guard me from the snare which they have
set up for me;
and from the obstacles of those who do iniquity.
10 Sinners shall fall by their own net;
I am alone until I pass by.

Psalm 142 (141) **When persecutors threaten**

[A song] of instruction. Of David, when he was in the cave. A prayer.

142:1 With my voice I cried out to the Lord,
with my voice, I made my petition to the Lord.
2 I shall pour out my petition before him;
I shall announce my distress before him.
3 When my spirit was fainting within me,
and you knew my paths;
in this way in which I was journeying they hid a snare for me.
4 I looked to the right, and I saw that there was no one who recognised me;
flight failed me, and there was no one who looked after my soul.
5 I cried out to you, O Lord; I said,
'You are my hope, my portion in the land of the living.
6 Pay attention to my entreaty, for I am brought very low;
deliver me from those who hunt me down, for they are mightier than I.
7 Lead my soul out of prison, to give thanks to your name, O Lord;
the righteous shall wait for me, until you repay me.'

141:2 *Let my prayer be directed before you like incense:* the reader may be reminded here of Zachariah praying in the Temple (Luke 1:9-10).

141:4 *offer empty pretexts:* literally, 'to excuse excuses'.

141:5 *in their friendship:* this is a possible reading of the Hebrew, which is more likely to mean 'in their evils'.

142 **Heading:** *when he was in the cave:* the reference here is either to the cave of Adullam (1 Samuel 22:1) or to the cave in the Engedi desert (1 Samuel 24:3).

Psalm 143 (142) The seventh 'Penitential Psalm'

A psalm of David, when his son pursued him

143:1 O Lord, hear my prayer,
　　 give your ear to my entreaty in your truth;
　　 in your righteousness, hear me.

2 And do not enter into judgement with your servant,
　 for no living person shall be justified in your sight.

3 For the enemy has hunted down my soul,
　 has humiliated my life down to the ground,
　 made me sit in dark places, like those who have been long dead.

4 And my spirit was grieved within me,
　 my heart was troubled in me.

5 I remembered the ancient days,
　 and I meditated on all your deeds,
　 I meditated on the works of your hands.

6 I spread out my hands before you,
　 my soul like a waterless land [thirsted] for you.

Interlude

7 Hear me quickly, O Lord; my spirit has failed;
　 do not turn your face from me,
　 or I shall be like those who go down into the pit.

8 Make me hear of your mercy in the morning;
　 for I have hoped in you.
　 O Lord, make me know the way on which I shall walk,
　 for to you I have lifted up my soul.

9 Rescue me from my enemies, O Lord,
　 for I have taken refuge in you.

10 Teach me to do your will, for you are my God;
　 your good spirit will guide me on level ground.

11 For the sake of your name, O Lord, you will give me life,
　 you will lead my soul out of [its] distress.

12 In your mercy you will destroy my enemies,
　 and you will kill all those who oppress my life;
　 for I am your servant.

Psalm 144 (143) A king's prayer of thanksgiving

Of David. With regard to Goliath.

144:1 Blessed be the Lord, my God,
　　 who teaches my hands for battle, and my fingers for war.

2 My mercy, and my refuge, my helper and my rescuer,
　 my protector, in whom I have trusted,
　 who subdues my people under me.

---

143 **Heading**: *when his son pursued him:* this heading is not in the MT. The reference is to Absalom's rebellion (see 2 Samuel 15:14ff).

144 **Heading**: *With regard to Goliath:* this is not in the Hebrew, so is presumably a late guess about the situation for which the psalm might have been composed. The story, of course, is the splendid tale that we find in 1 Samuel 17. The references to the poet's hands and fingers in verse 1 might have suggested the idea.

144:2 *my people:* this is the reading of both MT and LXX, but there are mss and versions that read 'peoples', which is perhaps more to be expected. The idea of an Israelite king using violence on his own people is perhaps a little jarring.

3 Lord, what are human beings, that you are made known to them,
or mortals that you take account of them?

4 Human beings are like emptiness;
their days pass like a shadow.

5 O Lord, bow down your heavens and come down;
touch the mountains and they shall smoke.

6 Make your lightning flash and you will scatter them;
send forth your arrows, and you will throw them into disarray.

7 Send forth your hand from on high;
deliver me and rescue me from many waters, from the hand of foreigners,

8 whose mouth has uttered vanity;
and their right hand is a right hand of injustice.

9 O God, I shall sing a new song to you;
I shall play to you on a ten-stringed lyre,

10 to the one who gives salvation to kings,
who redeems David his servant from the evil sword.

11 Deliver me, and rescue me from the hand of foreigners,
whose mouth has uttered vanity,
and their right hand is a hand of injustice,

12 whose children are like plants grown to maturity while still young;
their daughters adorned, decorated like the appearance of a temple.

13 Their treasuries are full, overflowing on every side,
their sheep prolific, multiplying in their streets,

14 their cattle fertile,
no broken-down hedges, no gaps in the walls, no crying in their squares.

15 Happy the people who has these things,
the people whose God is the Lord.

Psalm 145 (144)   God's greatness and goodness

Praise. Of David

145:1 I shall exalt you, my God, my King;
and I shall bless your name for ever, and for evermore.

2 Day by day I shall bless you,
and I shall praise your name for ever, and for evermore.

3 The Lord is great, and very much to be praised,
of his greatness there is no end.

4 Generation upon generation will praise your works,
and proclaim your power.

5 And they shall speak of the glorious majesty of your holiness,
and recount your wonders.

6 And they shall tell of the power of your awesome deeds,
and recount your greatness.

7 They shall pour forth the memory of the abundance of your goodness,
and they shall exult in your righteousness.

144:3 *what are human beings:* there is an echo here of Psalm 8:4, grimly parodied in Job 7:17.

144:6 *scatter them:* the 'them' here has to be human beings, rather than 'mountains', which was the last to be mentioned.

144:7 *foreigners:* here the translator has rendered a bit over-literally a Hebrew expression which means 'children of strangers'.

144: The LXX seems to suggest these words still refer to
12-15 foreigners, but the Hebrew makes it clear they refer to 'our sons', i.e. Israelites.

145 this is an alphabetical psalm, each verse starting with a different letter of the Hebrew alphabet.

145:4 *Generation upon generation:* there may be an echo of this verse in Job 8:9.

8 The Lord is compassionate and merciful,
slow to anger and rich in mercy.
9 The Lord is good to all,
and his compassion is on all that he has made.
10 Let all that you have made give thanks to you, O Lord;
and let your holy ones bless you.
11 They shall speak of the glory of your reign,
and tell of your might
12 to make known your might to all people,
and the glorious majesty of your reign.
13 Your reign is a reign for all the ages;
your sovereignty is for generation after generation.
The Lord is faithful in all his words,
and holy in all his deeds.
14 The Lord supports all those who are falling down,
and restores all those who are broken down.
15 The eyes of all hope in you;
and you give them their food at the right time.
16 You open your hand,
and you fill every living creature with pleasure.
17 The Lord is just in all his ways,
and holy in all his deeds.
18 The Lord is near to all those who call upon him,
to all who call upon him in truth.
19 He will satisfy the desire of those who fear him;
he will listen to their entreaty, and save them.
20 The Lord guards all those who love him;
but all sinners he will exterminate.
21 My mouth shall speak the Lord's praise;
and let all flesh bless his holy name, for ever and for evermore.

Psalm 146 (145) Praise the Lord

Halleluiah. Of Haggai and Zechariah

146:1 Praise the Lord, my soul.
2 I shall praise the Lord all my life;
I shall sing to God as long as I live.
3 Do not trust in rulers,
nor in mortals, in whom there is no salvation.
4 Their spirit shall depart, and they will return to their earth;
on that day all their thoughts shall perish.
5 Happy are those whose helper is the God of Jacob;
their hope is in the Lord their God,
6 who made heaven and earth, the sea, and all that is within them,
who keeps truth for ever,

145:9 *good to all:* some Greek manuscripts here add 'who wait' or 'who endure'.

145:13 *The Lord is faithful . . . in all his deeds:* the verse beginning with the Hebrew letter 'nun' is missing in the MT, but it is in the Greek, and can be reconstructed, and turned back into Hebrew.

146 Title: *Praise the Lord:* in the MT, this is part of the psalm, which is the first of the five 'praise' psalms that end the collection. For some reason the LXX links this with Haggai and Zechariah, possibly recalling their work to rebuild the Temple.

7 who does judgement for those who are wronged,
who gives food to those who are hungry,
the Lord sets prisoners free.
8 The Lord restores those who are broken down;
the Lord gives wisdom to the blind;
the Lord loves the just.
9 The Lord guards the stranger,
will take up the orphan and widow;
he will blot out the way of sinners.
10 The Lord will reign for ever,
your God, O Sion, to all generations.

Psalm 147 (Psalm 146–147) Praise the Lord

Alleluia. Of Haggai and Zechariah

147:1 Praise the Lord, for it is good to sing a psalm.
Let praise be sweetly sung to our God.
2 The Lord builds up Jerusalem;
he will gather the scattered ones of Israel.
3 He heals the broken-hearted,
and binds up their wounds.
4 Who counts the numbers of the stars,
and calls each of them by name.
5 Great is our Lord, and great is his strength;
and there is no counting his wisdom.
6 The Lord lifts up the meek,
but humbles sinners to the earth.
7 Begin [the song] in thanksgiving to the Lord;
sing a psalm to our God on the harp,
8 who covers the heaven with clouds,
who prepares rain for the earth,
who makes grass grow on the mountains,
and greenery for humans to use,
9 who gives cattle their food,
and to the young ravens who call upon him.
10 He will not take delight in the strength of the horse,
nor does he take pleasure in a man's legs.
11 The Lord takes pleasure in those who fear him,
and in those who hope in his mercy.

Alleluia. Of Haggai and Zechariah

12 Praise the Lord, Jerusalem,
Praise your God, O Sion,

146:10 *to all generations:* the MT ends the psalm with 'Alleluia', which starts the new psalm.

147 **Title:** *Psalm 146–147:* here at last LXX and MT reunite. The Hebrew treats this as a single psalm, probably correctly.

147:8 *greenery for humans to use:* this half-verse is omitted in MT, but should certainly be restored.

147:10 *strength of the horse . . . pleasure in a man's legs:* the idea here is that none of the qualities on which human beings ordinarily rely (the psalmist today might speak of 'the speed of your car . . . your ability at football') is of any interest to God.

147:11 *Alleluia. Of Haggai and Zechariah:* this, of course, marks the start of the new psalm (147) in LXX.

13 for he strengthened the bars of your gates;
    he has blessed your children within you.
14 He makes your borders peaceful,
    and fills you with the very best wheat.
15 He sends out his teaching to the earth,
    his word will run swiftly.
16 He gives snow like wool,
    he sprinkles the mist like ashes.
17 He flings his ice like crumbs;
    who will stand before his cold?
18 He will send out his word and melt them;
    he will make his wind blow, and the waters shall flow.
19 He announces his word to Jacob,
    his decrees and decisions to Israel.
20 He has not dealt like this to any of the Gentiles;
    he has not revealed his decisions to them.

Psalm 148 Invitation to praise God

Alleluia. Of Haggai and Zechariah

148:1 Praise the Lord from the heavens;
       praise him in the highest.
2 Praise him, all you his angels,
   praise him, all his hosts.
3 Praise him, sun and moon,
   praise him, all you stars and light.
4 Praise him, highest heavens,
   and the water above the heavens.
5 Let them praise the name of the Lord;
   for he spoke, and they came to be;
   he commanded and they were created.
6 He established them for ever,
   and indeed for ever and for evermore;
   he gave a command; and it shall not pass away.
7 Praise the Lord from the earth,
   dragons and all you depths.
8 Fire, hail, snow, ice, stormy wind,
   all you things that do his word.
9 Mountains and all the hills,
   fruit-bearing trees and all cedars.
10 Wild beasts and all cattle,
    creepy-crawlies, and winged birds.
11 Monarchs of the earth and all nations,
    rulers and all judges of the earth.

147:14 *very best wheat:* both Hebrew and Greek here have 'fat of wheat', but this is what they mean.

147:18 *make his wind blow:* here the Greek has a Hebrew-sounding phrase that you might translate 'will blow his blow' or 'will wind his wind'; but the Hebrew actually uses two different words.

148:4 *highest heavens:* literally, in both Hebrew and Greek, 'heavens of the heavens'.

148:6 *a command; and it shall not pass away:* Jesus alludes, perhaps, to this in the Sermon on the Mount. See Matthew 5:18 'until heaven and earth pass away, not a single "yodh" nor a single "vowel-sign" shall pass away from the law'.

¹² Young men and maidens,
old men and youths.
¹³ Let them praise the Lord's name,
for his name alone is exalted,
his praise is above earth and heaven.
¹⁴ He shall exalt the horn of his people;
a hymn for all his holy ones,
the children of Israel,
a people who come close to him.

Psalm 149   Invitation to praise God

149:1 Alleluia.
Sing a new song to the Lord;
his praise is in the assembly of the holy ones.
² Let Israel rejoice in its Maker,
and let the children of Sion exult in their king.
³ Let them praise his name with dancing;
let them sing songs to him with tambourine and harp.
⁴ For the Lord is pleased with his people,
and will raise up the humble with salvation.
⁵ The holy shall boast in glory,
and exult on their beds.
⁶ God's praises shall be in their throats,
and two-edged swords in their hands,
⁷ to bring about vengeance on the nations,
and reproof among the peoples,
⁸ to bind their kings in chains,
and their notables with handcuffs made of iron,
⁹ to carry out the judgement decreed upon them,
this glory is for all his holy ones.

Psalm 150   The final doxology

150:1 Alleluia. Praise God in his holy places,
praise him in the firmament of his power.
² Praise him for his mighty deeds,
praise him according to the abundance of his greatness.
³ Praise him with the sound of a trumpet,
praise him with lyre and harp.
⁴ Praise him with tambourines and dancing,
praise him with strings and pipes.
⁵ Praise him with cymbals that please the ear,
praise him with loud cymbals.
⁶ Let everything that breathes praise the Lord.
Alleluia.

149:5 *beds:* this is what LXX has; but the Hebrew has 'couches', which could be for either sleeping or for banqueting.

150:1 *Alleluia. Praise God in his holy places:* this is the opening of the final psalm in the MT (LXX has, as we shall see) an additional one. This entire psalm functions as a doxology, similar to those we have seen above, ending each of the 'books' of the psalms (41:13; 72:18-20; 89:52; 106:48).

150:5 *cymbals that please the ear . . . loud cymbals:* these are clearly two kinds of cymbal. The first kind may be unknown to most of us.

Psalm 151   One last psalm

This psalm is in [David's] own hand. For David, and outside the number.
When he fought Goliath in single combat.

151:1   I was the smallest among my brothers,
and the youngest in my father's house;
I was shepherding my father's sheep.

2   My hands made an instrument,
and my fingers tuned a lyre.

3   And who will announce to my Lord?
The Lord himself – it is he who hears.

4   He sent out his messenger,
and he took me from my father's sheep,
and he anointed me with the oil of his anointing.

5   My brothers were handsome and tall,
but the Lord took no delight in them.

6   I went out to meet the Philistine,
and he cursed me by his idols,

7   but I drew the sword [I had taken] from him,
and took away the disgrace from the children of Israel.

151   **Title:** *One last psalm:* LXX adds a final psalm here; it
seems good to offer it to readers.

outside the number: so the editors know that it does not
belong with the regular psalms, but they are convinced
that it is worth including.

Goliath in single combat: for the story, see 1 Samuel 17.

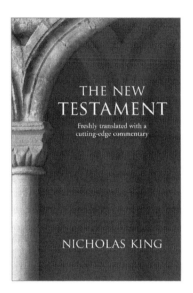

The New Testament

Keeps as close to the original Greek as possible, frequently incorporating idiomatic or grammatical peculiarities, resulting in an illuminating and faith-strengthening translation. To quote one reviewer: 'This is Dynamite.'

Paperback – 1500858

Hardback – 1500740

Pocket Paperback – 1500945

Pocket Presentation copy
Leatherette binding, gold edges and ribbon. – 150094

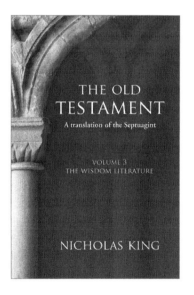

The Old Testament Volume 3
The Wisdom Literature

The first in a four-volume series, this cutting-edge translation includes Job, Psalms, Proverbs, Ecclesiastes, The Song of Songs, Wisdom and the Wisdom of Ben Sira (Ecclesiasticus).

Paperback – 1501199

Hardback – 1501129

The New Testament Study Guides

Interactive explanatory notes and commentary that explore the personalities, background, teaching, language, devices, style and syntax of the document writers, give the feel of the texts, explain trickier passages and highlight themes of special significance.

Matthew – 1500885

Mark – 1500886

Luke – Acts – 1500887

John – 1500888

Romans to Corinthians – 1500899

Galatians to Philemon – 1500898

Hebrews to Revelation – 1500890

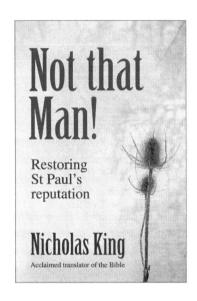

Not that Man!

Using Nicholas King's own translations, this book covers controversial topics such as Paul's attitudes to women, slavery and sex, delving into the mystery of this extraordinary character and helping you to get to know him better.

1501183

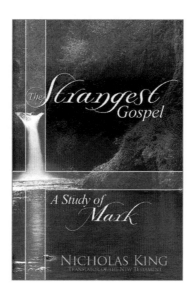

The Strangest Gospel

Be prepared to look with fresh eyes as Nicholas King unfolds the truths and oddities of Mark's Gospel, addressing two fundamental questions: 'Who is Jesus?' and 'If Jesus was so, what must his disciples be like?'

1500949

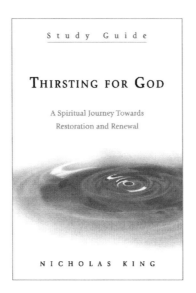

Thirsting for God

An excellent course for groups or individuals alike, particularly suited to the season of Lent, when 'our soul is athirst for God'.

1500653